John M. Palmer, c.s.c.

John M. Palmer, c.s.c.

THE
WINDSOR
Style

By the same author

THE ROYAL JEWELS

THE WINDSOR *Style*

Suzy Menkes

GRAFTON BOOKS

A Division of the Collins Publishing Group

LONDON GLASGOW
TORONTO SYDNEY AUCKLAND

To my sister Vivienne,
who loves Paris

Grafton Books
A Division of the Collins Publishing Group
8 Grafton Street, London W1X 3LA

Published by Grafton Books 1987

British Library Cataloguing in Publication Data

Menkes, Suzy
  The Windsor style.
  1. Windsor, Edward, *Duke of* – Biography
  2. Windsor, Wallis Windsor, *Duchess of*
  Biography
  I. Title
  941.084'092'2   DA581.W5

  ISBN 0-246-13212-4

Designed by David Driver

Picture origination by Adroit Photo Litho Ltd, Birmingham

Photoset in Linotron Baskerville by
Rowland Phototypesetting Ltd,
Bury St Edmunds, Suffolk

Printed in Great Britain by
W. S. Cowell Ltd, Ipswich

Contents

PREFACE

I CAME to the Duke of Windsor through his elegant, eccentric clothes and to the Duchess through her flamboyant jewels.

As a Fashion Editor, I had always been fascinated by the Windsors as a quintessentially stylish couple. The Duchess's sleek 1930s 'cocktail shaker' chic is part of a vanished world where Paris designers created *haute couture* clothes in an ambience of sophisticated glamour.

The Duke, as Prince of Wales and King Edward VIII, set a standard for English style that made him the idol of his generation and a totem for our own. His Prince of Wales checks, Windsor knot, Oxford bags, plus fours and dashing hose all look extraordinarily contemporary.

Not until I unfolded the monogrammed shirts or examined the misty check tweed suits did I realize how studied that style really was: the discreet tab behind the jacket lapel to hold the natty carnation buttonhole; the trousers cut high in the waist to emphasize a board-flat stomach; the unlined tweeds as an escape – metaphorical and literal – from the starched shirts, morning dress and royal court uniforms of what the Duke called a 'Buttoned-up childhood in every sense'.

There is no question of the Duke's fascination with fashion. In his slender book *A Family Album* – published in 1960 – he discusses trouser and tie widths, hatmakers and haberdashery, with an energy he had once applied to the state of the empire.

Wallis, I discovered, was the epitome of self-improvement. She was a plain woman who worked hard at being chic and enjoyed her quest for fashion perfection. Her 'accomplices' – especially her good friend Hubert de Givenchy, and her dressers and fitters at Yves Saint Laurent and Dior – reveal a woman with an eye for fashion, a clear understanding of her own image and a sense of fun.

Her famous wit is elusive. Friends from the Windsors' charmed circle in Paris, who tell so much of this book in their own words, found it impossible to recreate the Duchess's droll responses and rallies of repartee.

A strand of wit runs through the clothes and the jewels: the extravagant jewelled flamingo the size of a breastplate, the menagerie of jungle gems, the Schiaparelli dress printed with a blush-red lobster.

I found echoes of the wit, too, in the Duchess's whimsical bathroom and in the pillows embroidered with quirky mottoes that she scattered round her home.

That house, hidden like an enchanted folly in the Bois de Boulogne, was a shock. I visited it when every precious object and royal memento was still in place. I had been expecting a spare ocean-liner style of decoration, used as a background to the treasures, just as Wallis made her deceptively simple couture dresses a canvas for her jewels.

Instead there was a riot of elegant décor – a 1950s version of eighteenth century France – all marbled walls, rococo gilding, tasselled mouldings and fancy furniture.

As I researched the house and the Windsors' former homes, I was able to read the taste of the Duke and Duchess: her sweet-tooth for colour, flower paintings, china ornaments and trinkets, overlaid with a fascination for eastern exotica and the Southern Belle's nesting instinct.

The Duke brought to the house a royal heritage of commemorative objects and family mementoes. I took tea in the salon, sitting under Queen Mary's portrait, and I soon realized that the Duke's royal mother – but not his father – was a recurrent image in his home in exile.

So were the pugs. Those dogs who snuffled through the salon, showing off like spoilt children for dinner party guests, were commemorated in paintings, pictures, models and photographs throughout the house, and especially in the Duchess's bedroom where the pets were laid out on a plastic cover on her bed each night as carefully as her silken negligee.

The Duchess made the Duke's bedroom a shrine to the life he abdicated to marry her. He made it a shrine to his wife, covering every surface with the same photographs that stood on chairs round his bed in an empty hotel room the night he left England for exile. Those poignant half-forgotten 1930s pictures of Wallis Simpson – the chinoiserie portrait by Man Ray and Cecil Beaton's elongated, elegant photographs and sketches – are reproduced in this book.

The cornucopia of illustrations – over half of them never before published – is designed to introduce the reader to the world of the Windsors, where the intricacy and perfection of domestic detail turned living into an art.

Friends and servants painted pictures for me in their words, especially recollections of the luxurious dinner parties: wall candles casting an eighteenth century glow on the fabulous gold boxes – all now vanished without trace; the table linen hand embroidered to copy exactly the priceless porcelain; the hot crunchy surface of the glacial Camembert ice cream; the kitchen boy sorting salad leaves to match them for size; the Duchess's neat feet dancing, dancing, dancing; and the Duke singing, with pale, moist eyes, the Viennese songs of his mother's childhood.

Other fascinating stories introduced me to the Windsors at play, in their sumptuous Riviera villa, where the gilded bath was a double headed swan, or on their social sorties from their suite in New York's Waldorf Tower.

With the help of Lady Mosley, I managed to see the Moulin de la Tuilerie – the Windsors' tumble of country cottages tucked in a green valley near Orsay, where the Duke of Windsor created an empire of larkspur, lupin, delphinium and sweet pea that was forever England.

Historians, who have sifted exhaustively through the political evidence of the abdication period, have been baffled and distressed by the years in the wilderness of their golden-haired boy King who, I discovered, put iodine on his locks to keep their colour.

Edward VIII's biographers have searched for an intellectual justification for the monarch to give up his throne, and have insisted on casting Wallis Simpson as a temptress and castigated her for filling an empty life with frivolity.

Yet all my evidence suggests that the style was the substance for the Duke and Duchess of Windsor, who both relished, as the French do, the minor arts of exquisite living, dressing, cooking, entertaining.

Although Wallis may have been briefly bored and frustrated in the 1950s and the middle decade of her own life, the Duke seemed a contented man – and never more so than when his kingdom had been reduced to a tiny self-sustaining world of chandeliered salon, an acre of green garden and Thou.

In their own words, the Duke and Duchess of Windsor give nothing away. The ghosted Windsor memoirs are polite, correct and passionless. Any friends in whom the Duke might have confided are dead and their secrets with them. None of the Duchess's companions in Paris or New York claim to have been *intime* with her. Even in widowhood, she did not discuss her life or make a considered judgement on an extraordinary story.

The conclusion must be that the Duke and Duchess of Windsor shared their innermost joys and disappointments only with each other or, as Grace, Countess of Dudley suggests, they wanted even 'to spare each other' from that unpeeling of the outer skin.

The recently published Wallis and Edward letters show a couple incapable of deep and coherent expression of their emotions.

But objects can sometimes speak louder than the banal and childish words in which the Duke expressed his historic love. The sensual jewels reveal in their rounded stones, torrid colours and animal shapes, a seam of passion. Beneath the stylish surface of the home that Wallis made for her King, we sense that the Duchess fulfilled a need in the Duke to be cherished and cosseted.

In the rows and rows of shoes and bags and clothes – 117 pairs of identical gossamer fine stockings – we can see a self-absorbed woman with a memory of growing up poor and a sense of duty about making the best of herself.

And it was with a sense of shock that I realized that the blue and silver salon, with its gold boxes, seals, family photographs, jade elephants and fine porcelain, was a mirror image, created quite unconsciously by Wallis, of the taste of her husband's beloved mother.

ACKNOWLEDGEMENTS

With especial gratitude to

MOHAMED AL-FAYED
For generous permission to research the Windsor archives in Paris and to reproduce pictures from the collection
THE BRITISH EMBASSY, PARIS: Sir John and Lady Fretwell, Diana Neill, M. James Viane
MICHAEL BLOCH
LE BARON ET BARONNE FRED DE CABROL
For generously allowing me access to their albums
The late LADY DIANA COOPER
CARTIER
For putting their archives at my disposal. In Paris: M. Alain Perrin, Mme Gilberte Gautier, M. Philippe Bessis *et tout particulièrement* Mme Betty Jais. In London: Anthony Marangos, Joseph Allgood, Caroline Neville, Teresa Boxford
CHRISTIAN DIOR: M. Marc Bohan, Mme Alexandra Tchernoff el Khoury, Mme Agnès Bertrand, M. Claude Laurent
GRACE, COUNTESS OF DUDLEY
GIVENCHY: M. Hubert de Givenchy
PAMELA, LADY HARLECH
HORST
For generously allowing me to use unpublished photographs of the Windsors
VALENTINE LAWFORD
For kind permission to publish extracts from his letters to his mother
MUSEE DU LOUVRE: M. Daniel Alcouffe
LAURA, DUCHESS OF MARLBOROUGH
METROPOLITAN MUSEUM, NY, Costume Institute: Jean Druesiedow, Katell le Bourhis
THE HON. LADY MOSLEY
NATIONAL PORTRAIT GALLERY: Terence Pepper
LA PRINCESSE DE POLIGNAC
LA VICOMTESSE DE RIBES
HOTEL RITZ, PARIS: M. Frank J. Klein
YVES SAINT LAURENT: M. Saint Laurent, Mme Gabrielle Buchaert, Mme Danielle Porthault
SEVRES, MUSEE NATIONAL DE CERAMIQUE: Mme Hallé, Conservateur
SOTHEBY
For kind permission to reproduce photographs of the Windsor jewels. In Geneva: Nicholas Rayner, Ines Schwarzenbach. In London: David Bennett, Fiona James; Lydia Cullen for Beaton archives; Kerry Taylor
VAN CLEEF & ARPELS
M. Jacques Arpels for permission to reproduce archive material and M. Canavy, *avec tout remerciements*
CHATEAU DE VERSAILLES: M. Daniel Meyer
HUGO VICKERS
For permission to reproduce from his archives

With my warmest gratitude also to the following in London, Paris, New York, and to those who have helped me anonymously:

ALEXANDRE DE PARIS: M. Alexandre, Mme Vigoreux; Jean Amory; PIERRE BALMAIN: M. Erik Mortensen; BBC TV: Martyn Gregory, Elaine Thomas; Janice Blackburn; Maître Suzanne Blum; Nino Caprioglio; CONDÉ NAST: Alex Kroll; COUNTRY LIFE: John Cornforth; Joanna Cummings; Mme Hebe Dorsey; M. Olivier Echaudmaison; Susan Farmer; Anne Goodchild; Gerald Grant; HAMILTONS GALLERY; Mme Nora Harper; HARPERS & QUEEN: Suzanne Von Langenberg; Nicholas Haslam; Sydney Johnson; Sandra Kaspar; M. Gerard Van der Kemp; Kenneth J. Lane; Lord Lichfield; LIFE: Gail Ridgwell; Mary Lou Luther; Patricia McColl; M. Gerard Mare; Hon. Rosamond Monckton; Lord Monckton of Brenchley; Michael Nash; Michael Parkin; M. Philippe du Pasquier; Countess of Romanones; Kenneth Rose; M. et Mme Georges Sanègre; Ingrid Seward; Oonagh Shanley-Toffolo; Mme Pierre Schlumberger; Anne Slater; VALENTINO: Valentino Garavani, Giancarlo Giammetti; Gordon Watson; M. Paul-Louis Weiller; HARRY WINSTON: Mr Laurence Krashes.

My grateful thanks also to:

Grafton Books, for all the help I have been given by my editor Richard Johnson, Anne Charvet, Janice Robertson and Marianne Taylor; to David Driver for his art direction, encouragement and understanding; to my agent Mike Shaw at Curtis Brown; to Rebecca Tyrrel at the office; to my three sons Gideon, Joshua and Samson; and most especially to my husband, David, for his unstinting support.

CHAPTER

—— 1 ——

AT HOME

*'If I am ugly, and I am, I am going to make everything around myself beautiful.
That will be my life. To create beauty! . . . And beautiful things are faithful
friends, and they stay beautiful, they become more beautiful as they get older. My
lovely house, my lovely garden – I could steal for beauty, I could kill for it.'*

ELSIE DE WOLFE, LADY MENDL
in LUDWIG BEMELMANS: *The One I Love the Best*

D INNER at the Windsors, Thursday, 17 October 1956. First there is a
rain-soaked drive through Paris streets; then a leafy avenue; a slate
roof breaking over the trees; iron gates decorated with gilded crowns;
a pillared mansion ahead.

Round the edge of the porticoed doorway comes a pair of disembodied
white gloves, followed by the scarlet and gold livery and ebony face of the
Bahamian servant, Sydney. We could be in America's Deep South, but for
the autumn rain dripping on the Bois de Boulogne. The 'Bwaa de Boollone'
the Duke of Windsor calls it in his Churchillian French.

The former King of England is standing in the doorway smiling his 'dentist
smile' as the cars arc round the gravel drive. A pair of footmen open car doors
with a twin flourish. The invitation is for 8.45 pm.

'The guests can wait for dinner, but my chef doesn't wait for the guests,'
the Duchess says.

The first sight of the grand entrance hall suggests, as the American Diana
Vreeland says, a much larger house. White arum lilies on the sweeping
staircase are banked up, up, up towards the exuberantly painted ceiling, a
great vault of puffy clouds and flying geese framed by an Italianate balustrade.
The Duchess favours decoration that deceives the eye.

Curly wrought-iron banisters circle the landing, from where the Duke and
Duchess will beckon friends into their upstairs boudoir on more intimate
occasions. Over the stairwell hangs a pennant, a dull red and gold remembrance of kingly things past. The silk brocade banner, once placed proudly
in St George's Chapel, Windsor, hovers over the Duke and his guests below.

The Duke of Windsor, at 62, is sprightly, 'very silken and natty and
well-arranged', as James Pope-Hennessy observes. Above the ink-blue dinner
jacket with its wide black satin lapels, the melancholy Hanoverian countenance
is illuminated by his welcoming smile.

The butler, Georges, correct in black tailcoat, asks guests to sign the visitors'
book. It lies open on the table, beside the red leather box the colour of fresh
blood, lettered in gold THE KING. Two French-farce maids, all starched white
collars and aprons, tangle with the pugs on their way upstairs with the coats.

What makes this sombre, spacious hall seem so exotic? Is it the towering
sunflowers on the gilded spread-eagle tables? Or the chinoiserie screen, its
miniature imperial figures echoing the red and grey-green servants' livery that

*Sydney Johnson in his dress uniform opens the
door of the Windsors' Paris mansion on to the
glowing entrance hall and the salon beyond.
With him, a Spanish footman, butler Georges
Sanègre and a posse of pugs.*

The porticoed front entrance and miniature park at 4 Route du Champ d'Entraînement in the Bois de Boulogne. The Duke of Windsor took the slate-roofed mansion over from General de Gaulle in 1953.

the Duke himself has designed? Or the limpid light from the glassed-in candles?

'The hall would glow, with pools of light and the white flowers,' says the Princesse de Polignac, an elegant and vivacious visitor to the Windsors' charmed circle.

'It was like going back to the eighteenth century,' says the American jewellery designer Kenneth J. Lane. 'The lights were out of eyesight and cast an extraordinary glow.'

'The Windsors spelled glamour,' says Grace, Lady Dudley, a true friend who was to accompany Wallis on the desolate journey to England for the Duke's funeral.

The elongated silver-blue salon, flanked by a small room at either end, is the heart of the house that the Duke and Duchess took over, by grace and favour of the French government, from General de Gaulle in 1953.

The sunlight pours in here all afternoon, dancing on the diamond-encrusted gold boxes, or pinpointing the jewels embedded in the silver frames with their portraits of Queen Alexandra, Queen Mary and the fresh-faced young Duke as Prince of Wales.

Every available surface is covered with a profusion of precious objects – daggers, seals, enamel, porcelain.

'The Duchess was not one for an empty space,' comments Joanne Cummings, widow of the American collector Nathan Cummings, who was to acquire so many of the Windsor treasures in the Duchess's twilight years.

'It manages to be chic and frightfully cosy,' said the decorator Fleur Cowles as she surveyed 'immense bouquets of forced spring blossoms' among the

objets d'art. 'Cozy', with its American spelling and sense of warm intimacy, is used also by the Countess of Romanones to describe the Windsors' home.

The Duke and Duchess at home with their favourite pugs: Trooper, Disraeli, Imp and Davy Crockett. 'We did have one called Peter Townsend,' says the Duchess. 'But we gave the Group Captain away.'

The curtains in the salon are gossamer light, a translucent bone white silk stippled with stylized roses. They are drawn tonight, but on summer evenings the French doors will be flung open on to the terrace for drinks and for dinner at the three round tables set with festive table cloths embroidered with bottles of champagne.

If this is your first visit to the Windsors, you will be offered now a glass of chilled champagne, a whisky (the Duke drinks only G & B), or a thimbleful of vodka. For the seasoned guest, your favoured drink has been noted by your hostess and is already at your elbow, presented by the footman on a silver tray that gleams in the candlelight. 'As though it had arrived from Cartier that morning,' says the Baron de Cabrol, one of the intimates of the Windsors' Paris set.

'It was the only household where the water in the vases was always crystal clear,' his wife says.

The flowers are magnificent, for the Duchess of Windsor understands the 'poetry of flowers', in the words of her faithful hairdresser Alexandre, who came today as her *coiffeur* comes every single day for 30 years, to dress her sleek, dark chignon. Upstairs, on the dressing table in her fondant pale bedroom, there are just three single carnations in an elegant vase. But here in the salon, the consoles and *guéridons* are heaped with pyramids of densely packed white lilies and orchids, plucked from the three hothouses at the end of the garden.

Cecil Beaton had described Wallis's exotic tastes when he visited her

13

'Come up to the boudoir,' the Duke and Duchess will call from the top of the curving staircase. The red and gold royal banner, showing the arms of the Prince of Wales, belonged to the Duke's grandfather Edward VII and hung at Windsor.

OPPOSITE: The imposing painted marble entrance hall is lit by candelabra. Dinner guests sign the book on the central table which holds the red leather despatch box marked 'THE KING'. On the landing is the Munnings portrait of the Prince of Wales on Forest Witch.

London home in 1936: the 'bleached olive' of the 'trailing ivy, intertwined with green orchids', offset by 'the mauve orchids and crimson roses . . . and the pink in Mrs Simpson's cheeks'. Wallis had 'discovered' the avant-garde florist Constance Spry, who created 'towering vases' of lily-of-the-valley and white peonies for the Windsors' wedding.

'Many orchids and white arums' recorded Sir Harold Nicolson in his diary when he visited the flat in Bryanston Court, near London's Marble Arch, where the Simpsons first entertained the Prince.

If you look carefully at the flowers tonight, you will see that, as the frosty blue and silver salon gives way to the golden yellow library at one end, the bouquets of white lilies are interleaved with ivory yellow cattleyas. At the other end, bronze petals stud the vases towards the blue and coral dining

room. This is a skill that the Duchess and her friend and mentor Lady Mendl learned from Stéphane Boudin, President of the Paris decorating firm of Jansen and the man responsible for the silver tasselled walls, the painted *boiserie* and the Louis Seize furniture.

'It's terribly, terribly Elsie de Wolfe,' claims the author Hugo Vickers of the Duchess of Windsor's decorative house in the Bois. Elsie de Wolfe, who married the British Embassy's press attaché Charles Mendl, was an American actress-turned-decorator who weaned American society hostesses in the 1920s from heavy Victorian drapes and introduced them to the pale elegance of French eighteenth-century furnishings.

'Lady Mendl taught the Duchess everything she knew,' agrees Paul-Louis Weiller, the Airforce Commandant and wealthy industrialist who leased to the Windsors a house in the rue de la Faisanderie.

'Go on! Buy it! It might come in useful someday,' Lady Mendl would urge if Wallis hesitated over a furnishing purchase.

'Elsie naturally had wonderful taste,' says Diana Vreeland. 'But what Elsie Mendl had was something else that's particularly American – an appreciation of vulgarity. Vulgarity is a very important ingredient in life . . . a little bad taste is like a nice splash of paprika.'

After a formative year in Paris attending Elsie Mendl's lavish parties at her house near Versailles, the Duchess complained to young Nicholas Lawford, Third Secretary at the British Embassy, that the classical furniture the Duke had brought with him into exile was 'too masculine'.

'French furniture is more elegant, don't you think?' she said.

At the house in Neuilly, her Petit Trianon furnishings, the Louis Seize chairs with their spindly legs, rounded backs and plump embroidered seats (that she will leave on her death to the Palace of Versailles) contrast artfully with grand English portraits.

The long main wall facing the garden is dominated by a formal painting of Queen Mary in her Garter robes, staring out at the salon she never visited and her son's wife whom she did not choose to meet. 'I send a kind message to your wife' was the warmest response, in a letter to the Duke from an indomitable Queen.

On the other long wall is the Duke as Prince of Wales in his robes of the Garter – a pantomime rig of white hose and velvet cloak bestowed on him in 1911 at the age of 16. In the 1960s, on a sudden whim, the Duke will try on the robes again at their country house, shouting 'Look, it still fits me like a glove,' as he cavorts across the garden of the Mill.

Beneath this portrait of a Prince born to be King, sits Wallis – although no-one this evening will address her as anything but Duchess. The Duke will say 'Her Royal Highness', and speak to her as 'darling' and 'sweetheart'. 'They called each other "darling" a great deal,' noted Nicolson.

The Duchess of Windsor looks formidably frail as she sits, straight-backed, against the shell-patterned cushions, her legs tucked at right angles to the silk *canapé*. 'She does not curl up, but somehow dismantles herself, so that she looks like a puppet lying in the wings of a toy theatre,' observes James Pope-Hennessy.

Her ink-blue faille dress is short and chic.

'She invented the fashion for the short evening dress. She made it smart,' Diana Vreeland says.

'She had good legs and she wanted to show them off,' says Ghislaine de Polignac.

The dress is a Dior, cut in a spiral on the bias 'in that subtle way of haute couture,' as Grace Dudley describes it. Her wrists are stick thin and as pale and translucent as the barrel of the carved jade gun on the grand piano by the window. Round one wrist is a heavy bracelet, curving like a snail shell and set with rubies, sapphires and emeralds. Her eyes are sapphire blue. 'So very large and pale and veined,' says Pope-Hennessy.

'She had oil-drilling eyes. They went right through you,' says Anne Slater, whose mother-in-law Martha played hostess to the Windsors in her Long Island mansion every Easter.

Those eyes, mesmeric and compelling, beam out from the portrait by Gerald Brockhurst that is hung over the mantelpiece in the library, and took pride of place in Government House in the Bahamas during the Duke's wartime stewardship. It may have been true, when Cecil Beaton saw it in 1939, that it was *nothing* like her'. Like dog and master, the Duchess has grown to resemble her portrait.

Beside her on the *canapé* are Trooper and Disraeli, one sleek and shiny as a rat, both pale beige. The Duchess is so fastidious that her sheets have to be taken off the bed and freshly ironed each night. ('Her Royal Highness would never think of having a wrinkle on her bed,' say her maids.) Yet she is indulgent to the dogs, who run wild before dinner, like children brought down from the nursery to show themselves off. They nuzzle and nestle and snuffle around the salon, leaning their heavy weight against the legs of the dinner guests. Outside on the manicured lawn, the Duchess will watch her dogs dine off solid silver bowls.

'I always sit here,' says the Duchess, 'to protect them.' She is referring to the litter of priceless porcelain pugs on the red lacquer *commode* behind her – one of an antique pair of chests that will also end up, without the pugs, in the Palace of Versailles. Portraits of her darling pugs are hung in gilded oval frames on the library walls in the Petit Salon next door: Disraeli on an orange cushion, Trooper on blue velvet and Diamond rampant. On one of the fantastically decorated gold boxes displayed in the salon is a miniature enamelled picture of Madame de Pompadour's pet spaniel, cushioned on red velvet.

The Windsor pugs are enshrined in paintings, photographs, porcelain and sculptures all over the house.

'Those dogs were substitute children,' says Joanne Cummings. 'They ran about all the time, I wonder if the Duke and Duchess ever went to other people's homes where dogs behaved like that.'

Nancy Spain watched the Duke and Duchess comfort Trooper when noisy peals of laughter scared him. 'And both of them bent down to whisper in his ears just as though they were speaking to a well-loved child,' she says.

'Naughty boy,' Wallis will scold Disraeli as he scrambles over the silken sofa.

The dogs are part of the private language King Edward VIII used in his love letters.

'The Babies send you eaunum flowers,' he wrote in September 1936.

'A pat to Slippy Poo,' begged Wallis for her cairn terrier Slipper, nicknamed Mr Loo, which the Prince of Wales gave her for Christmas 1934.

'He sends you a million of dog kisses and thanks you for the pat you sent him,' replied the Duke.

Slipper was killed by a snake bite at the Château de Candé, in France, where Wallis and her David – the family's name for him – were married.

'He was our dog – not yours or mine but ours. Now the principal guest at the Wedding is no more,' wrote an anguished Wallis. A diamond-encrusted

Caught in a shaft of sunlight is the Duke's mother, Queen Mary, painted by Sir William Llewellyn in robes of the Order of the Garter. At night, wax candles at eye level, and an upper tier of electric candelabra, cast a warm glow. In the foreground, a sculpted pug on a Louis XVI two-tier table.

slipper, embedded in a medallion inscribed 'Our Mr Loo', commemorated the dog's death. The only trace of their occupation of a Riviera villa which they rented is a grave marked 'Preezie, A faithful Little Friend of Edward and Wallis, Duke and Duchess of Winsor, 1938-1949.' When the Windsors sold up their country house, the Mill, they insisted on a clause protecting the graves of their dogs.

The Duchess has not grown to look like her dogs. Her head is large above a bird-like body. She looks both older and more lively than photographs suggest. The frown that cleaves her forehead ('as though she'd been hit by an axe' says Anne Slater), is removed in pictures by a retoucher's skills.

'We couldn't afford the best photographer – they are so dear,' complained Wallis to her American aunt Bessie Merryman in 1931, when she was still plain Mrs Simpson and longing to record her presentation at Court.

Even the great society photographer Cecil Beaton could not capture the

mobility of her face, with its 'great giglamp smile', in James Pope-Hennessy's telling phrase. She is smiling, laughing, pulling droll faces as she puts at his ease a young man of only 21 visiting the Windsors for the first time. The Duke and Duchess both draw energy from the company of youth.

'I can't stand people my age. Old people like me are such bores,' says the Duchess.

'You are so lucky to have children,' she says wistfully to her friend Lady Mosley. 'They bring young people into the house.'

The Duchess's laugh, harsh, slightly vulgar but very infectious, reverberates though the room. 'She did not have a nice smile or a nice laugh and she laughed at her own jokes,' Lady Dudley admits.

Cecil Beaton described 'the sudden explosion of her broad firework laughter'.

'Her gaiety is contagious,' he said.

The Windsors and their brood of pugs near the entrance to the library. Arranged on the marble top of a red lacquer Louis XV commode, decorated with birds and flowers, is the collection of Meissen pugs. 'I always sit here,' says the Duchess, 'to protect them.'

Cole Porter will tinkle on the piano in this corner of the salon. A pair of Louis XVI chairs with medallions of Chinese silk embroidery flank a table with a photograph of the Duke in his investiture robes as Prince of Wales. 'What would my Navy friends say if they saw me in this preposterous rig?' he asked.

A long view of the silver blue salon looking towards the dining room. The chandelier and Louis XVI furnishings are French château style. The two-tier central table decorated with gilded bronze was donated by the Duchess to the Palace of Versailles. The carpet is woven with a Prince of Wales feather motif.

She is at her most lively and charming at this cocktail hour – as she was when Mrs Simpson in London invited friends round for what she then called in popular American slang 'KT's'. 'We have yet to have a dinner,' she wrote to her aunt Bessie Merryman in November 1933. 'I have however had people for KT's quite often.'

The ex-King is solicitous of his guests, turning his pale blue eyes round the room. He no longer 'prepares the potions with his own poor hands' as he used to for Duff and Lady Diana Cooper at Fort Belvedere, his English hideaway on the Windsor estate. 'He was always doing the waiting, although one didn't know why,' said Lady Diana. 'He once gave me some wine, and she flew at him saying, "You can't give Graves – it's the commonest wine in the world." She had very high standards.'

Now only at the Mill, the Windsors' tumble of stone houses and barns in the Chevreuse valley outside Paris, will you see the Duke of Windsor role-playing host, passing the potted shrimps and the cucumber sandwiches as the Duchess presides, more uncomfortably than the Mad Hatter in *Alice in Wonderland*, over a large teapot.

The Duchess is crumbling one small dry cocktail biscuit, discreetly laid out on a porcelain plate, while her guests dip into the domed silver dish, 'like a lottery drum', says Erik Mortensen, friend, protégé and now design director of Pierre Balmain, the Paris fashion house.

The guests exclaim over the latest délice and delight – tiny bacon pieces frizzled with brown sugar, a recipe brought back from the Bahamas that makes Count Nicholas Palavacini wet his lips at the memory.

'A variety of fastidiously presented hors d'oeuvres, grapes stuffed with cream cheese, diminutive chipolatas . . . appears and disappears as quickly as the banquet in *Scheherazade*,' said Cecil Beaton of Wallis Simpson's entertaining.

'It was not at all French to have the cocktail food,' says the Vicomtesse de Ribes, who was taken up in her early twenties by the Windsors. 'In France you are expected to save yourself for dinner.'

You can spoil your appetite tonight on mouthwatering puffballs of cheese, fried mussels, an aromatic dip for freshly peeled prawns that are offered stuck like a pink-quilled porcupine in a green cabbage.

'She cared a lot about the colour of her food,' says Nicholas Lawford, who visited the Windsors after his Embassy days with his friend the photographer Horst.

'Chefs are curiously colour-blind,' warned the Duchess when giving hints on entertaining. 'Leave them to their own devices and you may end up with an all-rose dinner – Crème Portugaise, Saumon Poché with Sauce Cardinal, Jambon with Sauce Hongroise and Bombe Marie-Louise.'

The Duke stabs a silver spoon into a bowl of caviare.

'Take a big spoonful. It's only good when there's a lot of it,' he says to Fred de Cabrol.

'Son Altesse Royale est servie,' announces Georges in the formal French style at precisely 9.15 pm.

There is a faint *frisson* among the guests at those three words: 'Her (gasp) Royal (shudder) Highness (and not one eye dared meet the other),' said Harold Nicolson. Although the Duke's brother, the new King George VI, had refused to give Wallis royal rank, the Duke insisted that his staff treated her with due respect.

'I curtsied to the Duke and then kissed him hello,' says Aline de Romanones, an American married to a Spanish Count. 'I did not curtsey to the Duchess. I never did . . . I was too American at the beginning, and then it became a habit not to.'

Wallis is queen of her dining room. Sydney Johnson, the Duke's valet, who doubles as a footman at formal dinners, has watched her slip downstairs after her bath, a slight figure lapped in a brief towelling bathrobe, to survey her domain.

The decoration is a very personal combination of French grandeur, Southern comfort and Eastern exotic. The room is small – even by the standards of her grandmother's neat Victorian house in her childhood in Maryland, or the apartment house in Baltimore where Wallis Warfield's vivacious mother would take in paying guests for dinner and feed them far too well on 'terrapin, squab, prime sirloin steaks and soft shell crabs'. Her daughter has inherited this luxurious extravagance.

'Why does the Duchess spend so much money?' The Duke asked her aunt, Mrs Bessie Merryman.

'Well Sir, you spoil her so,' came the reply.

The dining room in Neuilly is a deep blue, the colour of Chinese *cloisonné*. Its walls are decorated with chinoiserie panels taken from a château at Chanteloup and depicting the willow pattern world of hanging gardens, arched bridges, watery vistas and latticed pavilions. It stirs in Wallis memories of Peking and a temple 'with a tiled roof of many colours and vermilion eaves from which hung tiny bells that tinkled in the wind'. After separating from her first naval officer husband, Wallis had spent a 'lotus year' in China which left an indelible impression.

An exotic eastern theme is impressed on her French mansion, with its lacquered chests, screens, jade elephants and oriental treasures. 'And leopard print cushions,' says Erik Mortensen.

The architect of the dining room is trim, moustachioed Monsieur Boudin, who accompanies the Duchess on forays for furnishings. Wallis will recall in her memoirs the pleasure of these 'endless afternoons given to combing the antique shops and the art galleries of the Left Bank, picking up here a piece of Sèvres or Meissen for a table or a *vitrine* . . .'

'He was her accomplice,' says Alexandre of the dapper interior decorator who always managed to find to hand (and at a price) the treasures to realize his clients' dreams.

Stéphane Boudin worked in the French classical style and became a favourite society decorator in the 1930s – especially for sophisticated Americans in Europe.

'It will be a symphony in blue and silver,' said Sir Henry 'Chips' Channon of the new dining room which Boudin designed for the Channons' London home, and where King Edward VIII dined on the night he told his brother that he would marry Wallis Simpson.

'My Duchess,' Boudin would say self-importantly to Grace Dudley, once he had been taken up by the Windsors. He had established the same relationship as showman-cum-salesman with another ex-patriate American – Lady Baillie at Leeds Castle in England. The 'Boudin weekends', when a three-ton truck would arrive at Leeds Castle laden with antiques, resulted in a bedroom with bright blue *boiserie* and Louis Seize furnishings very like this Windsor dining room.

For his Duchess, Boudin has orchestrated deep blue panelling (scrubbed with a wire brush, glazed and the colour rubbed in dry). He has painted the

ABOVE: *These oval portraits of the Meissen pugs in Louis XIII gilded frames are matched by three more pictures of the Duchess's own dogs. The entire set is hung in the petit salon.*

RIGHT: *Each pug has a solid silver bowl and the Duchess feeds them herself on the lawns of their Paris home.*

ceiling in his favourite *trompe l'oeil* with trailing ribbons and flowers. A washed Chinese carpet in glowing silken coral reflects the fanciful lacquer clock and oriental ornaments.

Two tiny *loges* ('like the film of *Les Enfants du Paradis*,' says Diana Vreeland) are built into the upper corners of the walls. The Duke's velvet cloak (his own design) and his pale kid gloves are thrown over the side for effect. For one special dinner party, the 'opera boxes' will be filled with an entire orchestra of monkeys, copied in balsa wood from the Meissen originals.

It is a world away from the harsh glaze covering a French pastoral wallpaper that Wallis Simpson tried in an earlier decorating experiment. That was when she was entertaining her Prince in London at Bryanston Court, where the white leather-seated chairs were designed by the fashionable thirties decorator Syrie Maugham, wife of the novelist. The dining table then was mirror-topped.

'It contributes to the gaiety of meals,' Wallis said.

You are sitting now at one of two round tables of eight, for the Duke and Duchess prefer intimate dinners to large ones. They are set with fine linen table cloths, embroidered with delicate birds' nests in an exact copy of the lattice of twigs and upturned beaks of the Sèvres porcelain at the table centres.

In the laundry room next to the staff quarters on the top floor of the house

24

are drawers of table cloths, each matching a dinner service, embroidered by Madame Porthault of the renowned French linen house.

'The Duchess got all the linen out herself, rather than expecting the *lingère* to do it,' Grace Dudley recalls. 'She relished the feminine arts.'

'It was an awful lot of ironing, and everything washed by hand,' says her maid.

The Duke and Duchess of Windsor each host a table, and it is a mark of honour that Humbert des Lyons de Feuchin, a young French aristocrat on his first visit, is seated on the right of his hostess. On the Duke's left is the Baronne de Cabrol with her cool aristocratic profile, a lineage that can be traced back further than that of the Hanoverian Kings of England, and one of the few in the Windsors' Paris set to come, as Lady Mosley puts it, from '*le gratin*' – France's upper crust. Alone of this circle, Fred and Daisy Cabrol will be invited to pay their last respects to the Duchess when her slight body is laid out on her bed upstairs in April 1986.

Cole Porter, on one of his trips to Europe, is a guest from the entertainment world who can combat the quick wit of the hostess. Sheet music of his haunting songs 'I've Got You Under My Skin' and 'Let's Do It', is propped up on the piano in the salon.

ABOVE: *The pugs are displayed in family snapshots throughout the Windsors' home.*

TOP: *A pair of eighteenth-century Meissen pugs. The male, with rose pink collar, turns to look at the female and her young. The Duchess gave the sculptures to France's National Ceramic Museum at Sèvres.*

LEFT: *The Duke, spectacles in his hand, plays with his favourite pug. 'Just as if he were speaking to a well-loved child,' says a guest.*

ABOVE: *One of the pair of musicians' galleries, lit by ostrich-egg candelabra and set in the corner of the dragged blue panelled walls. In the mirrored alcove: a Vigier clock on an Italian gilded red console table.*

TOP: *Far pavilions and hanging gardens are painted on panels taken from the Château de Chanteloup and installed in the dining room by the decorator Stéphane Boudin of Jansen.*

On his right is Mona Bismarck, her feline face and emerald eyes above three rows of globular pearls. Her fabulous collection of jewels will be sold up at Sotheby's saleroom in Geneva in the spring of 1986, just one year ahead of the Duchess's collection.

A Windsor dinner may carry echoes of the Duke's former life: Sir Oswald Mosley or the ex-King's cousin and friend Lord Louis Mountbatten. His clumsy attempt to wheedle a royal inheritance out of the bereaved Wallis immediately after the Duke's death in 1972 will cause a spectacular fall-out. 'He wanted me to make out a will right there and then, giving everything to the Duke's family and, of course, some to himself,' the distraught and confused Duchess will tell Aline de Romanones.

Her husband Luis listens politely while the Duke practises his Spanish. Next to the Count of Romanones is the young Vicomtesse de Ribes, with her proud Nefertiti profile and upswept chignon. Years later, when the Duke is back at home in an English garden in the mausoleum at Frogmore, Jacqueline de Ribes will set up as a designer of elegant Parisian dresses.

There are no flowers on the tables, only porcelain and the Duke's 'truly magnificent collection of old silver' that Wallis had first seen tumbling out of crates on the lawns of the Villa la Croë, that the Windsors had rented in the South of France.

'The table was always simply covered with things – little gold boxes, cigarette boxes, candelabra in *vermeil* – silver gilt – so much so that you could

26

The exotic dining room with its cloisonné blue silk curtains, the Chinese panels and coral silk carpet. The chairs are in dragged aquamarine wood with white damask seats. Three Meissen pots in the 'Flying Tiger' pattern are mirrored on the black marble-topped table. For her dinner parties the Duchess installs three round tables for eight.

hardly see the table cloth,' says Jacqueline de Ribes. 'And it was all laid English style with the wine glasses at the side and so much cutlery you never knew what to pick up.'

The dinner service tonight is royal porcelain: a William IV pattern with gilded embossed oak leaves and the Royal Arms. Below stairs, stacked in the institutional cream cupboards beside the servants' hall, is more ancestral china – the eighteenth-century Copenhagen sérvice from the Duke's Danish grandmother Queen Alexandra; George IV's Lowestoft and the fabulous Meissen 'Flying Tiger' that once belonged to the Elector Frederick August II of Saxony, King of Poland.

'Not those old people,' Wallis would complain across the tables when she heard the Duke discussing his royal past.

The Duchess's own taste in porcelain is for nature run riot. She has collected dishes lapped with china leaves, her sculpted pugs, prancing lions or whimsical birds of paradise. There are candlesticks shaped as proud cockerels, and the magnificent covered soup terrine has a surface crawling with finely sculpted insects and whorls of snail shells that match the Duchess's striking shell earrings.

The most sensual and intimate of the porcelains are the twisted monkey sculptures found in the apricot boudoir that separates the first-floor bedrooms of the Duke and Duchess.

There the Duke will watch football on television while the Duchess leafs through saleroom catalogues; and in their declining years they will spend more quarrelsome evenings over a bottle of whisky.

'They had nothing and no-one. They were just two lonely old people,' says Sydney.

Dîner

Mousse de Homard Froide
Concombres à la crème

Perdreau rôti sur canapé
Bread sauce
Riz sauvage aux petits pois
Céléris branches au beurre

Salade mâches et betteraves

Bombe glacée aux fraises

Petits gâteaux

Savoury hollandaise

TOP: *From the Duchess of Windsor's collection of fine china: a 1740 Meissen flowered plateau and terrine, the knob on its lid a child pouring from a horn of plenty.*

CENTRE: *Delicate table linen embroidered with the Duke's royal crowns and crests.*

BELOW: *A pair of early nineteenth-century Meissen baskets in decorative white porcelain.*

The first course at a Windsor dinner is never soup.

'After all those cocktails, it's just another drink,' says the Duchess.

The lobster mousse is delicious. The six different kinds of bread make a conversation piece. There are rolls plain, seeded or flavoured with cumin in silver lattice baskets; toasts, breadsticks and Ryvita in solid English silver dishes; in an elegant silver gilt basket is a hot, crusty baguette. In front of each guest stands an individual Sèvres butter pot and porcelain-handled knife.

'A little surprise for my guests,' says the Duchess as she lifts a lid.

Surprise is an essential ingredient at her dinners.

The historic dinner services stacked downstairs on the kitchen table: eighteenth-century Copenhagen from Queen Alexandra; George IV's Lowestoft with crown and cypher; William IV's Lowestoft with the Royal Arms and gold oak leaves; Meissen 'Flying Tiger' plate made for Elector Frederick Augustus II of Saxony, King of Poland. Nineteenth-century Meissen baskets filled with painted fruit, candlesticks and table centres.

'It wasn't just good food, it was always amusingly prepared,' says Ghislaine de Polignac. 'The Duchess would make us dishes from Maryland, chicken with tiny corns and bananas, or English grouse with gravy in a silver boat and breadcrumbs.'

'She served very good fish and birds, birds, birds,' says Lady Dudley.

Tonight's dinner is a succulent mix by chef Lucien Massey of fine French cooking and the English tradition. Instead of the lobster mousse and game with bread sauce, you might have had a tender faux filet served with a feather-light Yorkshire pudding; or marble-sized new potatoes stuffed with melted butter and caviare; or the Princesse de Polignac's favourite, roast beef sliced and interleaved with foie gras.

Or perhaps there will be exotic recipes discovered by the Duchess during her days in China and the Bahamas, or delicacies from her native Deep South.

'The cooking from Maryland and Carolina is exquisite, rich, spicy, done almost entirely by the negroes, who have a special skill in preparing the most aromatic dishes,' Wallis explained to the readers of French *Vogue*.

Her very first dinner party for her Prince had been a Southern Belle's offering: 'black bean soup, grilled lobster, fried chicken Maryland, for the sweet a cold raspberry soufflé, and . . . a savoury of marrow bones.'

The young Prince of Wales had also tried his hand at a savoury – serving up tadpoles fished out from a pond on toast as a trick on his French tutor, who had expressed a liking for frogs' legs.

The staff glide through the door under the musicians' box in the right-hand corner. There are two servants at each table.

'The secret of all this smooth perfection . . . was the system of having the equivalent of a man and a half for every job,' the Duke said of his father's royal household.

Behind the servants' door is a pantry. But the dishes are all prepared in the large, workmanlike kitchen exactly below this exotic dining room. On the kitchen table, above the blue and white tiled floor, the sous chef is sorting out the salade mâches – lamb's lettuce – into leaves of exactly the same size, on the orders of the perfectionist Duchess.

'Do all American women insist on having their meat and fish in matching sizes?' asked a bewildered British poulterer after searching for half a dozen identical birds.

'I had my own fixed ideas about food,' Wallis admits.

The second kitchen boy might be running from the kitchen to the pantry with its two catering-size cold stores to fetch the Camembert ice cream, one of the most famous of the Windsor savouries that are served, English style, at the end of the meal with port. 'They never served cheese,' says Jacqueline de Ribes. 'I never saw one piece of it in their house.'

'She took out the flesh of the Camembert and mixed it with cream and other cheeses,' says Daisy Cabrol. 'Then it was reformed, with breadcrumbs coating the outside, and frozen, then served with a hot crusty outside and the icy inside. I never did get the precise recipe.'

Like any renowned hostess, Wallis is not eager to part with her culinary secrets, although in earlier days she had begged Aunt Bessie for recipes of 'entrées and egg dishes especially'.

When the Duchess asked the Baronne de Rothschild for her recipe for *chaud-froid de poulet*, the reply was gracious but firm: 'Madame . . . I cannot go so far as to cut off my arm. Yet without my hand, the receipt is useless, even to the most eminent chef.'

The Duke is taking a second helping of the roast partridge that his father, King George V, used to shoot in their thousands on the royal Sandringham estate. He has had nothing to eat since breakfast, apart from two cups of china tea at the golf course, freshly brewed, and a bowl of stewed plums.

'I married the Duke for better and for worse, but not for lunch,' is one of Wallis's favourite quips.

All his life the Duke retains his nursery passion for stewed fruit. When his cancerous throat is so painful that eating is a major effort, he will whisper a request for a cooked peach on the night he dies in his bedroom upstairs in May 1972.

The Duchess's table gusts with laughter. Her legendary wit is hard to pinion and often as flat as a fallen soufflé in repetition.

It is like a good rally at tennis,' said Cole Porter. 'She always returns the ball.'

'Wallis's wit was rebarbative,' says Joanne Cummings. 'It depended a lot on pace and timing.'

'She was *quick*, which after all is part of cleverness,' says Lady Mosley.

Wallis inherited her sharp Warfield wit from her lively mother, who, when asked why her second marriage to John Freeman Raisin had produced no children, quipped that he was a 'seedless raisin'.

The Duke is not 'heir conditioned', the Duchess replied to a similar question. Wallis is not above repeating her own *bon mot*.

'Oh, Sir, that would be too much of a Wallis collection,' said Mrs Simpson winsomely in face of the King's desire to order all of Cecil Beaton's photographs – the same pictures that crowd the desk top and occasional tables in the Duke's bedroom today.

Five years before, she had sent Aunt Bessie 'two poses of me alone to add to the Wallis collection'.

'What a pity it isn't in the Wallis collection,' says the Duchess 30 years later when Pierre Schlumberger showed her a Louis Seize table that matched her own.

Her wit is sharp, crisp, delivered in the rasping Baltimore drawl with a comedienne's timing.

'I just love your pansies,' said a guest at the Moulin de la Tuilerie, looking at the Duke's herbaceous borders.

'In the garden or at my table?' replied the Duchess.

When another guest surveyed the two dining tables at the Mill smothered with yellow pansies and repeated the joke to the Duke, there was only a frosty, regal stare.

The Duchess is giving intimate attention to her elderly neighbour. 'She was always charming with older men. She was a Southerner with very good manners,' Grace, Lady Dudley says.

'I remember . . . the extraordinary gift she had, so pleasing to men, in that she immediately found out what one's interests were, and they were immediately hers for the next ten minutes,' said Lord Monckton of Brenchley, son of Sir Walter Monckton who steered the Duke through the Abdication crisis.

'Wallis,' the Prince of Wales had said, 'you're the only woman who's ever been interested in my job.'

She is keeping half an eye on the Duke. 'She was very tender and thoughtful when the Duke's eyes started to give him trouble,' says couturier Hubert de Givenchy. 'She would get up at dinner and move the candles in case the light was hurting his eyes.'

RIGHT: *The Duchess of Windsor and her dogs by the window in the library. The brocaded sofa was designed by Wallis, its red velvet embroidered cushion made from a cardinal's cape.*

BELOW: *Butler Georges Sanègre, who was with the Duchess to the end, beneath her portrait and beside the elephant clock on the mantelshelf.*

'The Duke would ask for the candles at a dinner to be moved so he could see her all the time,' says Laura, Duchess of Marlborough, the former wife of Lord Dudley. 'He was mesmerized by her.'

When the Duchess is at one end of a long table for 16, she will pause briefly in mid-anecdote to find a word or a name of lady so-and-so that the Duke is missing.

'They had such close antennae, and you could sense it,' says Erik Mortensen.

Before they were married, Wallis had confessed to Honor Channon that she 'always kicks him under the table, hard when to stop and gently when to go on. Sometimes she is too far away and then it is difficult.'

Another wary eye is on the staff.

'She was dignified as a hostess, never sending messages to the kitchen,' says Diana Vreeland. 'But she was very proud of her chef and she would say "none of you have mentioned my asparagus soufflé. Isn't it the best thing you have ever had."'

Downstairs in the servants' hall, beside the zinc tubs where the pugs are washed and groomed, the staff are putting away the china – a ring of felt between each ancestral plate. There are 18 indoor staff, including young Georges Sanègre, who, with his wife Ofélia, will nurse the Duchess and her treasures to the end.

The chef, Lucien, has his assistant chef, two kitchen boys and a pastry cook, who has to make the Duke's favourite Sacher torte, oozing with apricot jam under the dark chocolate, or the crunchy ginger biscuits that the Duchess lays out in her guest rooms.

One of the kitchen boys, James Viane, who went on to become chef of the

The library or petit salon, lined with books and
dominated by the compelling portrait of the
Duchess painted by Gerald Brockhurst in 1939.
On the red marbled chimneypiece are a pair of
flamboyant cockerel candelabra and a Louis XV
elephant clock. In the foreground, an antique
lacquered wood chair covered in sunshine yellow
velvet, matching the brocade sofa. At the far
angle, an ebony Louis XVI corner piece.

33

British Embassy in Paris, remembers the rigid hierarchy of the kitchen when he was the *commis* chef and allotted the task of cleaning the massive silver in the underground strong room.

The pecking order in the kitchen is matched in the housekeeper's domain, where the *lingère*, Anna, has four housemaids who are quite separate from the Duchess's two personal maids, just as the butler has his underman and two footmen, and the Duke his valet and secretary. Tonight, the footmen are two nervous young Spanish boys, sent to the Windsors from the estate of the Countess of Romanones.

As Wallis Simpson, struggling through the Depression on tightened purse strings, she filled her letters to her aunt with the hiring and firing of domestics.

'Am in such a gale over domestics – you know how I go to pieces,' she wrote to Mrs Merryman in 1931. 'As for cooks, it's too awful – and wages are going up each day.'

The Duke, contemplating his large household, or complaining about the staff bills, knows that when he was Prince of Wales the cavernous royal kitchen at Windsor Castle 'kept sixty souls busily employed'.

Dinner is over.

'Now don't stay chatting too long, David,' says Wallis as she leads the ladies out.

She is not always so gentle, and her occasional acid comments to her husband can embarrass guests.

'Come on, David, it's time for bed,' she says reprovingly when they are at a party in New York.

'She said it like a nanny,' said Nicholas Lawford.

'She was like a governess,' says Horst.

Lady Mosley saw a different side to Wallis: 'I can't explain enough how courteous the Duchess was to the Duke,' she says. 'She never took the smallest liberty but always treated him in public, among friends, as *King*.'

You never forgot, at a Windsor dinner, that this was a King, and especially not at this moment over the port. Just as his father George V had done before him, the Duke talks power politics and finance, puffing on his cigar. (Wallis, as Mrs Simpson, had scandalized society at the opera by making the Prince take his cigar out of his breast pocket, with the nanny-like reproof: 'It doesn't look very pretty.')

'You must always remember your position and who you are,' the rigid, authoritarian George V said to his son.

'You realize,' said the Duke of Windsor to James Pope-Hennessy, 'that there are only three completely royal persons alive now. My sister, my brother and myself.' By the absolute standards of monarchy, even the Duke's niece, Queen Elizabeth II, had her royal blood diluted because her mother was originally a 'commoner' rather than a royal Princess.

The port is passed among the gentlemen. A glass of G & B has been brought in discreetly on a silver tray and placed beside the Duke. His conversational style is royal male: a salvo of questions fired out; a long discourse on politics by himself; a silent response to another point of view, occasionally punctuated by 'That's quite right! Absolutely true.'

'He is not a *thinker*. He takes his ideas from the daily press instead of thinking things out for himself,' King Edward VIII's Prime Minister Stanley Baldwin said. 'He never reads – except, of course, the papers. No serious reading: none at all.'

Nicholas Lawford, working at the British Embassy in Paris in 1938, described to his mother a musical evening at Lady Mendl's when the male members of the party were 'being held forth to by the Duke of Windsor.'

'HRH was in a marvellous mood and made me come and sit beside him and tell him every detail of my (rather humdrum) life. Thus:
' "Were you at Oxford?
' "How old are you?
' "Is this your first post?
' "Where were you at school? . . . Good old school.
' "What's your second language?
' "Where did you learn German?"

'I've never been so cross-examined in my life, but it was all done very quickly, and he certainly has a sort of charm.'

'There wasn't much conversation,' says the Baron de Cabrol. 'The Duke didn't talk about much. He wasn't an intellectual. He used to talk to me about gardening.'

Golf and business were the other topics that filled the ex-King's life. In his green marbled bathroom, where the Duke always takes a shower, the tub is lidded with a wooden slab, its surface piled higgledy piggledy with financial papers. 'It was piled with papers, papers . . . papers PAPERS!' says Diana Vreeland. 'Bills, little things to do with golf.'

'This happens to be *my* bathroom, and that happens to be *my* table,' she heard the Duke say to his meticulously tidy wife. But when the pile of yellowing newspapers threatens to overwhelm him, the Duchess quietly destroys them.

The 'noospapers', the Duke says, with an American inflection.

'Hallo! It's the Dook here,' he will announce on the telephone.

You are in the downstairs cloakroom to the right of the entrance doors. The taps on the capacious marble basin are gilded swans. When the Duke and Duchess first set up residence at La Croë, their rented house near Antibes, the gilded bathtub in the shape of a double-headed swan caught the imagination of the public. The sybaritic lifestyle of the exiled Windsors is now expressed by the paper in the lavatory, which has been unrolled and cut into prepared squares by the staff. The washstand holds a phalanx of fine linen hand towels, each embroidered with the W & E insignia.

'God bless WE,' the King wrote to Wallis.

The ivory candles in the hall are burning low. In the leaping shadows it is easy to imagine the towering Christmas tree that will soon stand in the corner of the hall.

'On Christmas day, their Royal Highnesses would always be alone, just with us and our families,' says Sydney Johnson. 'And the dogs would be running around getting presents too.'

It is an attempt to recreate the annual Christmas festivities at Sandringham, where the royal clan would gather round the tree with its shimmering candles, tinsel and glass baubles. Outside in the stable yard 300 servants – 'the gamekeepers, gardeners, foresters and stable hands' – lined up to receive the royal bounty.

The Duchess of Windsor chooses the presents for the staff, just as she did when she was the King's favourite.

'I have just completed the shopping for HRH, 165 presents for staff and this weekend have been busy wrapping them up,' Wallis wrote to Aunt Bessie in December 1935.

'She was kind to us,' says former kitchen boy James Viane. 'She brought

A 'Wallis collection' of portraits surround the Duke of Windsor as he sits at the table at the foot of his bed.

ABOVE: *A sketched portrait of the Duke.*

OPPOSITE: *Honi soit qui mal y pense – evil be to him who evil thinks – the motto of the Order of the Garter, is on the imposing wall-hanging. Beside the ex-King's bed are pictures of Wallis, a needlepoint pillow telling him to 'Take it easy' and pug models. To his right, the chimney-sweep doll which Queen Mary made her son is the Duke's lucky talisman.*

me back a transistor radio from America, and when she saw the staff kicking around a tennis ball, she gave us a football.'

'I'm sorry, John, but until the Mill has been sold, I'm afraid we can't afford a present for you,' the Duke will tell his faithful secretary John Utter in 1968.

Each Christmas Day, no matter where or when, the Windsors will sit down to listen to Queen Elizabeth II broadcast to the Empire turned Commonwealth.

The hall is scented with pine, but a quite different, pungent fragrance fills the nostrils as you re-enter the salon. The writer Nancy Spain, visiting the Windsors, will finally trace the 'pervading sweetness in the air' to 'an outsize scent bottle with a perforated cap behind the door'.

'Walking through that house was a sensuous experience, because every room had its own perfume burner with its own distinct perfume,' says Aline de Romanones.

It is fun time. There is no sitting around after dinner in a post-prandial stupor, parrying polite exchanges until it is the right time to depart.

'Oh, not one of those dull French dinners where you have to sit and talk for hours,' the Duke will complain about the formal dinner party.

The Duchess is full of 'pep', that particularly American word which expresses precisely her energy and gaiety.

'If you accept a dinner, you have a moral engagement to be amusing,' she told Ghislaine de Polignac.

When a guest sat sunk in silence, the Duchess voiced her annoyance, her social philosophy.

'Nobody has the right to come to a party and sit there like a piece of furniture,' she says. 'I resent intelligent, worldly people who won't make an effort. They're just parasites, relaxing while other people entertain them.'

The entertainment tonight is a young pianist, who sits down at the gleaming black Steinway, beneath a fine flower painting and Eugène Boudin's blush-pink view of Antibes. The repertoire is chirpy Broadway musical numbers: 'Put on a Happy Face', 'Bye Bye Birdie' and Cole Porter's 'I Get a Kick out of You' that will be played over and over again on doctor's advice to the comatose Duchess, in the hope of striking a flicker of memory in the blank blue eyes.

She keeps up with the latest trends in popular music.

'I'm sure *you've* never *heard* of Liberace,' she says accusingly to Lady Mosley.

The Duke's taste is a little more sentimental. His eyes water over at the mellow, full voice of the singer Richard Tauber, and when an Austrian trio sings familiar Viennese tunes, Nicholas Lawford sees him tapping them out 'rather pathetically, on his knee'.

It was awkward to admit in the post-war years, but the German language was for the Duke 'the *Muttersprache* of many of our relations'. His fondest childhood memories are of times when, his authoritarian father preoccupied with his stamp collection, Queen Mary would regain her youthful spirit in a sing-song round the piano with her children.

The Duke is dancing. Just as he will lead the Duchess out on to a ballroom floor for a graceful waltz, he is now partnering her in the cha-cha, his creased face smoothed into a smile. He loves dancing, and with his high-spirited brother Prince George used to roll back the rugs at Windsor Castle and fox trot until 'the ancient walls seemed to exude disapproval'.

His exhausting tours of the Empire as Prince of Wales were punctuated every evening by formal dances with colonial wives and colonel's daughters. As the great London houses were opened up again after the First World War, the London season was, in the Prince's words 'an almost continuous ball from midnight until dawn'.

'I danced with a man, who danced with a girl who danced with the Prince of Wales,' was a bitter sweet melody of the 1920s.

In the nightclubs of the Jazz age, the Café de Paris, Quaglino's and the Prince's favourite Embassy Club, there were the new dances.

'For a brief period,' said Prince Charming, 'I counted the music of the Charleston and the Black Bottom among the foremost American exports to Great Britain.'

The ex-King is light on his feet in their black patent slippers with silver buckles. His dancing shoes are lined up on rails in a cupboard in his dressing room.

'Don't mention it – the other foot is jealous,' the Duke says gallantly to a dancing partner who treads on his toe.

His most unlikely partner is the playwright Noël Coward, who dances a sailor's hornpipe and the Charleston with the Duke, at a Windsor party that has 'a blonde lady (French) pounding the piano and everyone getting a trifle high'.

'Princesse Sixte de Bourbon was definitely shocked,' says Coward. The sailor King George V ('You must always remember your position . . .') would certainly have said, with his grandmother Queen Victoria, 'We are not amused.'

The Duchess also loved 'to move and dance', says the Princesse de Polignac. 'She was very energetic.'

Wallis leads her guests in a conga round the delicate furniture. It is 12.30 am and she has slept a scant four hours the previous night. She never rises until 10.30 am, but insomnia and a nervous recurrent ulcer plague her all her life.

The Duke is singing now, standing by the piano with one hand tucked nonchalantly into his double-breasted dinner jacket as he leads the assembled guests in the chorus:

'Come on and hear, come on and hear, Alexander's Ragtime Band.'

The first guests are starting to leave. When a dinner breaks up early, the Duchess may drive the remains of the party on to a nightclub, to continue the fun.

You will be torn abruptly from the charmed circle of glamour and refinement that has lapped you for the last four hours, bundling into the cars outside where the chauffeurs have been waiting for their masters like faithful hounds. The Duke's driver Ronald Marchant (whose 20 years of nightly vigils will bring him severe kidney troubles) chooses the Cadillac limousine from the Windsors' four cars, and brings it round.

'After a while I *longed* to escape,' says the Duchess of Marlborough. 'I didn't want any more flowers and perfume and jewels. It was too claustrophobic.'

It *is* a shock to exchange this house bathed in its warm golden glow for the nocturnal tinseltown of champagne and cabaret. The Duke, increasingly unwilling to keep up with all this pep, will stay behind, a slight figure with a crumpled face waving from the doorway.

But Wallis may be seen on the nightclub dance floor with Woolworth's heir, the drunken, outrageous but entertaining Jimmy Donahue. His spiteful homosexual wit is sharp, brittle and a match for her own. It seems to be part of an attraction which her friends find difficult to understand or forgive.

When their relationship is ruptured by the displeasure of the Duke and Donahue's excesses, Jimmy will reply insouciantly to gossip mongers who ask after the Duchess:

'I've abdicated.'

'Are you fond of the Duchess?' Jimmy Donahue asked Laura, Duchess of Marlborough, unexpectedly at their very first meeting in Paris. 'If she ran away with me, who's side would you take?'

Tonight, the party comes to its natural end at 1 am, and the Duke and Duchess together say goodnight to their guests, before going upstairs – two small, neat silhouettes against the vast marble staircase and its massed orchids.

'You children go upstairs to your dreary attic,' says the Duchess, as Aline and Luis de Romanones take the lift hidden behind the Chinese screen in the hall. They are on their way to the two small guest rooms on the top floor: hers enlivened by a fantastical chest of drawers painted by Boudin with pastoral views and rococo bows; his adorned with military helmets on bedposts and chairs. The furniture has been brought by the Duke of Windsor from the Fort and was used as his own bedroom suite at their earlier rented home in the Boulevard Suchet.

'He has a passion for little helmets,' Nicholas Lawford wrote to his mother. 'His chairs have helmets at both corners of the back; and his bedside-clock is enclosed in a helmet of metal and mother-of-pearl.'

On the other side of the guest landing is a door that leads through to the

39

TOP: *On a flowered table top in the Duchess's bedroom, her menagerie of mementoes: a wise owl, a litter of pugs and a ferocious frog – part of a frog collection the Duke bought for her.*

ABOVE: *A sketched portrait of the Duchess of Windsor.*

corridor of staff bedrooms, where Sydney, in a bare and simple room, is sleeping below a pair of paintings of his native Bahamas. At the age of 19, Sydney, with his 'angelic coffee-coloured face' joined the Duke's staff at Government House. Now he wears scarlet and gold livery, travelling with the Windsors and staying with them each winter season in New York at the Waldorf Tower.

'It was hard work travelling with all that luggage,' he says. 'We were away for three months at a time, as many as 120 bags, His Royal Highness to look after, his breakfast to make, and the dogs and the shopping.'

The Duke of Windsor remains a hero to his valet. The Duchess will dismiss him after 27 years of service with a slam of the door, because he dared ask to go home earlier than usual to look after his four small children after his wife's sudden death.

The Duke and Wallis are having a nightcap upstairs together, as they pick over the party.

The apricot boudoir and the Duke's bedroom next door are as solidly English as the salon below is daintily French. The Duke and Duchess sit in the comfortable armchairs, covered in golden yellow velvet to match the silk-fringed curtains. Between them is a squashy sofa with leopard print cushions – a whisper of the exotic beside the wholesome dark English oak bookstand and footstool. The Duchess's *coiffeur* Alexandre will perch nervously on the edge of the canteloup-coloured sofa when he is invited by the widowed elderly Duchess to stay for tea.

Here too, Grace Dudley or Aline de Romanones will be entertained by the

Wallis's graceful lavender blue bedroom with its gilded wheatsheaf mouldings, watered silk walls and frothy curtains. Every little object has its allotted place on her dressing table. Golden chrysanthemums, pots of azaleas and one hothouse orchid fill her room with flowers. To the right is her bed and the entrance to the dressing room and bathroom beyond.

41

ABOVE: *On a table in the boudoir are photographs of the Duke's hero Winston Churchill and of the Duchess at her Red Cross work in the Bahamas.*

RIGHT: *The Duchess of Windsor's Japanese bureau in the upstairs boudoir, where she writes letters, instructs her secretary and runs the household.*

Duchess, or take tea poured from a silver teapot by the Duke himself. He sits back in his armchair, puffs on his pipe and imagines himself back in an English drawing room.

On the low coffee table, or stacked under the television on the far wall, are the books the Windsors read – not the gold-tooled regimental histories, daunting tomes of royal diaries or the *British Bird Book* in eight volumes that you will find in the library below.

'I remember arriving to photograph the Duchess at the Ritz in the Windsors' suite and seeing all those mountains of bags and not a single book,' says Horst. 'There was just one catalogue of Revillon furs on the mantelshelf, beside a framed photograph of Queen Mary and another one of the Duke and Duchess with Hitler.'

Lady Mosley admits that 'novels and whodunits' were Wallis's palliative for insomnia and that the daytime hours were spent on newspapers and magazines.

But the catalogues are now of culture rather than clothes: Sotheby's glossy Art at Auction books; Christie's sale of Important German and Ormolu-Mounted porcelain; an exhibition of seventeenth-century Italian painting in a Paris museum.

The Duchess, in Lady Dudley's words, has developed a 'good eye' for *objets d'art*. She will never be an aesthete or intellectual.

'Beautiful, but I wonder what use could be made of them,' said Wallis,

looking at Picasso's sensual, twisted vases of mythological beasts at an exhibition in Vallauris.

'I met her in the Paris bookshop Galignani,' says Nicholas Lawford. 'She was buying the books that people were talking about.'

A Gore Vidal or the latest Philip Roth will be on the bedside table in the guest room. For the Duke, she will buy *Jennie*, the biography of Lady Spencer Churchill. Her son Winston was steadfastly loyal during the abdication crisis and remains one of the Duke's heroes.

'The Duke's love for her is one of the great loves of history,' said the noble statesman and romantic, whose eyes filled with tears as he said goodbye to his King on the steps of Fort Belvedere.

A signed photograph of Winston, in wartime army uniform, is on the table facing the sofa, under the portrait of a sturdy child whom the Duke insists is Queen Victoria.

He judges books, like art, from a personal rather than a literary point of view.

'As far as the painter's brush is concerned, my true features will not unduly inflict posterity,' he says.

When, as Prince of Wales, he read Lytton Strachey's newly-published biography of Queen Victoria, 'he was in roars of laughter over the description of the Queen and John Brown.'

'She shouldn't have done it,' was the Duke's opinion of the 'U and non-U'

The Windsors' most intimate room is the boudoir separating their bedrooms. The Duke will pour tea for himself in this private drawing room, furnished English-style with comfortable armchair and sofa, and scattered with books and magazines. The exotic leopard-print velvet cushions were inspired by the Duchess's friend Lady Mendl. The delicate Saxe chandelier, smothered with white porcelain flowers, now hangs in the Palace of Versailles.

class controversy delineated with wicked wit by Lady Mosley's sister Nancy Mitford.

Piled on the footstool in front of the Duke and Duchess are *Time* and *Newsweek* (his), *Vogue* and *Jours de France* (hers). The Duke has not mastered the French language, but the Duchess is taking lessons and can speak relatively fluently. A framed poem in French is on the side table.

The Duchess has been leafing that afternoon through an illustrated book of Paris in the 1920s. The Duke referred to Fielding's *Quick Currency Guide for Europe*. Unread and unopened beside Wallis's Chinese escritoire, with its studied clutter of framed photographs and pens, are coffee table books about Egypt, New Zealand, Great Gardens and Great Palaces of Europe.

The purpose of the boudoir is to provide a private sitting room: a morning room where the Duchess can list instructions for the household, work with her secretary or write letters in her generous, dashing hand; an intimate comfortable place for evenings at home, which become less rare as the Duke withers into old age. The log fire burns lustily, while the mirror above the mantelpiece reflects the sculpted Meissen monkeys and the cluster of white porcelain roses that make up the magnificent central chandelier.

Their conversation is about the who and when and where of their lives.

'What do you and the Windsors talk about?' an American hostess was asked.

'Well, where they've just been and who they've just seen,' was the reply.

His friends and admirers fret for the Duke that the man who once ruled an empire has no occupation. He is, in the descriptive phrase the Windsors' secretary would use when typing out salient details about a guest, 'a gentleman of leisure'.

'I can't help feeling that he is sadly wasted,' said Nicholas Lawford, as he supplied the Duke with 'various English reference books'.

'His life had stopped with the abdication,' says Sarah Schlumberger, wife of the Duke's banker friend Pierre Schlumberger. 'It was especially sad for him that he had no role. And she did not occupy herself with a single charity. Nothing. It was an empty life.'

'They wanted to spare each other the fact that either of them was unhappy,' says Grace Dudley. 'A lot of the things she did were just to make the Duke feel wanted and needed.'

The Duke kisses the Duchess goodnight. Every evening, when they stay with the Dudleys, he would 'pick a flower from the garden and lay it on her pillow.'

'There *may* be a happier couple somewhere,' said the Duke on his eighteenth wedding anniversary. 'But I doubt it.'

The Duke's bedroom is designed to make believe he is still King, or, at least, a person of consequence. Wallis has made it a shrine to royal history, and the Duke has made it a shrine to Wallis, scattering her pictures over every surface: Man Ray's striking photograph of Mrs Simpson *à la chinoise*, her hair 'brushed so that a fly would slip off it', in Cecil Beaton's vivid phrase; the Duchess in mellow old age in the garden of the Mill, a sweet smile softening the hard sunlight on her face; the entire 'Wallis collection' of Beaton's fashionable photographs, including Mrs Simpson in a dress patterned with matchsticks and a pointed wizard's hat. 'To David from Wallis – June 1935' the dedication reads.

'He sleeps in a room . . . entirely devoid of anything personal except several large photographs of Wallis . . . the ex-monarch of the world has no possessions, nothing,' said courtier Lord Brownlow when the Duke had fled helter skelter from the throne into exile. Perry Brownlow described this vision of the 42-year-old Duke to Diana Vreeland: '. . . just like a little schoolboy, sound asleep, with sun coming across his blond hair. His bed was surrounded by chairs . . . and on each chair was a picture of his beloved Wallis.'

'It was an obsession,' said Perry.

The Duke's bedroom is a man's room, in the way of an English gentleman's club, with its leather-topped desk and its pictures of flags, soldiers and hunting scenes. They are as red-coated and view halloo as the energetic Munnings portrait of the Prince of Wales riding to hounds on Forest Witch that hangs outside on the landing at the crest of the stairs.

Royal insignia lie heavy on the room. The lion and the unicorn prance across the base of a china lamp which illuminates a portrait of a coy Wallis, photographs of the cairn terrier Slipper in a double wallet, and a formal picture of the Duke's sister Princess Mary.

A signed family group of a glowing Princess Margaret, her husband and tiny children will take pride of place on the table in the lobby of the room which serves as both study and bedroom.

More royal photographs of the Duke's bearded and moustachioed father, always in his naval uniform, and a majestic Queen Mary stand rigidly around the room.

Downstairs in the salon, the Prince of Wales feather motif is woven so subtly into the silver blue carpet that you might not realize that you are treading on the Duke's past. In his room, the three proud plumes – symbol of the heir of the throne of England – are embossed on hair brushes, inlaid in a miniature mahogany cabinet, painted on ashtrays or curl in rococo gilding above the mirror.

'I am being presented June 10th and I'm borrowing . . . Thelma Furness's . . . feathers and fan,' Wallis wrote to Aunt Bessie in 1931 of the presentation at court that was to mark the first stirrings of her royal romance.

The Duke of Windsor's room is dominated by his bed and his desk – which carries a line up of pipes. His relentless smoking – a tin of pipe tobacco a day – will contribute to his final fatal illness.

'It was the only thing he did which infuriated the Duchess,' says Aline de Romanones.

The bed has a hanging sweep of velvet, embossed with fleurs-de-lys and the royal coat of arms. The central medallion reads *Honi soit qui mal y pense* – evil be to him that evil thinks – the motto of the Order of the Garter. The ivory bedcover repeats the words round a symbolic ER – Edward Rex.

Beside the bed of England's one-time King is a menagerie of nursery toys: a forlorn stuffed donkey with white ears and nose; a coal black teddy with a ribbon round his neck; the chimney sweep doll that Queen Mary made for her son.

'It was the first thing I had to pack when we travelled,' Sydney Johnson says.

Beside the doll is a pin-cushion, embroidered by Queen Mary with the words: 'What is home without pleasure?'

The Duke abandons his clothes in the dressing room that leads off the bedroom – an ante-room to the veined marbled bathroom beyond.

'It's the kind of room where things are hung up on the floor,' says the Duchess.

Sydney has squeezed toothpaste on to the royal brush. The pyjamas are

RIGHT: *The Duke's masculine bathroom in veined marble is decorated with regimental prints. The bath tub was boarded over because the Duke always took a shower. The lavatory is in the corner concealed by a screen.*

BELOW: *'Papers, papers, papers . . . PAPERS,' said a guest when she saw the higgledy piggledy pile on the Duke's tub.*

laid out on the bed, where Grace Dudley will hear him groaning in agony in his final illness.

'She used to go in and hold his hand, and he was quieter. That was proof enough for me that he loved her,' she says.

In the certainty of his love, and after looking at the soldier prints on the walls of his dressing room for signs of slovenly dress, the Duke of Windsor falls into a sweet sleep.

The Duchess's bathroom resembles a circus tent. Its ceiling is painted *trompe l'oeil* with marquee stripes and hanging tassels. On the walls is a fantastical mural of ballet dancers, ribbons and flowers created by the artist Dimitri Bouchène – the French equivalent of Britain's stage designer Oliver Messel.

Flowers flutter patchily across the walls in a shadowy blue. The *cabinet de toilette* fitted into the corner of the room beside the bath has a floating vision of a blindfold maiden with weeping hair – an Ophelia drowning in her bath. Above the curving tub is Cecil Beaton's sleek portrait of Wallis in a chrome yellow evening gown.

'A charming, feminine setting,' was Beaton's description of her home. The same could be said of this bathroom with Bouchène's ballet costume pictures framing the doorway and its curving commodes carrying framed pictures of people or pugs. Reality, in the shape of the heavy, insistent weighing scales behind the door, or the memory of the griping pains of the Duchess's recurring

ulcer, is sublimated to this fantasy. The effect is not so much romantic as droll.

The Duchess is undressing in the cool aquamarine area between her bathroom and bedroom. In front of her is a professional wide-angle, full-length mirror where she stands patiently for dress fittings or while her maid bustles out of the door on to the landing and into the ironing room.

'You can wear a dress that is 20 years old, but it must be immaculate,' Wallis tells Aline de Romanones. The Duchess's dresses are conspicuously this year's models. In the cupboards that wall the little dressing area are the bags, the shoes, the hats, the all-in-one stretch corsets and the gossamer fine flesh stockings that are the tools of her trade.

It is late, and the Duchess has told her maid not to wait up.

'She was considerate in that way,' says Lady Dudley.

But every single night, no matter how late, or how wild the party, or how many thimblefuls of vodka she has drunk, the Duchess of Windsor will act out the same loving ritual with her clothes. Her dress is taken off, put on a padded hanger, and suspended from the pale bentwood coat rack beside the latticed Chinese pagoda stand in her dressing room.

Each night, however late, her make-up, including the false eyelashes that her *maquilleur* put on so delicately that no-one knew, will be removed with Elizabeth Arden's cleansing milk. On her dressing table, in sharp focus and close-up, is a picture of the Duke with his puckish smile.

The Duchess's fantasy bathroom, the ceiling painted with stripes and swags like a circus tent. Over the bath a drawing by Cecil Beaton of Wallis in a yellow dress. Round the door theatre designs by Dimitri Bouchène.

ABOVE: *Chest and scales.*

47

No-one but her maid ever sees the Duchess without her make-up.

'I was staying at the Mill in 1969 at the time of the Moon landing,' says the Duke's friend Philippe du Pasquier. 'He was so excited and begged her to come down and watch, but she wouldn't appear in front of us without her make-up.'

Ten years later, an intrusive long tom lens will catch her face looking, in Diana Mosley's words, 'like the Greek mask of tragedy, her mouth a square, her dark and penetrating blue eyes staring out of the window'.

There are two windows in the room, both opening on to the miniature park and the tall trees of the Bois beyond.

'Isn't this a pretty park. I wonder who it belongs to?' the Duchess will ask the Baronne de Cabrol when her mind starts wandering.

Gilded flower and wheatsheaf mouldings gleam against the watercolour tints of pale blue, dove grey and mauve. There are clusters of flower pictures and Boudin's choice of Louis Seize chairs.

The Duchess's nightgown is laid out by her maid with a tucked waist and spreading skirt to suggest the imprint of Wallis's tiny form. It is an exquisitely fine slither of peach satin inset with *café-au-lait* lace.

Diana Vreeland remembers Mrs Simpson's taste for luxurious lingerie.

'There was one in white satin copied from Vionnet, all on the bias . . . The whole neck of this nightgown was made of petals . . . and when you moved they rippled.'

At the foot of her bed lie the pugs, who scorn the line-up of pug cushions on a dainty couch and choose instead a regal pose on the bed itself, which is protected by a plastic slipover.

Under it, the bedcover is moire silk in a watery blue – not the strong Wallis blue that she will make famous, nor the deep sapphire of her piercing eyes that are closed now, in fervent hope of sleep.

One ear listens for the soft footfalls that will herald the Duke's arrival tonight, as on so many other nights.

Across the breast of her nightgown, woven in a cobweb of diaphanous lace, is a crown of fleurs-de-lys above her entwined initials. In sleep, if not in life, Wallis Windsor is Her Royal Highness.

OPPOSITE: *The Duchess of Windsor's exquisite silk lingerie laid out on her watered silk bedcover. The peach satin is encrusted with lace and embroidered with her crowned monogram of WW for Wallis Windsor. In the alcove are Wedgwood medallions of George III and his family.*

CHAPTER
— 2 —

AT PLAY

I tried to hold the courage of my ways
In that which might endure.
Daring to find a world in a lost world,
A little world, a little perfect world.

VITA SACKVILLE-WEST: *The Garden*

THE Duke of Windsor is at war with the algae. He stands astride the millstream, his feet in stout leather brogues with tiny silver acorns swinging from the ends of the laces. The quivering surface mirrors a blur of checked tweed and a narrow, determined face. It is magnified by the water into a pale circle as he bends to stab at the grey-green primeval slime that has dared to invade his kingdom.

Behind him is a powder-grey drystone wall that the Duke has planted with purple flowering clematis, as enthusiastically as his mother Queen Mary would have stripped it off to reveal 'a naked wall'.

'My mother *loathed* the country. She was a Londoner,' says the Duke.

Down here at the Mill, on the Windsors' country weekends, he seems more the ex-King and much more English than in the hothouse salons of Paris. He is English in his eccentricity: the hairy tweed suits, inherited from his father; the 'yelps' of high pitched enthusiasm with which he masterminds the landscaping of the garden; his habit of stumping off to the top of the hill behind the house. 'Cardiac Hill', the Duke calls it, because the faint-hearted or those under doctor's orders will not attempt the climb.

From the top, you can see the cluster of buildings spread out below, their roofs on varying levels. There is the long central barn with a gaily striped awning over the terrace at the back. To the left, the guest cottages, called by the Duchess in her determined French '*les célibataires*' – bachelors' quarters. It is an ironic echo of the bachelor's cottage that the future Edward VII and Queen Alexandra built at Sandringham, and where their son George V was obliged to bring up his burgeoning family.

The mill house itself, a warm grey stone building with white shutters and a cobbled courtyard, was bought by the Windsors from the French painter Etienne Drian in 1952.

'Our first real home,' said the Duchess as she gutted the interior and recreated a glossier version of rustic charm.

In return, Drian presented her with a portrait of herself, a rose-tinted, romantic painting of the Duchess in an evening dress of sweet pea colours. The Duke was soon to dig up the kitchen garden and plant a 40-foot stretch of sweet peas and red and yellow dahlias, to feed his wife's voracious appetite for flowers.

'A source of supply for the vases which dot every room in the Mill,' he says.

From the top of the hill, the garden looks like an Impressionist painting –

ABOVE: *The gardening Prince, with three feathers in his hat, admiring his* Rosa Imperialis *– as seen by the humorous magazine* Punch *in 1934.*

OPPOSITE: *The King over the millstream: the Duke working in his water garden at the Moulin de la Tuilerie – literally 'tile kiln'. He diverted the stream and sent for plants from Windsor Castle. Behind him are the scattered buildings that make up his country home in the valley of the Seine.*

the cottage garden flowers in the herbaceous border are bright stipples of paint and the grey rocks in the stream below are Claude Monet's fat, flat water lilies floating on the water. Among those guests lunching today is Gerald Van der Kemp, who will become keeper of Monet's garden idyll at Giverny. Now he is curator of the Palace of Versailles, the man who has taught the Duchess of Windsor everything she knows about art, and who will persuade her after the Duke's death to entail her finest furniture on Versailles.

As the Duke landscapes the rock garden, with his gardening guide and mentor Russell Page, the one-time King will not be thinking of Impressionist painting, but rather of the Sandringham estate where he was brought up. Around the still lake in front of the re-named 'York' Cottage, the six royal children played at pirates and hidden treasure as they broke away from the constricting rooms and rigid discipline.

The Duke has erected round the corner of the house an antique sundial, instead of Sandringham's stone pelican of his childhood memory. 'It was a very wise old bird,' he says, 'Sometimes we used to put funny hats on his head, which was not very popular or approved of.'

The Duke is wearing a cerise felt baseball cap. It looks as rakish and out of place with his tweeds as it does with the leather gardening trousers and sweatshirt which he puts on for the heavy work.

As Prince of Wales, he started a royal dynasty of gardeners. His grandfather, he says, liked gardens 'in a grandiose sort of way'. His father preferred shooting and collecting stamps. But David and his brother Bertie took to real 'dirt gardening'.

'I longed to start with my own hands,' said the Duke, of the 'monotonous lawns and uninspired sprinklings of tropical shrubbery' surrounding Government House in the Bahamas.

While he was trying to coax 'bright flowers' from the thin coral-reef soil of the Bahamas, back home in England, the new George VI was nurturing cuttings of shrubs and flowers. The fronds of larkspur and delphinium that Bertie planted will be picked 40 years on and sent to the London home of his wife, Queen Elizabeth, the Queen Mother, at Clarence House. And the passion for creating a garden will be inherited by Prince Charles, great-nephew to the Duke of Windsor and England's future King, who will make his own idyll in the English countryside at Highgrove Manor in Gloucestershire.

The Windsors' country home is at Gif-sur-Yvette in the Chevreuse valley, near Orsay and half an hour in the Duke's Daimler from Paris. The Duchess's luggage and two maids follow in the long blue Cadillac station wagon, turning off the main road and down the dead-end lane, to where the Mill and its stream lie in a green bowl of trees.

'It is here that the Duchess and I spend weekends and most of the summer,' says the Duke. 'It is a very tranquil place where one can garden, as one should, in old clothes, with one's hands, among familiar plants.'

Before the Moulin de la Tuilerie there had been Fort Belvedere, a castellated folly in Windsor Great Park, where Mrs Simpson acted as hostess for her Prince and his friends on what his father called 'those damn weekends'.

'I created a home at the Fort just as my father and grandfather had created one at Sandringham,' he says. 'I loved it in much the same way as they loved the "Big House".'

'Don't you see, I must make a home for him,' the Duchess explained when she was refurbishing Government House in the Bahamas. 'The only one he ever had he made for himself at Fort Belvedere. He had to leave it – you don't know what that meant to him.'

At Fort Belvedere, the Prince dug out the 'muddy lily pond' (to replace it with an ocean liner of a swimming pool), planted a regiment of tulips and edged the flagstone paths at the foot of the toy-town battlements with massed irises and roses.

Smart friends, who would rather have been at the side of the newly constructed pool, were pressed into service as 'down came the encroaching yew trees to let in light and air.' With much the same obsessional enthusiasm, his mother, Queen Mary, set up a Wooding Squad of reluctant guests and ladies-in-waiting when staying at Badminton House in the war years.

'Lovely morning which we spent clearing ivy off trees – We watched a whole wall of ivy of 50 years standing . . . being removed. Most of it came down like a blanket,' Queen Mary wrote in her diary in 1939.

The satirical magazine *Punch* lampooned the heir to the throne in 1934.

'Our artist has portrayed HRH the Prince of Wales engaged in what we respectfully believe to be one of his favourite hobbies,' wrote the editor, showing the gardening Prince in shirtsleeves and characteristic Fair Isle sweater, clutching a watering can beside a red rose bush that could have come from the pages of *Alice in Wonderland*.

Queen Mary had a more regal attitude to gardens.

'My mother liked flowers and used to take me as a child to admire the famous herbaceous borders at Hampton Court, near London,' says the Duke. 'She liked them best in vases, in their cut-flower state.'

So it is with the Duchess of Windsor, who is standing at the edge of the herbaceous border, her face harsh and furrowed in the fitful May sunlight. She has on a tailored green corduroy suit, a trug basket over one arm, and the determined look of mistress of the house in search of floral decoration.

'The Duchess hopes,' says the Duke, 'that the Almighty can cover an outside wall with vines as fast as she can curtain a window.'

The vines on the sunny back wall of the house straggle too untidily for her taste, and the Duke is constantly called into service to keep them under control.

The pugs meanwhile – Trooper, Disraeli, Imp and young Davy Crockett – run wild. They treat the garden as one vast playground, holding 'wild chases' through the flowers and carrying off in their mouths like a prey the tags on which the Duke laboriously writes the names of his newly-planted flowers.

He enjoys flowers in profusion, rather than French formality. In the wide beds that border the lawn there are thrusting stems of delphiniums, paper-fine petals of sweet peas, upright blue lupins and fronds of deep pink valerian. In August a new wave of blooms rolls over the herbaceous border, changing the colours from 'bluish' to warmer colours – red zinnias and yellow dahlias.

'Meadow sage is one of the main standbys in the garden because it goes on flowering for weeks,' says the Duke. 'Though as a rule I do not care for purple flowers, it seems to set off other colours near it.' Behind the waving meadow sage, a Spanish broom glows like polished gold.

'At last that stinking golden rod is going,' wrote the Duchess to Major Gray Phillips, the Duke's former Comptroller, in September 1958. 'We should adore to have the delphiniums to plant in October . . . It is sweet of you to give them to me – at last I have something of my own in this garden.'

The Duchess's contribution is to nurture the guests when they come to stay, take tea on the terrace or tour the estate with the Duke and admire his present life's work.

House guests look out on a homely bed of white petunias, which will be replaced by golden yellow dwarf chrysanthemums in late summer. 'It was

LEFT: *The idyllic English country garden created by the Duke of Windsor. He is tying up a vine on the outside wall of 'the barn'. The pugs run off with the carefully labelled plant tags from the herbaceous border. In the foreground: delphiniums, lupins, stocks. Against the stone wall are pink valerian, meadow sage, zinnias. Yellow Spanish broom and marigolds challenge the garden's pink and blue summer colours.*

ABOVE: *The Duke with freshly picked asparagus. He gives over most of the kitchen garden to growing cut flowers for Wallis.*

like living in a loose box,' says Laura, Duchess of Marlborough, of the Mill's guest cottages. 'The old stable doors opened at the top, and the Duchess left them like that.'

Paul's Scarlet Climber rose and Clematis Imperialis compete to climb the roughcast walls of the guest-house and twine round its carriage lamp.

'Gardening is a mood. And my mood is one of intimacy, not splendour,' says the Duke.

This Ruritanian retreat needs princely attention. The Windsors pull rank to get cuttings sent from England: the alpine plants for the new rock garden have been despatched from Windsor Castle. The Duke will stand in military mode shouting orders in German to the two gardeners from Alsace, a bewildered Spaniard and a baffled French garden boy.

'As the Duke's German is sort of better than his French, he likes to talk German with them,' explains the Duchess.

The ex-King wielded a force of five gardeners to re-channel the millstream, hump the rocks for stepping stones and pump the water up to make a series of miniature waterfalls.

The uppermost cascade falls in straight white lines of water, looking like the shower of New York ticker tape that rained down on England's Prince of Wales from the 'shadowy, steep-sided canyon of Broadway'. On that momentous North American tour of 1919, the Prince was so overwhelmed by the 'beauty and grandeur' of the Canadian Rockies, that he bought himself a four-thousand-acre ranch, which he will keep until 1962.

At the Mill he is master of God's 26 lesser acres. 'They pulled every string to get the land round them scheduled as green belt,' Diana Mosley says. 'But when they came to sell the Mill they couldn't have cared less about the landscape and tried to have the order revoked.'

Wallis tells her friends that she has never seen the Duke happier or more content than when pottering around his land.

In the autumn, he can revert to royal type and go off shooting. 'My father's favourite recreation was shooting, what I used to call "banging",' says the Duke, remembering his boyhood at Sandringham.

The Duchess does not share his enthusiasm for country sports. 'This is the shooting season,' Wallis wrote in September 1958. 'Fortunately women are not often included. Yesterday the Duke left here at 8 am and returned at 9 pm! He had good sport.'

'The Duke loved horses,' says Laura, Duchess of Marlborough. 'When they were both staying with us in the country, I whispered to him one day, "Come out with me tomorrow if you want." But the Duchess was so angry when she found out she put a stop to it.'

The Mill slumbers in its secret garden behind an ivy-covered wall. You can see nothing from the narrow lane until the massive oak entrance doors under their tiled portico open on to the sloping cobbled drive.

'All our friends are quite unkind about our courtyard and paths,' says the Duchess. 'And when I twisted my ankle the other day, they didn't write one word of sympathy, simply "There now, it's those cobbles."'

Last Christmas, those friends received cards showing the Windsors standing in the covered porch of the main house, he in a dress tartan kilt, she in plainer plaid and Tyrolean jacket, with Trooper, the cream pug with an upturned black snout, at their heels. Wallis Windsor, she signed in her loose, strong handwriting. Beside it, the E of Edward slopes forward and then extends in a long flourish above a spidery 'Duke of Windsor'.

Now the front door of the Mill is a gaping mouth. Above it is an eighteenth-century sundial and a deep lichen-covered roof. The windows are lidded with white shutters. Inside, the sweet country idyll is salted by the Duchess who had her decorator Stéphane Boudin paint a *trompe l'oeil* fresco of a ribbon running through a mill wheel on the wall of the upstairs drawing room.

'I may not be the miller's daughter,' it reads. 'But I have been through the mill.'

The Duke's *jeu d'esprit*, carved into the stone pillar of the sundial in the garden, is an epigram by the poet Hilaire Belloc:

> I am a sundial, and I make a botch
> Of what is done far better by a watch.

The Duchess is always precise; her husband is always late – an indulgence he has allowed himself ever since the death of his punctilious father. On the night that George V died, the new King, in a frenzy of hysteria, ordered all the clocks at Sandringham – kept half an hour fast since his grandfather's reign – to be put back.

Guests arrive for lunch precisely at half past one. This is late by French standards of the sacred noonday break. But even in the days of Fort Belvedere, time was out of joint.

'Everything is a few hours later than other places,' said Lady Diana Cooper '. . . A splendid tea arrived at 6.30 . . . dinner was at 10. Emerald (Cunard) arrived at 8.30 for cocktails.'

Weekend guests are asked to the Mill for Saturday tea-time. The invitation comes first in a telephone call, then a card follows from the secretary, or a note from Wallis on her country writing paper. That has the address and royal crest – a frisky lion and unicorn leaping for the crown – embossed in grass green, in contrast to the more sophisticated dark blue of the Paris stationery. With the letter comes a map, drawn by the Duke from the Carte Michelin and hand-coloured by the Duchess.

'No excuses for going in the wrong direction' is engraved on the Duke's gold Cartier pocket compass.

You cross the cobbled courtyard to the barn, a 40-foot room with a log fire blazing, where the Duke holds court among his royal souvenirs and round tables are put up for large luncheons.

'This room,' says the Duchess in her Southern drawl, 'represents the Duke's life.'

Above the stone fireplace is a mighty map criss-crossed with his tours as Prince of Wales – 150,000 miles to 45 different countries in six years of the 1920s.

'My education was completed on the trade routes of the world,' he says.

On the bookshelves is a noble bust of himself as King Edward VIII; jubilee coins mounted on a pyramid of green velvet; regimental buttons marshalled in a wooden frame.

'Every button in the British Army during the First World War – many from regiments that have since been disbanded,' explains the Duke.

The exotic curved swords, the 'kukris' in their gem-studded scabbards, were gifts from Indian maharajahs to the grandson of Queen Victoria. They will go under the hammer at auction in Geneva for fantastic prices to buyers bidding for a piece of England's history. Standing on a mahogany plinth, sculpted out of solid silver, is a statuette of the mighty Queen Empress Victoria Regina, 'Gangan' to the Duke, who would visit her at her villa at Osborne on

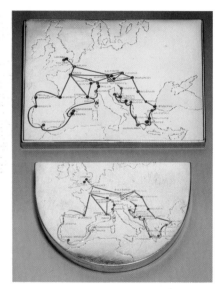

RIGHT: 'This room represents the Duke's life,' says the Duchess. On the wall above the fireplace is a map of the Duke's empire travels as Prince of Wales. Beside him is a table made out of the ceremonial bass drum of the Welsh guards. On the shelves, left to right: a silver statuette of Queen Victoria; the Prince's commission in the Royal Navy, signed by Winston Churchill; Indian daggers; a pig-sticking trophy and a green velvet obelisk set with royal sovereigns. At his feet is the variegated green carpet that his wife designed.

ABOVE: For Christmas 1935 Wallis gave the Prince a gem-set cigarette case on which the romantic holidays they had spent together were inscribed in enamel. The King gave her a matching half-moon powder case the next year.

ABOVE LEFT: *'Planning never stops,' says the Duke. He spends hours re-designing the garden with his advisor Russell Page.*

ABOVE RIGHT: *The Duke and Duchess find tranquillity in their country garden.*

OPPOSITE: *A stroll round the 26-acre estate takes in the wild meadow and weeping willows beside the Merantaise river that once turned the mill wheel at the Moulin.*

the Isle of Wight and watch her eat breakfast in a revolving hut that could be turned mechanically away from the gusting wind. All his life, the Duke of Windsor will be fascinated by gadgets, collecting silver whistles on a chain, fancy penknives, pipecleaners, bottle openers.

The Duke stands in the centre of the room on the tufted carpet in variegated shades of green the Duchess has designed.

'I call it my lawn,' she says. Visiting writer Nancy Spain finds the real lawn outside, bordered by the riot of English country flowers, riddled with weeds.

The Duke rolls back the map of his life 20 years. In this room ('the Duchess and I call it our Museum') stands the sturdy Chippendale table on which the King signed away his throne. A brass plate records the signing of the Instrument of Abdication, its time and date: '10.30 am December 10, 1936.'

The Duke of Windsor points out the documents in which he takes special pride: 'My commission in the Royal Navy signed by my father, Sir Winston Churchill as First Lord of the Admiralty, and my relative Prince Louis of Battenberg, as First Sea Lord.'

Beside it are his commission in the army and a mention in Despatches from the First World War, when the young Prince fought officialdom to be allowed to the front line in northern France.

The Duchess is not a countrywoman at heart. Her role at the Moulin is to invite guests to stay and entertain them. Behind her: one of the glowing flower paintings that dot the walls of the seventeenth-century mill house.

'The dead lie out unburied and in the postures and on the spots where they fell,' he wrote in his diary on 29 September 1915. 'Those dead bodies offered the most pathetic and gruesome sight . . . I have seen and learned a lot about war today.'

There are sporting trophies from the years spent in the saddle – for steeple-chasing and pig-sticking. A bronze statuette of a hunter is from 'Fruity' Metcalfe, the army captain who acted as the Prince's polo manager on the Indian tour of 1921 and became his close friend and ultimately best man. The Prince was a daredevil rider, but with an uncertain seat on his horse. His hair-raising point-to-point victories are commemorated in the 15 horseshoes nailed round the door.

'There was always so much fuss in the newspapers when he fell off,' says the Duchess. 'People don't seem to find it news when anyone wins anything.'

The Duke is pointing out three golf balls mounted in silver: 'To commemorate the three accidental occasions on which I made a hole in one.'

He taps his pipe in an ashtray lying on a drum of the Grenadier and Welsh Guards which has been silenced as a coffee table. So dear was his regiment to the Duke that he asked his brother, the new King George VI, without success, if he might keep his role as Commander in Chief after the abdication. The drums rolled home to Wales after the Duke's death.

'This is a cheerful room of ours,' says the Duke as he sits on the squashy tomato red sofa among the royal souvenirs.

'The King over the Millstream' James Pope-Hennessy calls him wickedly, as he watches the one-time Edward VIII, *Rex et Imperator*, barking orders in guttural German to the Alsatian gardener and passing round the potted shrimps at tea.

Tea is in the *orangerie*, as the Windsors call the covered porch at one end of the barn. Rain threatens to drizzle on the flowered table cloth that sprouts with *trompe l'oeil* china: two fruit plates with vine leaves lapping the rims; bowls sculpted as bunches of ripe purple grapes; cabbage saucers and squat tomato-shaped pots; a dish recreating a bunch of asparagus as it must have looked when Wallis Spencer, the 20-year-old naval bride, meticulously tied the green spears together according to *Fanny Farmer's Cook Book*.

The china will one day be on display in glass cases at France's National Ceramic Museum at Sèvres, with dry descriptions: ('Meissen: pair of baskets . . . Faïence: pot in the shape of a cabbage'). At the Mill, the collection is lined up in a leaf-green dresser or displayed with studied casualness on a tiled table on the terrace. More of Boudin's *trompe l'oeil* turns the cool green dining room into a conservatory, with painted fronds of greenery mounting the latticed walls.

The furnishings are not the comfortable, faded chintzes of an English country house.

'It was very bright with patterned carpets, lots of apricot and really more Palm Beach than English or French,' says Diana Mosley. 'It wasn't really like an English house,' Lady Dudley says. 'It was much more comfortable.'

'I wanted to have a fling with rich, bright colours,' says the Duchess. 'In the past I'd always leaned to soft pastels but the Mill was my chance to do something different.'

There are flowers, bright ones, splashed in red and green on chairs, and still-lives of fruit glowing like stained-glass windows against stone walls. Door knobs and finger plates are nineteenth-century English, redeployed from the Fort before it was taken over by the Duke's cousin Gerald Lascelles, the son of his sister Mary. Only the problems of transportation stopped the Duke from uprooting flagstones from Fort Belvedere. The stone floor at the Mill is ground and polished to a dull sheen, 'paved with gravestones stolen from cemeteries during the French Revolution,' explains the Duchess. Upstairs in the long drawing room loops and twists of ribbon pattern the tomato red carpet that would not have looked out of place in Queen Victoria's Balmoral.

'That carpet was a kind of tartan and I wasn't so sure about the taste,' says Hubert de Givenchy, the couturier who was to sit up with his workroom staff all night after the Duke died to make a black mourning outfit for the Duchess.

Cecil Beaton is cruel about the Mill, calling it 'overdone and chichi'. 'Medallions on the walls, gimmicky pouffs, bamboo chairs. Simply not good enough,' he said.

'The only thing about the Mill that was ravishing was one great room that had been taken almost verbatim from Fort Belvedere,' says the American interior decorator Billy Baldwin. 'Most of the Mill was awfully tacky but that's what Wallis had – tacky Southern taste; much too overdone, much too elaborate and no real charm.'

There are sudden flashes of nostalgia for Wallis's childhood in the American South. Cushions in a Star of Bethlehem patchwork – a sunset red centre shading out to a stormy blue – cover the garden furniture on the terrace, which is bricked in an intricate herringbone pattern like parquet flooring. Upstairs in Wallis's bedroom, pioneer homestead meets the American Dream in a pastel harlequin patchwork bedcover.

'A birthday present from my husband,' says the Duchess.

The same sugar-sweet lilac, blue, green and yellow stripe the silk that drapes the sloping ceiling like a circus tent.

'I'm going to do something dreadful,' whispered the Duchess to her hairdresser Alexandre. 'I'm going to paint those dreary brown beams white.'

The Duke is at his happiest among the solid English furnishings of his own quarters at the Mill. Both garden and barn are deliberate recreations of his country home in England – Fort Belvedere on the Windsor estate.

Tea is, in the words of James Pope-Hennessy, 'another serious perfectionist meal'. The Duchess is initiating the French guests into the delights of potted shrimps, which have become the conversation piece of the afternoon.

'You have to take the little grey shrimps, about a quarter of a pound,' she explains. 'Half a pack of butter, a pinch of black pepper, a teaspoonful of wine vinegar and one mint leaf. You put all the ingredients in with the butter and melt it, then add the peeled shrimps, mix it well in, and put it in the fridge so that you can serve it chilled.'

The tea may be laid out on the terrace or in the covered dining area beside the barn.

'I've stopped putting little tables out in the garden,' says Wallis. 'It makes too much mess.'

The maître d'hôtel is in a navy blue uniform with a red collar. He passes the tongue sandwiches and the hot savoury patties in a silver dish. The footman (in navy with a green collar) brings *petit beurre* biscuits on a silver platter for the pugs and offers guests two different sorts of jam. The Duchess pours endless breakfast-sized cups of tea for the Duke and educates her Gallic guests about cucumber sandwiches.

'Just one slice of bread,' she explains. 'And we don't cut it in rounds, but lengthwise, very fine, with all the pips taken out.'

'I could have imagined myself back in Virginia Water in Surrey,' says Nancy Spain, sitting on the terrace surveying the flower beds and 'the extremely wild meadow that begins where the garden ends'.

'Yes it *is* very English,' agrees the Duchess. 'Except for the lawns. The French don't understand lawns.'

ABOVE: *Southern comfort for the Duchess's bedroom at the Mill with its tented ceiling and pastel patchwork bedcover – a 56th birthday present from the Duke. The rocking chair in the left background came from Wallis Warfield's home in Baltimore.*

RIGHT: *The Duke's bedroom tucked under the eaves is stacked above his bathroom and dressing room. All his furniture came from Fort Belvedere. The drum table is from the Grenadier Guards, as are the prints on the walls. The red and green tartan theme reflects the Mill's bright colours.*

The entrance hall of the main house with its loud chintz and cheery colours. The Duke always sits in the studded leather chair. The flagstone floor was laid from gravestones stolen during the French Revolution. The rug is felt embroidered in floral squares. The stairs lead up to the large dressing room.

LEFT: The hall from the pantry.

The Duke leads a forward party off on a tour of the garden as the dying sun rims the hill. The other guests withdraw to the cottages – to exclaim over the care their hostess has taken to cater to every whim – literary, cosmetic or medicinal.

'There was always writing paper, postcards, stamps and telegram forms,' says Ghislaine de Polignac. 'We had all the newest books. And a television. Scent for the bathroom, Listerine, aspirins, pads for the eyes. It was like a little pharmacy in the bathroom.'

'The bathroom was loaded with scent bottles like a counter at a bazaar – a delicious sense of self-indulgence,' says James Pope-Hennessy.

'I shall never forget,' says Philippe du Pasquier, 'going into the bathroom and finding my toothpaste squeezed on to the brush.'

The Windsor staff have already unpacked in this little doll's house of a cottage, with its wall-covering of George IV coronation prints in the hall, and its black and white and blush-pink bedroom for the lady guest. When breakfast is carried in next morning, the strawberry design on the white breakfast china will exactly match the pink satin coverlet and embroidered insignia on the bed sheets.

'When I woke up, I found a crown imprinted on my cheek from where I had been sleeping on the embroidered pillow,' says the Princesse de Polignac.

Lord Dudley woke to a living nightmare in the sunshine yellow male guest room, where the bedside table was cluttered with pen, ink, cigarettes, bowl of cigarette holders, lighters and radio.

With an outflung arm, Eric Dudley had knocked over the Louis XV inkstand in his sleep, and woke to find a spreading Quink blue stain on the pale carpet. Quickly to the bathroom and to mop up the mess with the pile of fluffy almond-green towels, exactly matched to the chinoiserie wallpaper. Surveying the morning scene of absolute devastation, the Duchess (of whose sharp tongue Lord Dudley was afraid) gave him her most charming smile.

'I was just planning to change the décor,' she said.

Evening clothes are pressed and laid out precisely on the bed: tuxedo with handkerchief already folded in the pocket; dress shirts with studs already placed; socks rolled down.

'And a huge white woolly furry towelling bathrobe, as in a French hotel,' says Nancy Spain.

'Because she knew you liked daiquiris, there was a 1920s Cartier cocktail shaker, already frosted with your favourite drink,' says Anne Slater. 'There was lovely linen on the beds, it was all terribly comfortable and a feeling of being tended to. That was one of the things about her that charmed him.'

The main house is not an imposing building. 'It was just one of a cluster all put together higgledy-piggledy,' says Hubert de Givenchy.

'It's very quaint,' said the Duchess of Windsor's new maid, pursing her lips. 'I could see she thought it wasn't the place for a former King of England to live in,' Wallis says.

The Duke's room is small, tucked under the eaves, his sleeping quarters and dressing room stacked shipshape on top of each other. With its plain sofa bed and framed prints of the Grenadier guards, it seems to be a subconscious recreation of his father's study at York Cottage, Sandringham, where 'the walls were covered with a red fabric, the identical material that was used in the distinctive trousers worn by the French army of that period.'

The Duchess has mingled green with the red, tartan with bows, and underfoot the lion and the unicorn are rampant on a rug.

'He always lived in the simplest way,' says the Duchess of her husband. 'I mean, he always took the worst room in the house.'

Joanne Cummings and her millionaire husband 'Nate' are dressing for dinner in their guest cottage.

'I'll never forget seeing four maids, all in green uniforms, walking across the courtyard, carrying the freshly pressed organdie cloth over their heads,' she says.

'I remember pheasants in faïence from Strasbourg on the table,' says Grace Dudley.

'There was jelly, the real meat jelly, served after the cold cuts, on its own in a silver dish,' says Philippe du Pasquier.

The Windsors have a style for evenings at the Mill. He is always in a kilt, one of the dress tartans that hang in patches of muted colour in his closets. Long after his death, Prince Charles will take back the most emotive of the Scottish heritage.

'Prince Charles said the Duke's kilts were too small for him,' says Sydney Johnson. 'But I said to him, you've got two fine sons growing up. You take the kilts for Prince William and Prince Harry.'

The Duchess is in a caftan, a splash of pattern and colour as bold as the tartan ribboned carpet.

'She wore loose, slightly flowing things in the country with long sleeves,' says Lady Dudley. 'It was rather the Edwardian idea of a tea gown.'

'I shall use it as a tea gown for Sunday nights in the country. I haven't seen anything like it on this side and I love it,' Wallis wrote in 1936 to Aunt Bessie.

The big first-floor drawing room – its ceiling opened up to the rafters – is a riot of red and green, with splashy vermilion flower paintings and the Duke as Prince of Wales painted in vivid hunting pink.

'It was a very cheerful room,' says Lady Mosley. 'I always felt that it was the place to have fun and a good time.'

'I liked the Mill. It was a fun house; it was jolly,' claims the Duchess of Marlborough.

On the table in the drawing room is a jig-saw puzzle, a favourite royal pastime for Queen Elizabeth II and her house guests at Windsor Castle or Sandringham – and one of Mrs Simpson's earliest memories of weekends at Fort Belvedere.

'It's a very difficult one,' says the Duchess. 'All straight bits and so much brickwork.'

The Duke is in the bar, a small low room leading off the drawing room from beside the fireplace. It could be the snuggery of an English pub, but for the gouache map of the Bahamas, transferred from the walls of the Windsors' Bahamas beach hut to this country house in France.

Concealed in a cupboard outside the drawing room is a record player, its speaker crooning 'Bye Bye Birdie' through the cocktail hour.

'But you never forgot for one moment that he was a King,' says Anne Salter. 'People would come out from Paris for dinner, so there would be three tables of eight or ten, with two staff wearing white gloves at each table to serve. And then there were the regimental drums and things to keep the whole feeling of grandeur.'

The food is grand enough: a simple roast, but with a sophisticated purée of celeriac instead of potatoes; fresh trout, stuffed with mousse of trout and almonds; 'a Virginia ham of total perfection'.

The Sunday night suppers make the deepest impression.

TOP: *The misty green dining room with its painted trellis and leaves contrasts with the vibrant colours of the rest of the Mill. In the foreground: pheasant in Faience. On the mantelpiece: the Duchess's cabbage pots.*

ABOVE: *A Meissen plate in the shape of three leaves and matching pot and a cabbage and a bunch of asparagus in Faience.*

RIGHT: *The Duchess's collection of* trompe-l'oeil *china vegetables displayed on a Chinese escritoire in the first-floor drawing room.*

'It was all a completely new idea for us,' says Ghislaine de Polignac. 'Nobody in France had ever served the cold cuts with hot potatoes in their jackets and the meat jelly on its own in that way. It seemed wonderfully original.'

Dancing – to the latest American musical hits or to the Duke's bagpipe rendition of 'Over the Sea to Skye' – is part of the after-dinner ritual at the Moulin de la Tuilerie, just as it had been at Fort Belvedere.

'The Prince changed into a Donald tartan dress kilt with an immense white leather purse in front, and played the pipes round the table after dinner,' noted Lady Diana Cooper in 1935. 'We reeled to bed at 2 am.'

The Windsors and their friends – the Cabrols, the Dudleys, the Cummings, Ghislaine de Polignac – are competitive at cards, mainly bridge.

'We have been buzzing like bees for the past few weeks, many small dinners followed by bridge losses,' wrote Wallis to her Aunt Bessie of life in London with Ernest Simpson.

Poker was Wallis's game, learned in her uncomfortable time as a navy wife and honed during a period in Peking in the 1920s.

'I was not tempted to fill inside straights. I was not afraid to stand by good cards,' claimed Wallis. 'By the end of the game I had an impressive pile of chips in front of me.'

'We all liked to play canasta after dinner,' says the Duchess of Marlborough. 'That was her game more than bridge.'

Guests who have come out for the evening to dine eventually get up to leave for home.

'Even in the depths of winter the Duke would stand in a kilt, with his bare

ABOVE: *The Windsor style for evenings at the Mill is dress kilt for the Duke, caftan or tea gown for the Duchess and dancing to the record player hidden in a cupboard on the landing.*

RIGHT: *The Duke likes all the Hollywood musical songs and will croon along to the piano accompaniment.*

OPPOSITE: *The Duke of Windsor plays a mean hand at bridge. Poker is Wallis's game, or canasta among friends.*

70

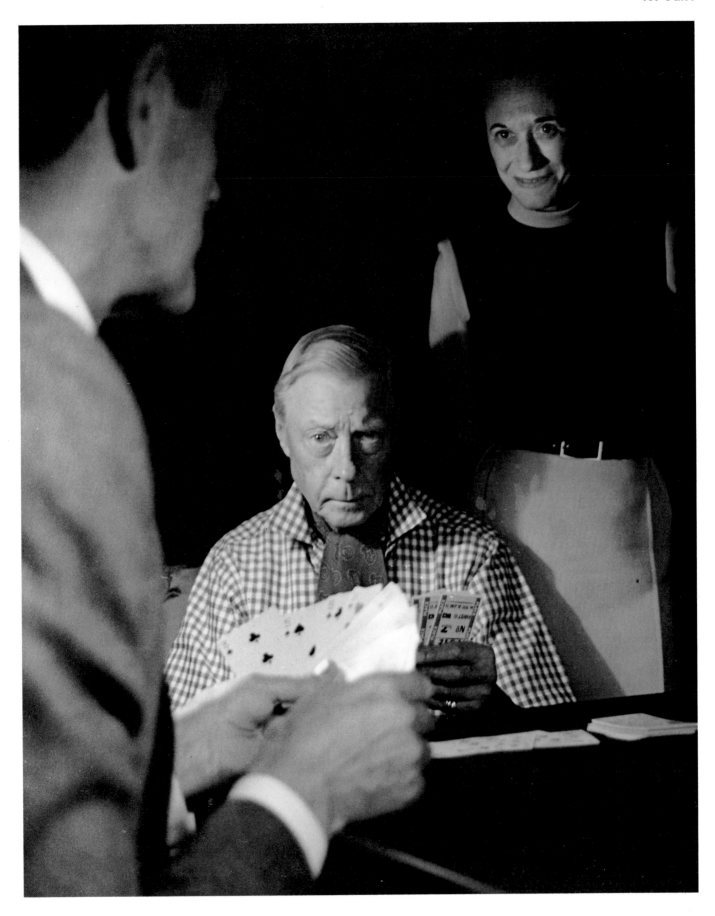

little knees, in the courtyard of the Mill to wave us off,' says Lady Mosley. 'He had such beautiful manners.'

Next morning, in the blustery outdoors, there are more games on the croquet lawn and on the pitch for the French game of *boules*.

'The Duke's love of competitive games is in evidence at the Mill,' says Nancy Spain. 'The Duchess, too, adores croquet and thinks it is a marvellous, vicious game.'

The Duke can practise his golf on the putting green, as he once did on the deck of the *Nählin*, driving 3,000 balls from the yacht into the open sea.

'Lots of our friends play golf and work up a good appetite for tea,' says the Duchess.

She likes most of all the swimming pool, when the temperature climbs up with the sun, and she can sit on the canopied *chaise-longue* and imagine herself back in the Riviera villa in the honeymoon post-war period of marriage.

At the Moulin, the Duke is always busy, pottering around the garden in his checked tweeds and plaid suits, looking eccentric, 'crumpled and happy'.

When the guests have left, the Duke and Duchess will walk together round the garden, through the gate at the back, up the hill and round the far stone wall of the estate, the pugs gambolling ecstatically behind them.

'After living in rented houses with other people's things for so long, we've gathered together in this enchanted spot our most cherished possessions,' says the Duchess. 'Like the garden we've planted here, we've put down roots.'

She feels at her most restless when the weather is bad and the mist closes in on the sopping meadows of the valley of the Seine. Her mind, says Nancy Spain, 'particularly can't be still on a rainy day.'

An illuminating vignette from Diana Vreeland on a visit to the Windsors:

'The rain was falling down and jumping off the ground, and I got in soaking, absolutely soaking, and I said, "Your country sir!" meaning that it rained too much there in France, or certainly at that moment, and his whole countenance changed.

' "*My* country?" He was furious at my suggesting that France was his country. Oh, he wasn't joking at all! Of course, immediately he recovered himself and was charming. But I had hit on something that was just about the *end*.'

OPPOSITE: *The elegant Baronne and Baron de Cabrol, Daisy and Fred, are close friends of the Windsors. They are standing in the drawing room in front of the Munnings portrait which is flanked by antique French hunting carvings. The Duke is wearing Royal Stewart tartan and his grandfather's Edwardian sporran. 'I wasn't sure about the taste of that tartan carpet,' says a distinguished guest.*

ABOVE: *The Duchess at the Cabrols' country house. The Duke in his father's tweeds with Daisy de Cabrol and Ghislaine de Polignac.*

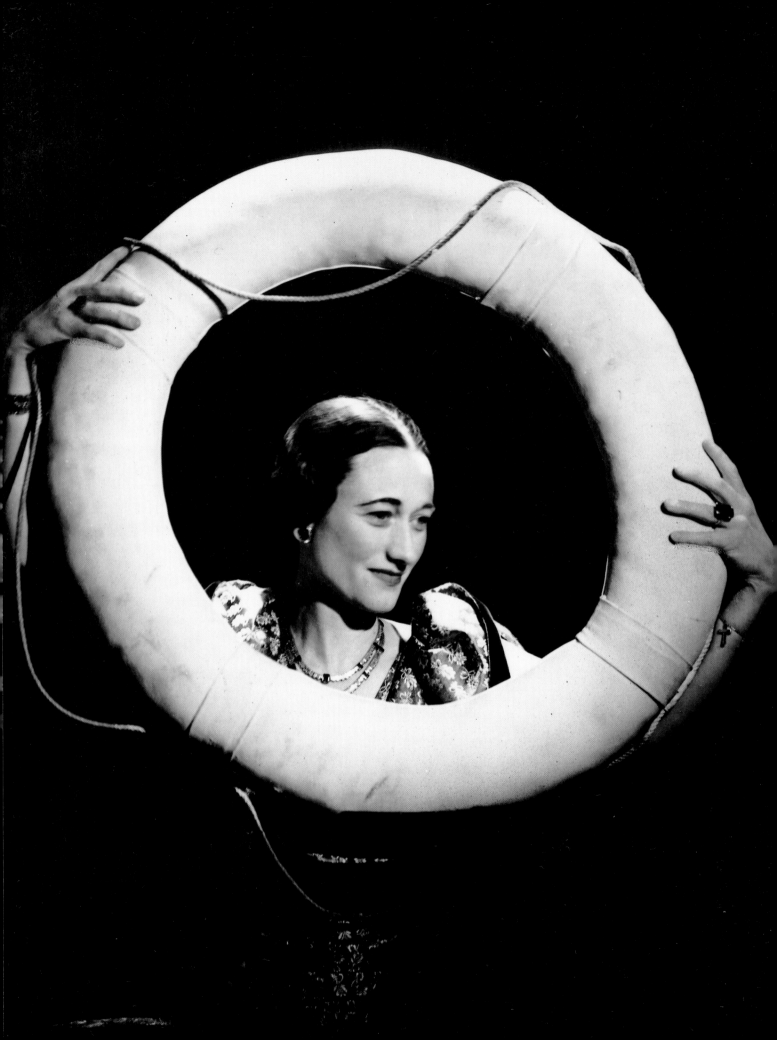

RIVIERA

'It really is the perfect holiday. I mean, the heat is intense, the garden lovely, the chair long and cool, the lime-juice at hand, a bathing pool there if one wishes to splash, scenery, books, gramophones, pretty people – and above all, the sense that it is not going on too long.'

HAROLD NICOLSON from Villa Mauresque, Cap Ferrat, 4 August 1938

A CONVOY of mottled brown trunks moves like a line of tortoises along the station platform. All around is the bustle and flutter of porters and stationmaster, maids and valet.

At the hissing head of steam are two tiny figures. The Duchess of Windsor is all in brown to match the square leather trunks, stamped in dull gold with LV for Louis Vuitton, the Paris cabin baggage maker. Sturdier gold letters by the leather handles declare the arrival of THE DUKE OF WINDSOR.

The 118 travelling trunks are the caravanserai of the Windsors' travelling years. Each lid is numbered. Inside each is a list of contents. Both maids carry the master list, with itemized outfits and accessories.

The mountainous baggage is a throwback to the Prince's empire tours. 'My travelling wardrobe was immense,' explains the Duke. 'I carried some forty tin trunks, each numbered and with its contents listed in a series of inventory notebooks.'

'They brought more trunks and suitcases than harassed customs officials could count,' said newspaper writer Adela St Johns when the Windsors arrived from the Bahamas for an American tour.

Later the trunks will be stacked in forlorn grandeur in the basement at Neuilly beside the pugs' zinc baths. During the Duchess's waning years, the priceless and historic luggage will melt away.

The Duke stands on Cannes station in this sunny post-war summer of 1946, a dapper figure in his tussore suit the colour of lobster bisque, rakish straw panama, two-tone brown and cream shoes, bumble-bee striped socks and silver-topped cane.

'I'll make a *boulevardier* of him yet,' says Noël Coward.

Even now, ten years after the abdication, the Duke of Windsor still expects the royal progress that made him, to Wallis Simpson, part of an 'enchanted world' in which he would send a plane to collect her Paris model dresses and she would fill it with '*langoustines* for him'.

'Trains were held; yachts materialized; the best suites in the finest hotels were flung open; aeroplanes stood waiting,' she explained.

'It was pathetic to see HRH's face. He couldn't believe it! He's been so used to having everything done as he wishes,' said Major 'Fruity' Metcalfe as the newly created Duke of Windsor started his post-abdication exile.

The stationmaster at Cannes is bowing low, reliving the glories of his nineteenth-century predecessors, who would receive commemorative medals from the Duke's great-grandmother Queen Victoria, when she descended with her entourage of household and servants on the Côte d'Azur.

Wallis is protecting herself from the scorching heat with a shady straw hat and her coiffure with a chiffon scarf, in preparation for the drive in the Buick estate car along the breezy corniches winding around the coast.

OPPOSITE: *In 1936 Cecil Beaton photographed a coquettish Wallis Simpson as a Hollywood bathing belle, framed in a lifebelt. On her left hand and wrist: her emerald 'engagement' ring and the bracelet of crosses.*

75

'She was always worried about the weather and her hair,' says her loyal hairdresser Alexandre. 'She would stay in her cabin for the whole of the crossing to America so that her hair would stay perfect.'

Studding the aquamarine water are the white hulls of miniature ocean-going liners – playthings for the rich.

'The Riviera has a cheap air about it . . . and the reputation of being the world's playground. It will be more dignified to be in the country,' said Wallis when she abandoned an earlier plan to marry in Cannes.

'Maybe WE can make the Riviera all right again together,' said the Duke, whose grandfather Edward VII had made fashionable the sweeping Baie des Anges at Nice with its spiky palms and wedding cakes of Grand Hotels lining the Promenade des Anglais.

The post-war summer visitors to Cannes fulfil snob society's worst expectations.

'The English people are beyond belief: they must all be black market profiteers. Most of them are Cockney Jews,' said Noël Coward. That was in the summer of 1946, when the Windsors re-opened the Villa de la Croë at Cap d'Antibes, which the Duchess had redecorated as their safe harbour after the abdication storm.

'Before I had fully grasped what was going on, the lawn had practically disappeared under an avalanche of crates, linen baskets, furniture, trunks of clothing, bales of draperies, chests of silver,' said Wallis on the day that the pantechnicons containing the contents of Fort Belvedere and her husband's royal history arrived at La Croë.

The sleek motor, announcing THE DUKE OF WINDSOR in metal letters on both forward doors, and its two following vehicles, swollen with luggage, circle Cannes harbour, spinning along the Croisette towards Antibes, where the wooded peninsula points a green finger into the sea.

'You can't imagine the sense of luxury at La Croë in that first summer after the war,' says the Baronne de Cabrol. 'It was a really grand villa, and to amuse us, the Duchess arranged to serve dinner in a different room each night over the ten days we stayed there.'

Noël Coward invited the Windsors to dine with him at Monte Carlo, in the first spring after the austerity of the Occupation. 'I gave them a delicious dinner: consommé, marrow on toast, grilled langouste, tournedos with sauce Béarnaise, and chocolate soufflé. Poor starving France,' Coward wrote mockingly in his diary in April 1946.

The 'plump, pigeon-shaped English chauffeur' draws up in front of the iron gates of the palatial residence.

'It gave the impression of a noble white vessel afloat on a calm sea,' says the Duke's ghost-writer, the *Time-Life* editor Charles J. V. Murphy.

'A dream-like place, cool, serene and aloof,' says the Windsors' secretary, Diana Hood.

'La Croë was really grand, all gold and white and mirrors, and right on the tip of Cap d'Antibes, near the Grand Hotel,' says Alexandre.

The commanding position was a major attraction when Wallis first found the ocean-liner of a villa, which its owner, the newspaper magnate Sir Pomeroy Burton, had built, complete with gilded swan-shaped bath, in the early 1930s.

'I have a terrible longing for the sight of the sea and something green,' said Wallis long before she was mistress of the sweeping green lawn rolling down towards the rocky sea at Antibes – and before an earlier visit to the Riviera was soured by the lesbian affair between her companions Gloria Vanderbilt and the Marchioness of Milford Haven.

OPPOSITE: *'I'll make a boulevardier of him yet,' says Noël Coward of the dapper Duke of Windsor, arriving here in his Riviera resort suit, rakish panama and co-respondent shoes, with pug as fashionable accessory.*

The scandal of that holiday Wallis took with four girlfriends to Cannes in 1931 was to reverberate through America three years later, when Gloria Vanderbilt fought to keep custody of her daughter. It was to taint Wallis with the accusation that she also had lesbian tendencies.

'I know for a fact that she had an affair with Elsie Mendl,' says a Parisian society caterer, although he cites no evidence.

'I should be tempted to classify her . . . as An American Woman, *par excellence*, were it not for the suspicion that she is not a woman at all,' says James Pope-Hennessy.

Wallis's flat, angular, boyish figure is most evident in a swimsuit, as she folds herself up on a sunbed under a striped awning by the pool at La Croë.

'A lovely villa *in the water* – our own rocks and all the privacy in the world,' Wallis said of the holiday she and her Prince shared at Golfe Juan in 1935.

For three years, their life together was a Never-Never-Land of sun-soaked holidays, culminating in the cruise round the Adriatic in the yacht *Nählin* in 1936, with the world's press in its wake.

'Existence on water is vastly restful to one's point of view,' Wallis recorded in flowing handwriting, in her Commonplace Book decorated with Prince of Wales feathers and filled with sayings and quotations. 'The past and the future are alike cut off; the present seems as interminable as the ocean itself . . . time stands still . . .'

It is time for lunch on the curving half-moon terrace, where the chairs are covered with bamboo-patterned cloth against the bright white of the pillared porch.

Inside the rooms, shuttered from the hazy heat, *trompe l'oeil* white clouds float across the high blue vault of a ceiling reflecting the sea view outside. A sunshine yellow pattern dances on the dining room curtains and splashes bright colour in the cool rooms. *Trompe l'oeil* effects of abandoned bags, trailing stockings and scattered jewels are painted on a chest of drawers in her bedroom – an earlier and racy version of the style of Wallis's later homes.

In a full dress rehearsal for the decoration of the Windsors' house in Neuilly, the Duchess has hung the royal pennant from the galleried entrance hall at La Croë.

The Duke – son of a naval father – has his telescope trained on the sea from the top deck of the villa, where the skylight of variegated glass makes a ceiling of the sky.

'My father never lost the nautical habit of consulting the barometer,' says the Duke. 'No matter where he was, on his way to breakfast or to bed, he would make a beeline for the instrument. He would peer at the glass, tap the case sharply to make sure the needle was not stuck, and set it again.'

The Duke of Windsor has re-christened his upper quarters at La Croë 'Fort Belvedere'. The sitting room is decorated with a crisp blue and white colour scheme and a ship's bell.

From the roof terrace he surveys the sea, just as once he stood on the bridge of the *Renown*, watching the 'Eddystone lighthouse thrust its white tower out of a calm sea' as the ship sailed into Plymouth Sound after an eight-month tour of India in the summer of 1922.

The ex-King of England now studies the detail of passing yachts and taps his late father's barometer to advise guests of the Riviera weather. The rest of his days is spent in dealing with his papers, nurturing his guests and trotting off to the golf course in his tropical shirt and bright trousers, while the rest are lunching in the shade.

'There's not one good golf course within motoring distance,' grumbles the

OPPOSITE: *The palatial villa La Croë, the Windsors' rented house in the South of France, with its green lawns sweeping down to the sea. The Baron de Cabrol made a collage in his album of the luxurious life on the Riviera in 1946 – the first summer after the war.*

OVERLEAF: *'Britons flung off their conventional clothes and started to dress like Mediterranean fishermen,' says the Duke of Windsor, pictured here with the Duchess in the Italian resort of Portofino in 1951.*

LA CROE
CAP D'ANTIBES
A.M.

LA CROE
CAP D'ANTIBES
A.M.

Séjour à la Croe 10 au 22 Avril 46

Duke, when the Windsors decided to give up their lease on La Croë in 1949.

Wallis lies like a lizard by the pool and comes to life at dusk.

'He was a man who liked a bit of an adventure, to jump into the sea or something,' says Lady Diana Cooper. 'She hated any form of adventure. She liked to sit quietly. They were not suited in that way.'

'She was *une femme de ville*,' says a Parisian acquaintance Sarah Schlumberger.

'*Une femme d'intérieur*,' says Wallis's friend Diana Mosley.

This is not strictly accurate at La Croë, where the Duchess, guided by society decorator Elsie Mendl, and with the help of her '*complice*' Stéphane Boudin, has done everything possible to bring the freshness of the seascape to the inside of the villa – and to make the outside terraces and poolside into an alfresco cocktail lounge.

White-gloved footmen manoeuvre silver trays across the lawn as the heat and the light fade.

'There was a lovely soft warm evening with that marvellous pink light among the pines,' wrote Harold Nicolson on the night the Windsors came to dine at the Villa Mauresque on Cap Ferrat with the author Somerset Maugham. 'The sun set over Cap d'Antibes. The lighthouses began to wink across a still purple sea. I stayed until the red oleanders became invisible and only the white oleanders shone in the moon.'

The languorous Riviera nights are spent in dinner jackets, cocktail in hand, like a stage setting for the latest Coward play.

'Two ice-filled silver buckets – sandwiches one bite big – again and again came the silver trays with fresh glasses of the bubbling champagne,' says Clement Puddleford reporting for the New York *Herald-Tribune*.

'A tiny white table for us four was set on the huge lawn,' says a guest at La Croë. 'There were rows of footmen . . . The night was furiously hot, but the Duke was in full Scottish regalia. I thought he was staging a production of some sort.'

Noël Coward himself, ostracized by the Prince of Wales in earlier years because of his rampant homosexuality, was tart about the man born to be King. 'All the charm in the world with nothing whatever to back it up,' he said.

'His face now begins to show the emptiness of life,' says Cecil Beaton. 'He looks like a mad terrier, haunted one moment and then with a flick of the head he is laughing recklessly.'

The Duke is in a nervous fidgety mood, his bagpipes wailing across the sunny terraces until it is time to dress for dinner.

'HRH was as if he was lying on a wet slab in a fishmonger's shop,' complained his friend Fruity Metcalfe. 'The same old greasy eye and limpness. He was not trying . . . even a comic interlude failed dismally to bring even a little smile to the face of our late (retd) Sovereign Monarch.'

'One cannot get away from his glamour and his charm and his sadness, though, I must say, he seemed gay enough,' said Harold Nicolson, after dining with the Windsors beside two cypresses and under the moon.

Wallis's evenings on the Côte d'Azur begin with the hairdresser, Alexandre, born and brought up in St Tropez, who arrives punctually at 6 pm each day.

'Except one day, when the Windsors were having a cocktail party and I fell asleep on the beach,' says Alexandre. 'I woke up at the time I should have been at the villa. So I dashed there, just in my shorts and beach clothes. As I bounded up the stairs, the Duke was standing at the top.

' "Where do you think you are going?" he asked.

OVERLEAF: *Life at La Croë centres on the swimming pool built into the rocks at the tip of Cap d'Antibes. The Baron de Cabrol's painted collage shows Wallis (far left) lying under the striped awning. The Duke (centre right) is in his 'Robinson Crusoe' clothes.*

OPPOSITE: *Guests at La Croë were entertained on the pillared terrace. Dinner was served outside by white-gloved footmen at a W-shaped table. This menu of Mediterranean red mullet followed by roast beef and Yorkshire pudding was chosen by Wallis in April 1946.*

' "To see Her Royal Highness," I replied.
' "Not dressed like that, you're not," replied the Duke, and sent me down to Georges to borrow a pair of trousers and a jacket before I could come up.'

'Is it raining in *here*?' George V had asked his fashion-conscious son, thinking that his trousers had been rolled up to cross puddles. When the Prince of Wales dared to wear trousers with turn-ups, it was the first of many sartorial rebellions against his autocratic father.

Tonight, the Duke wears a dinner jacket of fine silk tussore. 'Take off that white jacket, you look like a waiter,' the Duchess complained to her husband at Palm Beach, when he was wearing his summer-weight tuxedo.

'The Duchess, who likes a man to "dress up", is inclined to be critical of the fact that nowadays he tends rather to "dress down",' says the Duke.

Wallis will change her style according to the resort, the season and the fashions of the time: beach pyjamas for Cannes in the early Thirties; Capri pants for Portofino in the 1950s; silk for Palm Beach and linen for Portugal.

'We didn't go out to restaurants much in those early years,' says the Baron de Cabrol. 'It was the grand life on the Côte d'Azur, dining with friends.'

Those friends include Willie Maugham, ex-King Leopold of the Belgians, the Aga Khan, Winston Churchill, Eric Dudley. Or the Windsors might dine at one of the grand hotels: the Hôtel du Cap d'Antibes; the Hôtel de Paris in Monte Carlo; then on to the casino with the Dudleys.

'Wallis and I gambled to 5 am,' says Coward. 'She was very gay and it was most enjoyable. The Duke sat rather dolefully at one of the smaller tables.'

Wallis is an extrovert gambler.

'You've thrown away three kings,' gasps one of her partners at gin-rummy.

'But I kept the best one, didn't I,' Wallis roguishly replies.

The Riviera years are the overture to a life of parties. From the Bal des Petits Lits Blancs, to the Red Cross Ball at Monte Carlo, the Windsors are roving guests of honour.

'He will go from resort to resort getting more tanned and more tired,' predicted American columnist Westbrook Pegler at the time of the abdication.

'I was like a man caught in a revolving door,' the Duke described his earlier round of empire travels.

'The governorship of the Bahamas was no more than the gift of a sunlamp between the twilight grandeur of his eleven-month reign and the long night of his banishment to the transatlantic social tour,' said the broadcaster and historian Alistair Cooke.

The Windsors' travelling years slow down only at the end of the 1960s as the Duke's health fails. The pallid shadows of the royal empire tours are designed to give form to a shapeless life.

Like his father, his grandfather and his royal great-grandmother before him, the Duke of Windsor now has fixed points in the turning year. But instead of Christmas at Sandringham, summer at Windsor, September at Balmoral in Scotland and the spring and autumn 'seasons' in London, there are Paris and Palm Springs, Cannes and Manhattan.

'There is a strong New York side to the Windsors' lives,' says James Pope-Hennessy.

'We spend part of every year in the United States, where David seeks out the company of men of affairs whom he questions searchingly about the latest developments in their fields,' claims the Duchess.

'I have my trousers made in New York and my coats in London,' says the Duke. 'It's an international compromise which the Duchess aptly describes as "pants across the sea".'

The Duke and Duchess of Windsor in the gilded and mirrored salon of La Croë – the start of a lifelong love affair with the Riviera.

NEW YORK

The Vanderbilts are waiting at the club
But how are we to get there? That's the rub.

IRVING BERLIN, *Easter Parade*, 1948
sung by JUDY GARLAND and FRED ASTAIRE

THE Duke of Windsor is climbing slowly aboard ship, his eyes shielded by dark glasses, clutching the rail as the deck pitches and rolls. The Duchess is dressed for travelling – 'very fresh and vase-shaped, in a tight white or cream-coloured costume with a vast pale fur collar'.

'I saw them at Le Havre when they were embarking for New York,' says Diana Neill, now secretary to the British Embassy in Paris. 'He had just had an operation on his eyes. I noticed her narrow ankles like little sticks and her globular eyes, and that she didn't have a nice voice. It was very harsh.'

The stately Cunard liner sails to New York on a wave of cocktail parties and dinners – with society columnist Elsa Maxwell to record the fun and the outrageous and gossipy Jimmy Donahue to create it.

Wallis Simpson had broken into the world of the Captain's Table and the cocktails when she sailed to America without her husband in 1933.

'The captain has been very nice,' she reported to her aunt Bessie Merryman. 'I went for KT but found him inclined to pinch, so never again.'

For the five days on board she treats the ship as home.

'When we were all crossing the Atlantic on the *United States*, my cabins looked awful, and hers were immediately wonderful,' says Grace Dudley. 'She would throw down a fur rug and a pug pillow. She had the knack of making a place into a home.'

'They had a suite of cabins, with two bedrooms leading off a nice salon,' says Diana Neill. 'The private secretary was carrying a cushion and the Duke was leading the dogs.'

The landing is always an event – steaming in a triumphal arc past the Statue of Liberty and Staten Island towards the stack of matchboxes that resolves into the high-rise towers of Manhattan.

The Duke will reminisce about his 'fabulous harbour welcome' of 1919. 'Scores of vessels blasted a welcome with their whistles,' he explains. 'All the way to the Battery, the barge was serenaded by a brass band identified as the musical unit of the New York Street Cleaning Department.'

The infectious warmth of an American welcome reverberates across the water when the Duchess of Windsor sails in with her royal prize on New Year's Day 1941 – two small figures with arms aching from waving.

'American vitality – it is a tangible quality,' says the Duke to a US friend. 'You can feel it in the air. You absorb it . . . Your blood begins to tingle; I have always admired the great natural energy of you Americans.'

The Windsors' home in Manhattan is apartment 28a that takes up an entire floor in the Waldorf Tower – a world of uniformed bellhops, dining and dancing to the palm court band and movie stars riding the elevators.

'We're a couple of swells
We stop in the best hotels,'

croon Judy Garland and Fred Astaire when *Easter Parade* is released in 1948.

The Duchess's bedroom is furnished with fashionable satinwood furniture,

Because the Duchess is frightened of flying, the Windsors sail each season to New York, arriving here on the liner United States.

and fresh yellow and green curtains swagging the graphic Manhattan skyline. Wallis will fill the suite with pale, exotic flowers and scatter needlepoint cushions, stitched with New York wit, on the curving *chaise-longue*.

'You can never be too rich or too thin,' says the most famous of her embroidered pillows; or 'Never explain, Never complain'; or 'If you are tired of shopping, you are using the wrong shops.'

'I could scarcely believe my eyes – the Prince of Wales doing needlepoint,' exclaimed Wallis, when she saw him, needle in hand, at Fort Belvedere, practising the skill he had learned from his Mother, Queen Mary.

Later, Nathan Cummings will lend the Windsors art treasures from his collection to furnish the Waldorf suite more gracefully.

'When I say tea, I mean Scotch, neat,' says the Duke to Joanne Cummings, as he arranges to come over from the Waldorf at 4 pm to see her husband.

In New York, the Windsors use all the right shops. Up past the brownstones of Madison; along Fifth Avenue from the elegant department store floors of Saks to the jewel box windows of Tiffany, taking in Bergdorfs and Harry Winston's latest diamonds on the way.

'It was atrocious driving up Park Avenue tonight,' the Duchess will complain to Joanne Cummings in the early 1960s. 'Where do they get all those blacks from? And why do they allow them on Park Avenue?'

'She grew up in the South, at a certain time, with certain prejudices,' Joanne Cummings says.

The Duke is walking from Park to Fifth, turning into East 59th Street for a fitting for a new dress suit in ink blue wool.

'A tailor named Harris, who had served his apprenticeship in London,' explains the Duke.

The Duchess is two blocks away, stepping out of the bank of elevators and into the salon of Mainbocher, where tiny mirrored tables and brown banquettes line the beige walls. She stands patiently for the fitting, looking up at the sky-blue ceiling with its floating painted white clouds that bring back memories of La Croë.

'The most serious clients have the intelligence always to wear the same kind of underwear,' says Mainbocher, as he fits the Duchess in a column of black crêpe with a line of satin bows down its bodice.

The Duke is off to Dobbs of Fifth Avenue to buy a pale straw panama to take to the Riviera. The Duchess is lunching at La Grenouille, where the cheques that the Duke so reluctantly writes out are framed on the wall.

'I took my mother there and the Duchess was sitting in a corner,' says the jewellery designer Ken Lane. 'She was wearing one of my belts, and she got up and chanted to us "Look, I'm Mrs Kenneth J. Lane."'

'How I hate leaving America where I have all my girlfriends to laugh and lunch with,' Wallis writes from Government House, Nassau.

When the Duke is back home in Paris working on his memoirs, Wallis will lunch with Jimmy Donahue, who has acted as court jester, and paymaster, to the Windsors ever since they met the Woolworth heir with his mother Jessie in Palm Beach in 1950.

'There was a little restaurant just off Park Avenue on 59th,' says the interior decorator Billy Baldwin. 'I heard an absolute roar of laughter from the entrance of the restaurant, and into the room, like two children, rushed the Duchess and Jimmy . . . to the farthest corner in the back back back of the room where there was practically no light . . . After lunch they would just quietly go to Jimmy's apartment.'

'I just want to tell you something about your little Duchess,' says Jimmy

ABOVE: *Apartment 28a in the Waldorf Tower – part of the Waldorf Astoria Hotel – is the Windsors' home in New York.*

OPPOSITE: *The Duchess of Windsor photographed in the imposing suite at the Waldorf Tower in 1943. Her bedroom has satin-wood furniture, yellow and green curtains, and is filled with exotic flowers. Wallis's severely plain crêpe dress decorated with bows is by Mainbocher.*

A 1949 Cartier brooch, featuring a 152.35-carat cabochon Kashmir sapphire, made under the direction of Jeanne Toussaint (far right) for the Duchess of Windsor (below right).

The Cat's Meow

THE SQUID, THE WHALE, and the dinosaurs get all the attention at the American Museum of Natural History in New York City. But George Harlow, curator of minerals and gems, puts forward a strong case for his department. "Minerals make life possible on the planet," he says. Harlow, who joined the museum in 1976, has been "politicking for the last 20 years" to overhaul the storytelling around earth and planetary sciences. He finally got his wish with the opening this spring of the rebuilt Hall of Gems and Minerals. The space now has room for temporary exhibitions designed to draw crowds in. First up is "Beautiful Creatures," which showcases spectacular jewelry from the past 150 years in the shape of wild animals, a nod to the museum's zoological collection. The scintillating menagerie on display will include starfish, flamingos, coiling snakes, countless butterflies.

And the jewel of the exhibition, so to speak, is a brooch made by Cartier in 1949: a panther (the company's unofficial mascot), in platinum studded with sapphires and diamonds, that perches on a hemispherical sapphire as if conquering the globe. The work of legendary Cartier design director Jeanne Toussaint (herself nicknamed "La Panthère"), it embodies the French house's élan following the end of the war. Ironically, it was commissioned for the Duchess of Windsor by her husband who, it has since been revealed, harbored Nazi sympathies. Yet the piece has been divorced from this legacy and now spends its time traveling the world. "It's the *Mona Lisa* of jewels," says the show's curator, jewelry historian Marion Fasel. "The Cartier pieces are really masterpieces. They're pillars in the exhibition that people are going to make pilgrimages to see." — *Julian Sancton*

Sign Up
for Newsletters

Delivered to your inbox weekly, our Dispatch and WorldWise newsletters keep you up to date on what's new in fashion, culture, technology, and more.

DEPARTURES

Sign up at
departures.com/newsletters

PALAIS ROYAL: HOW THE WINDSORS LIVED

IT TAKES ONLY FIFTEEN MINUTES TO DRIVE FROM THE front door of the Ritz Hotel to the Bois de Boulogne, where the Duke and Duchess of Windsor lived at 4 Route du Champ d'Entraînement. The *fin de siècle* white stone mansion, which is owned by the City of Paris, was their residence from 1953 until their respective deaths in 1972 and 1986.

The French government gave the duke a lifelong lease, tax-free status, and an annual peppercorn rent of £25. Now the government has rented the house to Mohamed Al-Fayed, the affable Egyptian businessman who owns the Paris Ritz and Britain's House of Fraser stores, including Harrods. Al-Fayed persuaded Maître Suzanne Blum, the blind, 90-year-old lawyer who is executor of the duchess's estate, to sell him everything left in the house for £2 million. And he is proud of having kept these pathetic remnants together for posterity.

The Windsors in 1957.

Al-Fayed has promised to renovate the house, restoring it to its fifties glory. It will be a memorial to the couple's tawdry little lives, reflected in the faded, tattered décor of their home. Al-Fayed, who has no set budget (his funds are apparently unlimited), plans to keep a suite on the top floor for guests.

The late Stéphane Boudin, of the legendary French firm Jansen, helped the duchess decorate the house in a style that could be called early precious. The furniture is decorative. The paintings are mainly of flowers or dogs, and many are hung on velvet ribbons. Porcelain objects—dogs, fruits, vegetables—abound. It's all very "fashionable" but definitely not "royal."

When Wallis Simpson was first introduced to the Prince of Wales, in 1930, by his mistress at the time, Lady Furness, they called him "the little man." And the scale of things throughout the house is little—small, high-ceilinged rooms, low tables and sofas, tiny stools, and surprisingly narrow beds.

The house is not at its best now. The unpredictable heating system (circa 1945) needs to be modernized. The slate roof is being repaired and the stone façade scrubbed. The tattered curtains and damaged upholstery have been sent off to be restored. The gilded moldings and cornices have dulled with time, and precious ornaments have been packed away in the basement for safekeeping. And there are no small pugs snuffling and snorting about as there always were in the Windsors' day.

The duke's bedroom, where he died in 1972.

The double-height front hall has a black-and-white stone floor and is dominated by a sweeping staircase with wide, shallow stone steps that run up the left-hand wall. Straight ahead are three rooms that run the length of the house. In the middle is the long, ice-blue drawing room, with French doors leading out to the green, tree-shaded lawn. There are sofas on either side of the fireplace, and a grand piano. Above a small side table is a formal portrait of the duke's indomitable mother, Queen Mary, to whom, it is said, he whispered his last words—"Mama, Mama"—on his deathbed. In one corner is the plain wooden table on which the duke signed the Instrument of Abdication in December 1936.

To the left, large double doors lead to the Chinese-papered dining room. Tiny minstrels' galleries were used by the musicians who entertained during formal dinner parties. The original marble-topped dining table, designed by Jansen, is one of the many items that have mysteriously disappeared from the house.

Curator Joe Friedman (left) with the Windsors' servants.

On a large table in the library, the English curator Joe Friedman, 28, has laid out a few leather-bound books with a royal provenance. Most touching is the small prayer book inscribed by the duke's Danish-born grandmother, Queen Alexandra: "Darling little David on his seventh birthday when he went to church for the first time. Sunday June 23, 1901. From his loving old Grannie."

Directly above these formal rooms is the suite that the Windsors occupied. Above the dining room are the duke's bedroom, dressing room, and large gray marble bathroom. Oddly enough, this is where he used to spend his mornings working. And because he only took showers, he had a bare, unfinished wooden top made for the tub, which he used as a worktable, spreading out his papers and correspondence so it was all at hand as he dictated to his secretary.

The "boudoir," as the Windsors always referred to it, is the large sitting room that separates the duke's bedroom from the duchess's. Here they had tea every afternoon (he drank it; she didn't) or dined when they were alone. He'd wear a velvet smoking jacket and black tie, and she'd wear an evening dress.

In one corner is the green painted *(continued on next page)*

Photographs: top, AP/Wide World; bottom left and right, Press Association, courtesy of The Al-Fayed Archive, Paris.

Japanese escritoire at which the duchess used to organize their life—paying bills, writing letters, answering invitations. A small cup still holds stubby, blunt pencils, old ballpoints, and Parker fountain pens whose ink has long since dried up. A glass-fronted vitrine set into the wall holds objets d'art, including a few pieces of Chelsea china that can't compare to the collection in Clarence House, the London home of the duchess's bitter enemy Queen Elizabeth, the queen mother. At the far end, a door leads into the duchess's surprisingly small bedroom, its color known as "Wallis blue," which the duchess wore on her wedding day. The top drawer of a large chest is filled with 30 to 40 empty Cartier jewelry boxes—tiny for rings, small for brooches, long and narrow for bracelets, big and square for necklaces. Their leather looks new and untouched. The drawer below holds dozens of neatly sorted hair ornaments: combs, clips, barrettes, and hairpins in tortoiseshell, ebony, and ivory. A door beside the small bed leads to the duchess's dressing room, which survives as a tribute to the dying art of the lady's maid. Behind one door are floor-to-ceiling rows of shoes, most of them by Roger Vivier; the soles were always polished so they'd look pristine when the duchess crossed her legs.

Another cupboard has wooden shelves with the duchess's handbags; most are emblazoned with a small gold crest, a W

Pug-dog pillows in the duchess's bedroom.

below a tiny ducal coronet. Each bag is lined with crunched-up tissue paper and wrapped with tissue paper, too, in the way you'd wrap a gift. The adjacent cupboard holds lingerie—pale-violet and black corsets from Christian Dior. Across the room, another cupboard holds maroon bags, which protect her scarves and an assortment of little cotton hankies. One door conceals a passageway to the landing, which the maids used to get in and out without disturbing anyone in the bedroom.

Next door is the duchess's bathroom, which is bleak-looking and old-fashioned. It has not aged well. The cabinets still have leftover bits and pieces of soap and cotton. In a chest, there's a selection of bedjackets and the little shoulder capes she always wore when her hairdresser made his daily visit to her suite.

WHEN THE DUKE DIED, HE LEFT EVERYTHING TO HIS WIDOW. When the duchess died, she left their furniture to Versailles, but all I could track down there was a white porcelain chandelier from the boudoir, which now hangs in the Dauphine's anteroom. The rest of the $50-million estate went to the Pasteur Institute, which leads the world in researching AIDS, a disease that the duchess, who spent the last eight years of her life vacantly staring at the ceiling above her bed, probably never heard of.
— LESLIE FIELD

BABY, IT'S YOU

"I WAS PREGNANT AND working on Wall Street," Christine LaBastille recalls, "and all I could find were frilly dresses that looked inappropriate at a conference or meeting. So I decided to open a store where women could buy decent outfits near their offices."

The Executive Mother, LaBastille's ten-week-old maternity shop at Third Avenue near 47th Street, will make it easier for women who work in midtown to combine breadwinning and childbearing. (Traditionally, maternity shops have

LaBastille helps a customer.

been located where mothers-to-be *live.*)

The sleek, bright store carries conservative, well-chosen clothes ($40–$250) for professional women.

"Luckily, designers have recently figured out that pregnant women need a professional wardrobe right up until their baby is born," says LaBastille, 38, whose son is 4. "Finally, manufacturers are using better fabrics and tailoring."

The Executive Mother also carries children's clothing (infant to 24 months), Beatrix Potter books, stuffed animals, and gift baskets, so a mother can keep shopping there once her maternity leave is over and she's back at the office.

Since looking good is important for executive women—especially when they're eight and a half months pregnant—all the oversize dressing rooms have special pillows that customers can tie around their waists while trying on the clothes.
— JENNIFER SEABURY

ONE AFTERNOON, I WENT TO pick up the eight-year-old girl for whom I occasionally baby-sit at her parochial school in Queens. When I arrived, she was jumping up and down on the sidewalk and announcing that she hoped there *would* be drugs in her school.

I was startled and tried to explain that she was confused and that she really didn't want her school to become drug-infested. But she told me *I* was wrong. She said she wanted drugs in her school so she could do what was right and "just say no."
— PATSY J. MURPHY

Donahue. 'She's the best I've ever known . . . She's always considerate and adorable, and she never hurts me as almost all the others do.'

In return, Donahue entertains the Windsors, throwing lavish parties, inviting them to benefits at the Pierre Hotel, where the French boudoir furnishings remind the Duchess of her Paris home. Jimmy will take them on a merry-go-round of night clubs or to dine at the Colony.

'Their Royal Highnesses never entertained in New York, except for a few receptions,' says Sydney Johnson. 'But all New York was entertaining them.'

The daily allowance of 'pocket money' for the Windsors' staff, who have their own small quarters at the Waldorf Tower, is $2.50 a day.

'I only buy about a hundred new dresses a year, and most of them cost only about two hundred and fifty dollars apiece,' claims Wallis when criticized for her extravagance.

It is June, and a private dinner party of exquisite taste and perfection is being given for Wallis's birthday by Estée Lauder, cosmetics queen, and a warm friend to the Duchess.

'Wallis only liked American women,' says Diana Vreeland, fashion editor at American *Vogue*. 'She was very much like all Southern women. She was a marvellous hostess, a marvellous friend, and she cared a great deal about her own four walls.'

In New York, the Duchess of Windsor is known not as a hostess, but for going to parties. No glamorous gala evening, no fund-raising benefit, no dinner dance, no society ball of the winter season is complete without the Duke and Duchess of Windsor.

'Wherever the Duke and Duchess go, the world goes,' says society columnist Elsa Maxwell.

'I remember when Elsa was giving a drinks party,' says London interior designer Nicholas Haslam. 'The Duchess and I both arrived at the hotel too early. "Let's hide in here until everybody comes," she said, and swept us both into the maids' broom cupboard where she chatted away until the party got going.'

'A fetishistic concern for trivialities was to inspire the Duchess of Windsor to organize her entertainments for café society,' said Cecil Beaton dismissively. But Beaton himself designed the décor for the Duchess of Windsor Ball in 1953 – the apotheosis of Wallis Warfield of Baltimore, who was first presented to society as a débutante in the winter of 1914, in a white satin dress. 'Made for me by a negro seamstress named Ellen'.

'To be presented at the bachelors' Cotillion was a life-and-death matter for Baltimore girls in those days,' she says.

At the Duchess of Windsor Ball at the Waldorf, Wallis is the toast of New York, as she leads a parade of fashion models, wearing a $1,200-dollar dress in white taffeta embroidered with coral to the strains of the 'Windsor Waltz'.

The Prince of Wales was born to be the beau of the ball. 'Midnight often found me with wearied brain and dragging feet, and the orchestra blaring out hackneyed tunes,' he said as one 'elaborate and expensive' party after another was held in his honour.

That party-go-round has now become a life sentence, and the Duke seems increasingly unwilling to sing for his supper.

New Year's Eve, 1953: a noisy nightclub party is carousing at El Morocco to see out the coronation year of the Duke's niece Queen Elizabeth II.

'Bring one for the Duke,' shouts the Duchess merrily, as paper crowns, cardboard travesties of majesty, are handed out on silver trays and the flashbulbs record the moment.

'The coronation's over,' she calls to the photographers as she leads the sheepish ex-King out into the chill Manhattan night.

'They began almost at once to go about in what was then known as café society,' says Adela St Johns, a leading writer with the Hearst newspaper group, as the Duke and Duchess reached New York on their American tour from the Bahamas in the autumn of 1941.

The same criticism had been levelled at the Prince of Wales, when he touched base briefly in London between his empire tours, and spent late nights and early hours at the Café de Paris and the Kit-Kat and Embassy Clubs.

'My father, never having been inside a nightclub, assumed . . . that these establishments must be dimly lit, smoky, disreputable dives,' said the Duke, whose royal parents never attempted to provide any social background, introductions or education for their children.

'The Windsors were café society, if there ever was such a thing,' says Billy Baldwin. 'In the end the Windsors didn't care whom they saw, and they would finally go any place if anyone asked them to come for a meal; they just had no discrimination whatsoever.'

They also have no compunction about acccepting invitations and then expecting and demanding that transport and accommodation be provided for them as well. Theirs is a royal progress through Long Island, Rhode Island and Palm Beach.

'They had a bad reputation in New York for accepting freebies,' says Jean Amory, an American who moved in the social orbit of the Duke and Duchess. 'They would even accept free tickets to go down to Florida. But then the Duchess had a Southern mentality, that her country had come through the civil war and been raped and she was going to fight to get her share.'

In 1947 Wallis posed for the photographer Horst for American *Vogue* in a Scarlett O'Hara taffeta dress billowing out, her face tough and determined.

January and February are spent in Palm Beach, where the Windsors established themselves as the pivot of fashionable society and Wallis is as good a guest as she is a hostess.

'She was a fantastic house guest,' says Anne Slater. 'When they used to stay with my mother-in-law in Long Island, she would bring her four dogs. They weren't always totally housetrained, but she trained her staff to clear up after the dogs.'

'They'd arrive with a valet, a maid, two pugs, and more luggage than you'd believe, including a fitted basket for the Duke's afternoon tea . . . and all this for one week's stay,' says a fellow guest at banker George Baker's shooting plantation in Florida. In New York, Edith Baker would keep a room in their upper Manhattan mansion ready.

When 'Wally' arrived in Boston five years after her marriage, the Duchess checked 31 pieces of luggage into the Ritz Carlton Hotel and her every change of wardrobe was breathlessly reported in the local press.

'So much travelling,' says Sydney Johnson. 'Four months of the year at a time in America. It was too much for maids with families in Paris.'

The Duchess gives good value at the dinners, balls and benefits staged in honour of the Windsors. In Washington, Margaret Biddle, wife of Ambassador Drexel Biddle and the friend who gave Wallis her favourite pug Disraeli, wrote her a dinner party tribute: 'The woman I most admire / Is worth an entire Empire!' The Duke plays golf, discusses business and finance and is charming and melancholy.

'Uneasy lies the head that wears the crown,' quips Wallis to Cecil Beaton, as a sequin crown lands on her head at an Epiphany party given for her and the Duke by the wife of the owner of the Folies Bergère in Paris.

For the Duke's 70th birthday in 1964, millionaire Nate Cummings will charter a Parisian *bateau mouche* for a dinner dance – and then put a giant birthday cake on a second floating barge.

'He had an enormous admiration – a kind of adolescent hero worship, really – for men of huge wealth,' said the Duke's secretary. 'The fact that they commanded such enormous assets simply entranced him.'

Noël Coward contrasted the global frivolity of the Duke and Duchess of Windsor with the style of England's new young Queen Elizabeth and her husband Prince Philip. 'True glamour without any of the Windsors' vulgarity,' he said.

The pattern of the Windsors' days, at home or abroad, is much the same. The Duchess will shop, lunch, prepare for the evening; he will play daily games of golf, or shop with her.

'You know what my day was today?' the Duke asked a Paris-based writer Susan Mary Alsop. 'I got up late and then I went with the Duchess and watched her buy a hat.'

Nights are always late.

'He stayed until 3 am and played the bagpipes for them and stood on his head,' wrote Wallis of her Prince.

'The evenings lately have been *dreadful*! He won't think of bed before 3 am and now has started playing the accordion and the bagpipes,' wrote 'Fruity' Metcalfe immediately after the abdication.

'The boredom is appalling but healthy after 2 years of 3 am nights,' said Wallis, when she was exiled from the Duke in Cannes, waiting for her divorce to be finalized.

'Sir, some of the others are . . . awfully tired. Why don't you pretend to say good night, drive round the block for a bit, and then come back after the others have gone,' begged a hostess in Palm Beach, where the Windsors insist on the royal protocol that nobody can leave a party before they do.

'Have you no *home*?' the Duchess chides as she drags a reluctant Duke away.

'I remember when they were staying with my mother-in-law and the Duchess was still having fun at 4 or 5 am,' says Anne Slater. 'The Duke suddenly appeared in his pyjamas and silk dressing gown. He stood at the head of the three steps leading down to the sunken drawing room, cocked his head on one side, and said very gently: "Yankee, come home!"'

Christmas – that crown jewel of the royal year – casts its own spell on the peripatetic Windsors.

'I suppose the gayest Christmases we've spent have been in New York,' the Duchess tells Nancy Spain. 'American Christmas is really something.'

'It's worth making a special trip to New York just to see one,' responds the Duke.

'And outside the Rockefeller Plaza they have a tree about a hundred foot high.'

'It's really beautiful. Park Avenue has a tree for every block, and its lights. And then there's the shops, and the shop windows.'

Their voices, says Nancy Spain, 'mounted and climbed one upon the other in their efforts to convince me of the high-class excellence of the American Christmas.'

'They are a happy couple,' says Cecil Beaton. 'They are both apt to talk at once, but their attitudes do not clash.'

OPPOSITE: *An ecstatic welcome for the Windsors in Miami on New Year's Day 1941 on the yacht Southern Cross for their first visit to America together. 'I have always admired the great natural energy of you Americans,' said the Duke.*

92

IN THEIR FASHION

'We do expect that you will not wear anything extravagant or slang, not because we don't like it, but because it would prove a want of self-respect and be an offence against decency, leading, as it has often done before in others, to an indifference to what is morally wrong.'

QUEEN VICTORIA to the future Edward VII, 1851.
A Family Album, The Duke of Windsor

'Good Americans, when they die, go to Paris.'

THE DUCHESS OF WINDSOR's Commonplace Book

'THE COLLECTIONS. Aaaaaaaaargh, the collections!' groans the Duke of Windsor, burying his head in his hands in mock horror.

'The Duchess loves Paris,' he quips. 'Because it's not too far from Dior.'

The Duchess is mounting the curve of the staircase to take her seat at the 1958 spring-summer couture collections. Her Royal Highness, as the staff respectfully address her, is wearing a trim cream bouclé suit, a small brown ocelot hat, taupe gloves in glacé kid gripping a brown lizard skin bag marked with her personal insignia – a pair of intertwined Ws for Wallis Windsor, surmounted by a gilded crown.

From her seat by the deep window, she looks down through the fuzz of spring green on the branches to where the limousines are scuttling like scarabs along the Avenue George V.

'Avenue Papa,' the Duke calls it with an arch smile. His French guests look politely puzzled, for George V, that most correct and staid of monarchs, is not much remembered in France. The Duke's grandfather, Edward VII, is a different story. *'Le bon boulevardier,'* the elder Parisians will say, and think of the expansive white waistcoats, the gleaming stickpins and the check tweed suits that the Duke of Windsor's style so triumphantly celebrates.

'This bright tweeded opulence of my grandfather and his friends, while out shooting at Sandringham, was always a wonder to me as a child,' he says; and his own style, unchanging, individual and confident, seems to flow from his royal past.

'In a world where men tend to look more and more alike, he seems more than ever endowed with the capacity to look like no one else,' says Nicholas Lawford, who knew the Duke in pre-war Paris.

The Duchess's dress is a product of rigorous effort, rather than inherited or natural taste; it is based on simplicity of cut and line.

'She elevated sobriety to an art form,' said the French magazine *Elle* on the Duchess's death in May 1986.

Half a century earlier, on the eve of the abdication, the North American

OPPOSITE: *New Look for Wallis, photographed by Horst in a strapless fuchsia pink taffeta ballgown with embroidered underskirt, sapphire and diamond fleurette necklace and evening gloves to hide the hands she hated.*

95

ABOVE: *'Her posterior subtly invites a bustle,' claimed Cecil Beaton when he sketched Mrs Simpson in the proverbial little black dress in late November 1936.*

OPPOSITE: *Wallis Simpson's 1930s cocktail-shaker chic. She posed for Beaton with her collection of antique bottles beside a display of exotic mauve orchids and crimson roses in her London flat by Regent's Park.*

Newspaper Alliance stressed this fashion austerity: 'The note that this reporter has always detected in Mrs Simpson's clothes is that of extreme simplicity, which Paris says is the hallmark of the really well-dressed . . . woman.'

'I began with my own personal ideas about style,' the Duchess tells society hostess Fleur Cowles in 1966. 'I've never again felt correct in anything but the severe look I developed then.'

On her fashion-show programme, the Duchess is noting down three of the plainest tailored outfits by Hubert de Givenchy, who will be such a warm friend to her after the Duke's death, driving her out to Orsay to lunch with Lady Mosley and squiring her gallantly for the last gasp of the parties.

'S.A.R. La Duchesse de Windsor' reads the lettering embroidered on the blue – Wallis blue – cover which Givenchy's fitter uses to hide new outfits from inquisitive society eyes.

'They all wanted to know what she was ordering,' says M. de Givenchy, who started to dress the Duchess in the 1950s. 'Everybody wanted to copy her, like her friend Mrs Gilbert Miller. Even women who didn't have her figure or style wanted to dress as she did.'

The early days – before her fairy prince settled her dress bills – were a struggle.

'The royalty stuff is very demanding on clothes,' Wallis complained to her aunt Mrs Bessie Merryman, as she sent off lists of ideas for inexpensive clothes from America:

'Something sophisticated with red blue black or combination of colours . . . and not over $59.50,' she begged in the early new year of 1934.

'Any cheap pale blue summer dress for country wear . . . about $20.'

'Send me the dress as soon as possible as I'm really naked.'

'My evening clothes will just make it.'

Wallis Simpson uses her ingenuity and style to make a lean wardrobe stretch through the social season: she substitutes one trim for another; she trades in old dresses for new:

'I have been selling the old ones . . . I only get $20 or $30 for quite a lot – about the price of two new ones.'

She makes the most of the essential little black dress: 'We all look like black birds. As I always wear so much black for economy I got into mourning with no expense,' she writes to her aunt at the start of Edward VIII's new reign.

'You have to wear black, ageing or not,' she will tell Fleur Cowles, 'because when the little black dress is right, there is nothing else to wear in its place.'

In later years the Duchess will use her deceptively simple *haute couture* dresses as a canvas for her fantastic jewels.

'She always chose from the Dior collection one *robe écran*,' says her dresser of 30 years Agnès Bertrand. 'There would be a black coat and dress for day or an inky violet at night.'

In the Christian Dior museum collection hangs a tiny black silk crêpe dress, small enough for a child, long-sleeved, high-necked, utterly simple except for bands of horizontal seaming.

'My sitter is at her best in a nondescript black dress that she makes smart by wearing,' says Cecil Beaton, as he sketches Mrs Simpson for an article in *Vogue* in 1936. 'She is the antithesis of pernicketiness, but she is tidy, neat, immaculate.' He draws her in a series of elegant watercolours: 'S'-shaped in a citric yellow evening gown; in dull black behind a collection of sculptural antique bottles; standing in elongated elegance in a plain black dress, hand on hip.

'Her posterior,' claims Beaton, 'subtly invites a bustle.'

Wallis breathes into this classic simplicity a whisper of the exotic – just as she will do later in the furnishings of her Paris home. The surrealist artist Man Ray photographs her in 1936 beside a terracotta temple statue, wearing a dark high-necked Chinese coat tipped with gilded braid.

'She has the dignity and fragility of a Chinese princess pictured on a priceless piece of porcelain,' says Edwina Wilson, Mrs Simpson's first biographer.

'I remember a dress made from a sari of thin Indian silk, absolutely plainly cut, rather high at the neck and long sleeves. Probably made by some "little" dressmaker,' Lady Mosley recalls.

'The Duchess looked too beautiful,' says Diana Vreeland, 'standing in the garden dressed in a turquoise djellaba embroidered in black pearls and white pearls – marvellous – and wearing all her sapphires. She was so affectionate, a loving sort of friend and very rare you know. Women are rarely that sort of friend to each other.'

June 1933. Mrs Ernest Simpson is at Ascot in the Prince's party, in a demure dress with a white piqué dickie at the neck.

'PW calls it my white tie dress,' says Wallis, whose Prince of Wales is conspiring with his brother Prince George to end the male fashion tyranny of boiled shirt and white tie.

'Have any of you ever stopped to think,' he asked in 1928, 'why we are all dressed up in these stiff armour-plated shirts?'

Among the English society ladies, with their fussy hats, floating chiffons and patterned silks, Wallis seems to belong to a different breed.

'She reminds one of the neatest, newest luggage, and is as compact as a Vuitton travelling case,' says Cecil Beaton.

'She was chic and worried about it,' says Lady Diana Cooper.

'She was very much a product of the 1920s,' says Diana Vreeland. 'She was *soignée*, not *dégagée*.' The French words express neatly Wallis's polished but unrelaxed style.

Wallis Simpson's recipe of absolute simplicity with a dash of wit started way, way back, when she was plain – very plain – Bessiewallis Warfield of Baltimore, and speared her hair with a peacock blue feather above a conventional evening gown; or earlier still when at her first adolescent party she insisted on substituting a red sash for a blue one on a white party frock.

It became a recurrent fashion theme.

'Mrs Simpson,' said Prince Paul of Yugoslavia to her in 1934, 'there is no question about it, you are wearing the most striking gown in the room.'

'It was a simple dress, designed by Eva Lutyens, daughter-in-law of the architect, but the violet lamé material with a vivid green sash made it outstanding,' Wallis explains.

Cecil Beaton photographed the newly-married Duchess of Windsor wearing a slither of white bias-cut crepe by Mainbocher, a sash of the sparkling striped lamé matching its jaunty jacket.

This simplicity of line will be taken up as a constant reprise by the designers who keep her on the Best Dressed List for 40 years.

'We had a conspiracy of fashion purity between us,' says Marc Bohan of Christian Dior. 'She liked everything as plain as possible and that was my taste too. She would look at me quizzically and say "Shall we take off the pockets?" and I would say "Yes".'

'The Yves Saint Laurent style is one of rigour – that's why she liked it so much,' says the Duchess's vendeuse Danielle Porthault.

April 1934, Fort Belvedere. The Prince is sitting on the padded window seat in the Fort's octagonal drawing room, looking out of its pointed Gothic window.

The first thing you notice is the flamboyant socks – waspish stripes of yellow and black banding his ankles, below the Prince of Wales check trousers with the turn-ups his father so despises. He has just changed out of his elephantine golfing plus-fours, but kept on his bright hose.

'HRH was dressed in plus twenties with vivid azure socks,' wrote Lady Diana Cooper from the Fort in 1935 to Conrad Russell, gentleman farmer nephew of the Duke of Bedford.

'An incongruous figure in baggy plus-fours, a thick sweater, hair tousled' was Wallis's first vision of the Prince at the Fort.

Ten years earlier, the idiosyncratic style of the Prince at play had impressed the Paris fashion designer Coco Chanel, who based her costume for one of Diaghilev's ballets on a snapshot of the Prince playing golf.

Her Golf Player in *Le Train Bleu* wore 'a white collar, tightly knotted tie and, along with his plus-fours, a striped sweater with matching socks'.

'Perfectly smart,' judged the Prince's friend the Duke of Westminster when asked if Chanel had got the extraordinary costume right.

'Both my father and my grandfather had worn a baggy type of knickerbocker,' says the Duke. 'Possibly my own fell a fraction lower . . . and it is this that attracted so much attention.'

His easy double-breasted suit, buttoned low, with a triangle of spotted silk at right angles to the breast pocket, is also making a sartorial statement.

No gentleman would have dared to wear a lounge suit in town and never ever in front of His Majesty George V, who wore his flannel sports suit buttoned high over a formal waistcoat.

'We had a buttoned-up childhood in every sense of the word,' admits the Duke of Windsor. He has an instinct to unbutton – metaphorically and literally – the formal dress that reflected 'my family's world of rigid social convention'.

'It was my impulse, whenever I found myself alone, to remove my coat, rip off my tie, loosen my collar and roll up my sleeves,' he explains. 'The Duchess likes to describe this process as my "striptease act".'

'The Duke was always impeccably dressed,' says Laura, Duchess of Marlborough. 'He wore perfectly tailored suits and never a hair out of place.'

'His Royal Highness was so fussy about his suits,' says the Duke's valet Sydney. 'They had to be hung in the closet in order and rotated. And I would iron his shirts just the moment before he put them on, or otherwise the Duchess would come in saying "Sydney, there's a crease."'

The Prince of Wales suiting, named after the future Edward VII, is his grandson's trademark as Prince and King.

'My father set few, if any fashions,' says the Duke of Windsor in the manual of style *A Family Album* that he wrote in 1960. 'The only respect in which I followed the sartorial tastes of my father was in the materials of his country clothes. He liked bright checks on his tweeds and so did I . . . But the cut of my clothes is thought more casual than his.'

His country clothes become increasingly eccentric.

'The Duke scampered in . . . wearing red trousers, a fur coat, and a peaked flying cap with fur ear flaps,' says James Pope-Hennessy, visiting the Windsors at the Moulin in 1958.

'I say, you saw a pretty quaint apparition just now,' admits the Duke. 'Why they put me in red pants I can't imagine.'

OVERLEAF LEFT: *Wallis in Schiaparelli's carbon blue silk jersey dress and jacket embroidered with baroque gilded scrolls, photographed by Beaton at the Château de Candé on the Loire just before her marriage.*

OVERLEAF RIGHT: *Man Ray caught the exotic, oriental taste of Wallis Simpson in this surreal 1936 study for Harper's Bazaar.*

99

ABOVE: *The young Prince of Wales followed the 'bright tweeded opulence of my grandfather' in his dog-tooth check sports jacket* TOP *and houndstooth coat and cap.*

OPPOSITE: *The Duke of Windsor's fashion hallmark was the double-breasted lounge suit in Prince of Wales check, worn here with two-tone shoes. Wallis wears a plain, chic dress with turquoise hat and the turquoise fleur de lys brooch the Duke bought her from Cartier for her 42nd birthday present in 1938.*

'He was quite loud, in the way he mixed his checks,' says Nicholas Lawford. 'But he represented style to his generation.'

An earlier eccentricity was the gaudy sleeveless sweater that the Prince wore first in saddlecloth yellow under his hunting pink.

'To take the place of the thick buttoned waistcoat which I never found comfortable for hunting,' he says.

For golf, earlier on this spring morning at the Fort, he was wearing a V-necked jersey in a mosaic of pattern.

'I suppose the most showy of all my garments was the multicoloured Fair Isle sweater, with its jigsaw of patterns, which I wore in the Golf Club at St Andrews in 1922,' says the Duke, whose mix of knit and check is as riotous as the border of massed spring flowers outside the Fort's mullioned windows.

'He has . . . his own manner of putting things together, contrasting checks with stripes, bold colour with bolder colour . . . all in a hundred combinations of improbable elegance,' claims American *Vogue*. The Prince had scandalized society by arriving in New York in 1924 wearing tan suede brothel creepers with a wide-lapelled double-breasted light grey suit.

'I noticed that my American friends were looking down at my feet with some embarrassment,' he says. 'Finally someone explained that the wearing of these shoes in America was regarded as effeminate, to say the least of it.'

October 1935. Mrs Ernest Simpson is lunching at the Ritz with Lady Cunard, the cultured society hostess who has taken up the new royal favourite. Wallis is wearing a 'purple and black sport costume', with matching violet ribbons snaking round her sleek, shiny hair 'like a coronet braid'.

'Her maid makes these bands, and she has them in many colours,' wrote Mrs Simpson's first biographer Edwina H. Wilson.

Wallis looks at her best in the smart 'tailormades' that she brightens with a jewel-coloured blouse, a crisp white collar or a bold clip.

'One of her favourites . . . was . . . a satin blouse in jockey colours, made with the colours alternating, as in a jockey's shirt,' says Mrs Wilson.

Despite the cauldron of gossip bubbling around her, Mrs Simpson's clothes are discreet.

'Trim messenger-boy's suits,' says Cecil Beaton.

'Clever woman, with her high-pitched voice, chic clothes, moles and sense of humour,' observed the usually acerbic diarist Henry 'Chips' Channon.

'Mrs Simpson,' claimed Harold Nicolson, 'is bejewelled, eyebrow-plucked, virtuous and wise.'

Long after the 1930s silhouette has shortened, or hardened or softened into sportswear, Wallis will continue to base her daytime wardrobe on trim tailoring.

'What she always wanted were little suits, with short jackets cut very close to the body,' says Marc Bohan of Christian Dior. 'She would pull a tweed tight to her shoulders and say "make it smaller here".'

'The Duchess never really cared for Mademoiselle Chanel,' says her coiffeur Alexandre. 'And Chanel would say dismissively to me "How's Mrs Simpson?" But when Her Royal Highness saw how Chanel would cut a shoulder, so small and tiny, she had to ask for an appointment.'

'I think of her at the Moulin wearing tweed Chanel-type suits,' says Lady Mosley.

'She wore tweed skirts and wonderful thick stockings with little brogues,' says Grace, Countess of Dudley.

No-one could fault Mrs Simpson's sober style – even when she and the

Cecil Beaton's romantic study of Wallis in
Schiaparelli's white organza evening dress
printed with a giant lobster and matching
flame red midriff panel. The royal bride spent
$5,000 on a trousseau of 17 outfits from
'Schiap's' Music Collection in spring 1937.
Her ruby and diamond necklace was made by
Van Cleef & Arpels in October 1936.

ABOVE: *The lobster dress.*

The wedding dress, draped into a heart shape at the bust, had a matching long-sleeved jacket. With it, the new Duchess wore a blue straw bonnet, trimmed with pink and blue coq feathers by Caroline Reboux and pale blue suede shoes by Georgette, both of Paris. The blue crêpe wrist-length gloves opened up on the ring finger of the left hand.

King paid a frosty visit to Royal Lodge, in Windsor Great Park, to show off a new American station waggon to Bertie and his wife Elizabeth.

'I looked at her with some interest,' says the sharp-tongued royal governess Marion Crawford. 'She was a smart, attractive woman with that immediate friendliness American women have.'

'She was always correctly dressed, never funny, never slouchy, never don't care, always right and wearing pearls,' remembers Lady Diana Cooper.

'You would never see her in a roll-neck sweater in the country,' says Erik Mortensen of Balmain. 'She would be in a smart two-piece with a cardigan jacket.'

'I never saw her in a blouse and skirt in the country,' says Givenchy. 'I remember her in a pearl grey suit with a white blouse and a good brooch on the lapel.'

'Wallis admirably correct and chic. Me bang wrong!' wrote Lady Diana from Fort Belvedere in 1935.

Criticisms aimed at the Duchess of Windsor are for her vulgarity and frivolity in behaviour – never the style of her clothes.

'The Duchess could be very loud and vulgar in the way she behaved, even the way she laughed,' says the Vicomtesse de Ribes. 'But she had rigour and restraint in dress.'

August 1936. Mrs Simpson is with the King on the yacht *Nählin*, wearing a severely plain white play suit, cut in one piece with short sleeves, wide-legged shorts and a zip front. On her head, protecting her skin from the sun, is a frilled baby's bonnet. She looks cute.

'England doesn't wish for a Queen Cutie,' observes Noël Coward waspishly.

'Her sports and play clothes are frankly boyish,' reported the breathless American press. 'Most of the time on board the yacht she spent in dark blue or white linen shorts, with a little silk open-weave sports shirt, no stockings and white canvas deck shoes.'

'She makes, rather than mars her daytime appearance by capping her essentially hard, strict clothes with a baby's bonnet,' said Cecil Beaton.

King Edward VIII is wearing very little. Just a pair of cotton drill shorts below a bronzed chest partly covered in a striped vest, and rope-soled shoes.

'He had no hat . . . *espadrilles* . . . little shorts and a tiny blue-and-white singlet bought in one of their own villages,' said Lady Diana Cooper as the locals try to guess which of the royal party is the King.

'I . . . began to enjoy "going native" in this relaxed and easy fashion,' he says. 'I used to lie out for hours in the sun, toasting my skin to a rich brown tan.'

The King's entourage is not amused.

'Do you think you could get the King to . . . put his shirt on until we get out of sight of the Greeks,' Lady Diana begged Wallis.

'I like my work . . . I enjoy getting round the country meeting new people. But I get very bored with all this dressing up,' the King grumbles to Wallis as he strips down to 'a pair of shorts, a shirt and sandals'.

Mrs Simpson is swimming in the still waters of a secluded sandy cove. The King, bronzed and bare-chested, drawing on a cigarette, is pulling on the oars of the ship's dinghy.

'There was about him – even in his most Robinson Crusoe clothes – an unmistakable aura of power and authority,' Wallis admits.

She is wearing a long, lean bathing suit, its overskirt drawn modestly over her thighs.

*Wallis chose a sapphire blue silk crêpe dress
and fitted jacket by the American designer
Mainbocher for her wedding at the Château
de Candé on 3 June 1937. An embroidered
tablecloth over a chest of drawers made an
improvised altar. The towers of white blooms
were by London society florist Constance Spry.*

'Plus-twenties with vivid azure socks,' said Lady Diana Cooper when she first saw the Prince in his sporting garb. He added a Tyrolean hat to his tweed knickerbocker suit for a ski-ing holiday with Wallis in Kitzbühel in February 1935.

'We have a swimsuit with a chaste little skirt designed by Lola Prussac for the Duchess of Windsor,' says Yvonne Deslandres, curator of the Paris Costume Museum. 'The Duchess was clever enough to build a fashion image of being well brought up and respectable.'

The King is pulling on a matelot sweater.

'Latins and Southern Europeans tend to dress more gaily than we Anglo-Saxons,' he claims, to explain why 'Britons started to dress like Mediterranean fishermen.'

Twenty years later, at the age of 60, he will still be strolling round the Riviera ports in striped sweaters, coloured pants and fancy socks. His flamboyant clothes and fascination with them feed the faintest breath of a rumour that the ex-King might be one of . . .

'Those fellers who fly in over the transom,' the Duke will say, making stagey flapping gestures with his hands. 'I won't have them in my house.'

'If only the Duke would have a "pansy" these complications would not arise,' wrote Wallis to Major Gray Phillips in 1949 about the problem of servants leaving to get married.

The Duke is a snappy dresser, rather than a preening peacock. 'In Florida I often have trousers . . . made of tropical weight corduroy in . . . light colours,' he says. 'But I remain in most ways conservative.'

The Duchess likes blue, 'Wallis blue', the colour of her eyes.

'Blue is her colour – particularly in off-shades that are unusually becoming, with her blue eyes, creamy skin and rich brown hair,' claims Edwina Wilson.

'She liked blue greys and red blues, raspberry and navy,' says Yves Saint Laurent. 'She knew exactly what suited her.'

'Mauvey blue rather than a greeny blue,' agrees the House of Dior.

'I remember her in a wonderful Cardin dress, predominantly blue, covered with paillettes and sequins,' says Grace Dudley.

In the summer, Wallis wears baby colours, powder blue, fondant pink and ivory beige.

'The thing I most remember about her clothes is that she dressed very young for her age, in pale pink from head to foot,' says the Duchess's former kitchen boy James Viane, now chef at the British Embassy in Paris.

'I lunched with her in New York and she was wearing a fluffy mohair coat in pink and white check,' says London decorator Nicholas Haslam. 'When the Duchess wore a swagger coat, it always had the most enormous swagger.'

Nino Caprioglio, the fashion artist, sketched the Duke and Duchess as they arrived in a waterside restaurant in Portofino in the 1950s, to have dinner with the Infanta Cristina of Spain and the actor Rex Harrison.

'She was wearing pale pink piqué, with a little sleeveless white cardigan,' he says. 'The Duke was in a yellow shirt with bright red trousers.'

The Windsors' secretary, Diana Hood, reported His Royal Highness's trotting off to golf each midday at La Croë, 'wearing crimson trousers . . . with light blue shirt and red and white shoes, and another day bright blue trousers with a canary yellow shirt and blue shoes'.

'In his liking for colour in clothes, my grandfather sometimes overdid the effect,' admits the Duke. 'A French newspaper described him at Marienbad as wearing "a green cap, a brown overcoat, and pink necktie, grey shoes, white gloves and knee breeches".' The British tailoring press made an instant response to this sartorial goulash: 'We sincerely hope His Majesty has not brought this outfit home.'

The Duke lounges on deck, just as he used to on the long chair beside the swimming pool at Fort Belvedere.

'He is utterly himself and unselfconscious . . . He does not *act*,' writes Lady Diana Cooper from the *Nählin*.

Wallis is sitting in a deck chair, a chiffon bandeau holding her hair in place, a cardigan round her shoulders over a trim checked dress. She is dressed for relaxing.

'She was chic but never casual,' says the Vicomtesse de Ribes. 'Other American society women like Babe Paley could be chic in blue jeans. The Duchess was a different generation.'

So is the Duke.

'Blue jeans . . . are not,' he confesses, 'the pants for me.'

May 1937. Cecil Beaton is photographing Wallis on a sunlit summer afternoon in the park at the Château of Candé.

In this month before her wedding, Beaton creates a romantic and ethereal vision of Wallis, wearing a diaphanous white Schiaparelli dress decorated with a large red lobster. Through the sheer white chiffon skirt can be seen the silhouette of her slim thighs.

Earlier, Beaton had described the mannish Mrs Simpson as 'a brawny great cow or bullock in sapphire blue velvet'.

'I thought her awful, common, vulgar, strident, a second-rate American with no charm,' he said.

Memories of her 'Lotus year' in China in the 1920s stayed with Wallis all her life. She wore a Chinese coolie pyjama suit for a fancy dress party.
The Duchess of Windsor dressed in a satin domino cloak by Dior for a Venetian carnival ball in Paris in 1958. Wallis disliked the vogue for costume parties. 'She had no sense of theatre,' says a Paris friend.

OVERLEAF LEFT: *The Duchess of Windsor in the square-shouldered 1940s silhouette, photographed by Dorothy Wilding. Her hair is crimped round the madonna parting. On her lapel, the sapphire panther clip bought from Cartier in 1949. Wallis's collection of furs came from Revillon in Paris and Maximilian of New York.*

OVERLEAF RIGHT: *The Duchess photographed by Horst in 1947 in a Scarlett O'Hara dress by Mainbocher. The austere high neck is balanced by the panniered taffeta skirt built out over an elaborate crinoline.*

109

Now Beaton captures in his lens the elegance, the chic and the wit of the bride for an ex-King, posing her in Schiaparelli's skinny carbon blue dress and jacket embroidered with gilded scrolls, beside one of Candé's baroque commodes gilded to match the dress.

'I have been delighted with the pictures – certainly the best that have been done,' said Wallis as her photographs were spread over six pages of American *Vogue*.

Elsa Schiaparelli, the artistic Italian dress designer, shares with the more sober American Mainbocher the credit for Wallis's new image. 'Schiap' – friend of the surrealists and part of the *avant garde* circle in Paris – expresses the exuberant side of Wallis: her wit, her pep, her sense of fun and impatience with convention; her strength of character and her independence.

'Wallis was . . . the most independent woman I had ever met,' says the Duke.

Schiaparelli's sophisticated chic and witty frivolity will fly high at her 1938 'Circus' collection, as models swing from tightropes or ladders slung from Schiap's salon windows above the Place Vendôme.

For her trousseau, Wallis orders a tweed jacket appliquéd with jet butterflies, which Beaton pinions in a photograph framed by the scrolled stone window at Candé. Even more striking than the lobster evening gown is a floor-length coat in open-work navy horsehair lace like a giant net trapping the butterflies painted on the plain blue crêpe sheath underneath.

The Music Collection is the name Schiap gives to her playful designs in that spring of 1937, when bees and birds are woven on to soft summer dresses and buttons are made in the shape of fish, violins, chessmen, butterflies.

ABOVE: *Six shelves of the Duchess of Windsor's closets are filled with her collection of fine leather bags, each decorated with her crest of entwined WW insignia and gilded crown. Her favourite colour was brown, in calf, crocodile or lizard. The sofa with pug cushions is at the end of her bed.*

OPPOSITE: *Wallis using the chic bag as the essential 1940s accessory to trimly tailored suits. The round-handled bag in the facing picture can be seen in close-up above.*

ABOVE: *A pensive Duchess in a severe 1940s suit with pointed felt hat.*

OPPOSITE: *Wit was an essential part of Wallis's fashion style. Beaton caught her spirit of fantasy in this 1930s photograph of a crêpe dress printed with matchsticks and Schiaparelli's Mad Cap.*

RIGHT: *Wallis Simpson's hat was chic and sleek when she was photographed by Beaton.*

For the cruise on the Nählin in the summer of 1936, Wallis wore a floppy sun hat with her prim short-sleeved shirt and tell-tale bracelet of engraved crosses.

An element of fantasy will be stitched into the Duchess's wardrobe for the rest of her life.

'The very first dress I ever made for her had monkeys in wool embroidered on white cotton,' says Hubert de Givenchy. 'I had copied it from eighteenth-century *boiserie* and the Duchess adored it.'

'I made her a fantasy,' says Marc Bohan. 'It was in the 1960s at the time of the Twist, and she had a dress made for dancing, with a fitted body breaking out into pleats at the hips.'

For the Paris *première* of the film *A King's Story* in 1965, the Duchess chose a different kind of Dior 'fantasy': a black coat with its deep hem smothered in tiny bows.

'The only "frou-frou" costume she ever owned was one in her summer wardrobe,' wrote Edwina Wilson, in 1936. 'It was a black crêpe evening gown, severely plain in front, with many, many tiny ruffles at the back, each edged with white, and spreading like a peacock's plumage.'

'I remember the Duchess choosing a very simple evening dress, decorated with coq feathers,' says Danielle Porthault of Yves Saint Laurent. 'Her Royal Highness's style was sobriety by day and fantasy and originality at night.'

Dressing up for a costume party is not part of Wallis Simpson's fantasies.

'Tonight is Bertha Grant's advertisement party. I am going as a tube of Odol toothpaste in blue oil cloth with . . . round silver cap,' she wrote in 1931. 'It's been a lot of trouble so I hope it's fun.'

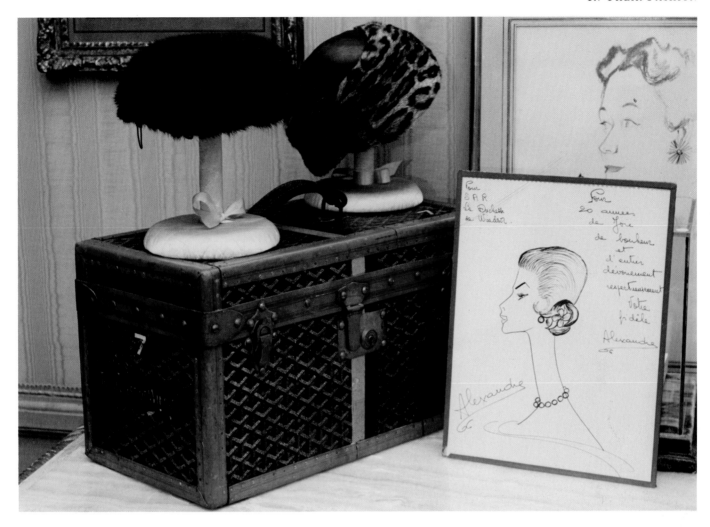

In the 1920s, she dressed up in Chinese pyjamas; with Ernest Simpson she went to a Naughty Nineties costume ball in rouge and a feather boa.

'My costume not bad. And the red wig fairly becoming,' Wallis said.

'For Alexis de Redé's oriental ball, I worked on my costume for three months,' says the Vicomtesse de Ribes. 'I cut up three couture dresses and a sable coat. The Duchess of Windsor did not look special at all. She was no good with fancy dress. She had no sense of theatre.'

'It is rare,' says Erik Mortensen, 'to see someone so famous, photographed so often over the years, who never, ever looked ridiculous.'

June 1937. The Duchess of Windsor has taken her marriage vows, framed by two cascades of white flowers designed by Constance Spry.

'I'm going to make the flowers as beautiful as I can . . . I'd do anything for her. I adore her,' says the society florist.

Wallis's dress is a vivid column of sapphire blue crêpe, long-sleeved, flute-necked, the skirt flaring out at the feet like a mermaid's tail. On the Duchess's head is a halo of blue straw overlaid with pink and blue feathers. Her shoes are powder-blue suede pumps with three-inch heels. Her gloves are pale blue crêpe and the fourth finger opens up – like a finger stall – so that the Duke can slide on the platinum wedding ring. 'Wallis 18–10–35 Your David 3–VI–37' it says inside, to commemorate the day the Prince asked her to wed him and their marriage date.

The Duchess of Windsor's neat head was outlined by her trim fur hats that were packed for travel in miniature trunks. The stylized sketch was a present from her 'faithful Alexandre' – her coiffeur for 20 years. Wallis framed the drawing and kept it on her dressing table with a sketch of her tiger lorgnette.

117

A pair of shoes to match every elegant outfit was the style of the Duchess of Windsor. Her exquisite evening shoes, jewelled, patterned and embroidered on satin and velvet were the work of Roger Vivier. He became couture cobbler to Christian Dior in 1953 and Wallis had some of his finest works of art at her feet.

The wedding outfit has been designed by the American Mainbocher as a slender dress and fitted jacket that is fastened with a line of covered buttons the size of shelled peas.

'Buttons were always a favourite with the Duchess,' says Marc Bohan. 'One of the last Dior dresses I made for her was a hostess dress in ivory crêpe with little buttons down the sleeves rather like that wedding dress.'

Both the jacket and its high-waisted dress are gathered into a soft heart shape at the midriff. But this is not a dress to stir the heart, for it is elegant and sophisticated rather than romantic. As it lies in a coffin of a box at the Costume Institute of the Metropolitan Museum in New York, the dress will fade to a dull cloud grey with just a glimmer of sky blue on the inside seams.

The Curator of the Metropolitan Museum's Costume Institute formally registered the wedding dress when it was given to the museum by the Duchess's friend Elsie Mendl: 'Dress is intricately cut on very simple lines; it is entirely cut on the bias. Dress is high waisted . . . shirred beneath the bust. The neck is very high, petal-like in front. Dress is about size 10 or less.'

'Somehow the preparations got done. Mainbocher made my trousseau. From his sketches I chose for my wedding gown a simple dress of blue crêpe satin. Reboux made a hat to match,' Wallis wrote in a terse précis of her wedding wardrobe.

'I didn't like the dress, and as for the hat, it was appalling,' says Lady Diana Cooper, who, like almost all the Prince's friends from the carefree Fort Belvedere days, was not there to see the Duchess wed.

'Wallis is today especially unlovable, hard, calculating and showing anxiety but no feeling of emotion,' Cecil Beaton noted privately in his diary. 'Her face broken out in spots and not looking her best.'

The exquisitely simple gown is part of fashion, as well as royal, history. For it is quintessentially 1930s – as frozen in its period as the Duchess's later full-skirted Dior New Look dresses, or the 1960s trouser suit, with its daisy chain of open scalloping running down the 70-year-old Duchess's legs.

Bias-cutting is the fashion hallmark of the 1930s, and Mainbocher has made slithers of sensuous fabrics the essence of Mrs Simpson's evening style, ever since Horst photographed Wallis in 1935 in a Madame Récamier pose, stretched out on a *chaise-longue* with her flat body moulded by shimmering fabric.

That dress was a Mainbocher creation in soft lamé, the bodice lapping her bosom, the skirt bias-cut, and more uncovered than Wallis's usual discreet style.

'Mary's clothes are rather naked for here – more nightclub types,' she said disapprovingly of Mary Kirk Raffray, the woman who was ultimately to marry the cast-off Ernest Simpson.

Main Rousseau Bocher, the elegant, Europeanized American with a suave smile and plump, soft hands, had established his Paris fashion house after editing French *Vogue*. Self-groomed like Mrs Simpson, he is the first designer to appreciate Wallis's rigorous elegance.

'Mainbocher was responsible for the Duchess's wonderful simplicity and dash,' says Diana Vreeland.

He has come down to Candé on six successive Saturdays to complete the weddding dress.

'I have to have Paris come to me,' Wallis tells Aunt Bessie.

'I would go to Paris for clothes if I had the cash,' she had told Mrs Merryman in 1931.

For her trousseau, Mainbocher makes Wallis a bias-cut white crêpe dress, topped by an edge-to-edge striped cardigan jacket entirely worked in sequins. Two years later, in 1939, more exotic embroidery in red, gold, white and green, lit with mirror glass, sequins and pearls, swathes the bust and hips of a black evening gown. In 1947 he will make the Duchess an austere, high-necked taffeta dress built over a spreading underskirt.

This stark evening gown could not be in greater contrast to the puffball crinolines of satin and lace created for England's new Queen, Bertie's wife Elizabeth.

'If she hadn't learned to iron a crinoline, what had she learned?' sneers Wallis to James Pope-Hennessy, after describing the inadequacies of the English maid she had inherited from Buckingham Palace.

'Women of the world were little absorbed in the conventional satin gowns of England's new Queen,' reported Life magazine on the eve of the Windsor wedding. 'What Mrs Wallis Warfield Simpson would wear, however, roused their avid curiosity.'

Wallis can now indulge for 35 years in Parisian simplicity and rigorous elegance.

'I remember a wonderful black Balenciaga dress that spiralled round the body,' says Grace, Lady Dudley.

'We arrived at La Croë on a stifling hot evening,' says Laura, Duchess of Marlborough. 'It was the first time I met the Duchess, and she was standing at the end of the green lawn, wearing a sleeveless black dress, long, absolutely plain and unadorned, except for her white fan of Prince of Wales feathers.'

A decade later, Wallis will dunk the same fan into an enormous bowl of red roses which Jimmy Donahue has put on the table at the Paris nightclub Scheherazade, squealing in front of the embarrassed guests: 'Look, the Prince of Wales feathers and Jimmy Donahue's roses.'

'The Duke said, "Laura, get me out of this," and I took him home to the Bois,' says the Duchess of Marlborough. 'In the car on the way back, he just sobbed and sobbed and sobbed.'

Sydney is packing for America in the autumn of 1958. On the table in the upstairs pressing room is a Mont Blanc of striped shirts, each with the monogram E on the left breast, a crown arched above like an eyebrow. Around him on the floor gape the trunks, from Vuitton and Goyard, to be stuffed with the tissue paper that lies in another mountainous drift on the table.

'Finally I said to His Royal Highness, "Why are we packing up twenty-seven trunks each winter to go to New York? You should keep the clothes you want to wear in America over there."

'"That's a good idea, Sydney," His Royal Highness said. "I don't know why we didn't think of that before."'

Twenty years of packing and unpacking are behind Sydney as he folds deftly into one trunk the Duke's massive greatcoat. It is ankle-length, fur-lined, so heavy that only the Duke's upright regal bearing stops his slender frame from buckling under its weight.

'His father's coat,' says Sydney proudly, smoothing the curly astrakhan collar like the hair of a rumpled child.

'In fact, it was given to me in the 1930s by my old friend and equerry, General Trotter,' says the Duke.

It seems a relic from the expansive Edwardian era, hanging in generous folds from the waist and swooping down to the ankles 'as low as those overcoats which London cabbies used to wear in my youth,' says the Duke.

'Her Royal Highness was always telling him to get it shortened,' Sydney

OVERLEAF LEFT: *The Duke and Duchess on one of their rare visits to London in 1946, staying with Lord Dudley at Ednam Lodge, where the Duchess's jewellery was stolen. Wallis is wearing Parisian country chic: a dog-tooth check coat, pleated woollen dress and elegant lace-up shoes. The Duke is in a pin-striped lounge suit, the jacket tailored by Scholte of London's Savile Row, the bottom half by Harris of New York. The Duchess calls it 'pants across the sea'.*

OVERLEAF RIGHT: *'In Florida, I have trousers and jacket made of tropical-weight corduroy in light colours,' says the Duke. On holiday in Biarritz in 1951, he gives his lobster-bisque cord suit an English style. The Duchess protects her ageing skin from the sun with a dainty parasol.*

says. 'But he wouldn't let me cut it off. He said, "It will soon be back in fashion;" and it was.'

'Now this, David, is the sort of coat you should have,' says the Duchess, modelling herself James Pope-Hennessy's stylish 1950s overcoat in the guest cottage at the Moulin.

The Duke sticks to his father's line: 'A short overcoat, he used to say, is only half a coat.'

For mellow autumn days, the Duke wears his cloth coats, generously cut from a raglan shoulder line, falling to mid-calf length and made from russet tweeds that disappear like camouflage into the surrounding park when the Duke strolls out with the pugs.

'Shepherd's plaids' the Duke calls them, explaining to the Parisians the cloth's Scottish origins.

'Tweed has nothing to do with the name of the river,' he insists. 'Tweeds derive from "tweels" or twills . . . The name was misread one day on an invoice.'

His own favourite country suit is a hairy pinky-grey tweed, overchecked in blue, black and green, made from fabric given to him by the Sutherland family when he was Prince of Wales.

For New York, Sydney packs the Duke's lightweight worsted formal suits, tissue paper in each sleeve and inside the trouser legs, so that they look like dummy bodies as they are lifted into the trunk.

'The unheated houses and palaces of my mother's and father's day called for an extra weight,' explains the Duke. 'Today however I possess no such thing as a "winter suit".'

He has another fur-lined coat for the New York winter, grey patterned tweed and so heavy that Sydney grunts as he lifts it.

'The hat-check girls wince and wilt when they lift it off my shoulders,' admits the Duke.

The inside is lined throughout with nutria pelts. 'From one of the Duchess's discarded fur coats,' the Duke says.

The Duchess treats her furs as fashion, leafing through the catalogue of the stylish Parisian furrier Revillon or New York's Maximilian and trading new minks for old. Balenciaga makes her a skinny fitting black broadtail suit that she wears with a perky white ermine hat.

'Wallis, what is the most expensive kind of fur?' Prince George asked, when discussing a wedding present for his wife Marina.

'Chinchilla,' replied a knowing Mrs Simpson.

'I bought . . . with the $200 the Prince gave me . . . some leopard skins which I think will make a lovely sports coat,' she told Aunt Bessie in October 1934.

She posed for a holiday snapshot in Kitzbuhel the following February in a three-quarter-length mink with a fashionable scarf tie. The Prince is in a pale tweed knickerbocker suit, its baggy plus-fours blooming above stem-thin ankles.

'Can't say I couldn't live without winter sports,' says Wallis, after her first ski lesson.

The Duke's tweed sports jackets are laid out on the table: all unstructured, unlined, and as soft as a shirt to wear. The most striking is in a yellow, burgundy and taupe check, single-breasted. The label inside the breast pocket says 'H.R.H. The Duke of Windsor 1947'; the gilt buttons read 'Duke of Cornwall's Light Infantry'.

The Duke explains to his American friends that he is a member of the

The Prince of Wales was seldom seen without a hat, especially in formal clothes. As a young man, he followed the style of his grandfather and dressed as an Edwardian dandy in a tall top hat and bow tie.

'Button Club' in Palm Beach, where antique dealers do a brisk trade in old livery and uniform buttons.

'That gave me an idea,' the Duke says. 'I selected some of my old regimental and hunt buttons, which I had sewn on my sports jackets. I returned to Palm Beach . . . remarking "Here are some real buttons. Buttons I am entitled to wear."'

'I do hope the Duke will keep quiet about his buttons or he will ruin my trade,' the dealer pleads with the Duchess.

A packet of ten Provost Marshal's buttons, three Coldstream Guards buttons, medal ribbons and rank badges sell at the Geneva jewel auction in 1987 for £8,000.

'I call his style "*chic fatigué*" – a kind of easy, casual stylishness,' says Katell le Bourhis, a curator of the Costume Institute in New York, where the most historic of the Duke of Windsor's suits now hang in air-conditioned racks. Once they were lined up in his closets in Paris, beside the framed regimental prints. 'The Duke picked things from English country life and turned them into fashion for the city,' says le Bourhis. 'And from the point of view of

LEFT: *The Duke's hats photographed against the worn red leather despatch box marked* 'THE KING' *and a green velvet obelisk set with royal medallions. The British bowler and the silk 'topper' are shown with a Tyrolean felt which the Duke wears on country weekends in the winter.*

RIGHT: *Summer straws. In the foreground, the Duke's golfing hats by Lacoste and from his favourite golf club at St Germain-en-Laye outside Paris. At the back, panamas from Dobb's of Fifth Avenue against an impressionistic portrait of the Duke.*

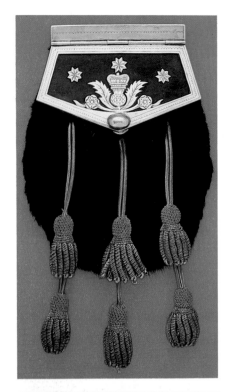

RIGHT: *The Duke's closets at the Mill are filled with tartan and tweed, buckled shoes and embroidered slippers. The kilts include Royal Stewart, Hunting Stewart, Rothesay, Lord of the Isles and Balmoral, all made at Oban in the West of Scotland. Prince Charles chose from these kilts for his sons the princes William and Harry.*

TOP: *A sealskin dress-sporran, mounted in silver with silver tassels and the cypher of the Duke's father George V.*

ABOVE: *A tooled leather and silver tasselled sporran. The Duke keeps his cigarettes inside the pouch which he wears with his dress kilts at Fort Belvedere and at the Mill.*

fashion history, he was the first man to dress in unstructured clothes with no stiffness or interlining.'

'Did he have style?' says Diana Vreeland, an advisor to the Costume Institute. 'The Duke of Windsor had style in every buckle on his kilt, every check of his country suits; in the way he put together sports clothes.'

The drake green check suit that Horst remembers the Duke wearing at the Mill is being packed for Palm Beach. It is double-breasted, all four buttons covered with the suit fabric; four more smaller buttons are on parade on cuffs that are cut like the sleeve of a shirt. The buttonhole for the Duke's carnation is bound with neat overstitching and at the back of the lapel is a loop of tweed to hold the stem of the flower. On top of the folded jacket go two identical pairs of tweed trousers:

'Always two pairs, because they wear out quicker than the jacket, and I had to rotate them turn by turn,' says Sydney.

The pants are pleat front, but high rise and cut with no waistband.

'They are for a man who wants to be seen to have a flat stomach,' says Katell le Bourhis.

The Duke's flamboyant red sports trousers, made out of melton cloth as bright as the walls of his father's Sandringham study, are edged at the waist with just a narrow band of satin ribbon.

The pants are labelled 'H. Harris, 43 East 59th Street'.

'I gave him a pair of my old London trousers and he copied them admirably,' explains the Duke. 'Since then I have had my trousers made in New York and my coats in London.'

For 40 years, from 1919 to 1959, the jackets are tailored by Mr Scholte of Savile Row.

'Scholte has rigid standards concerning the . . . cut of a coat to clothe the masculine torso,' explained the Duke, when his friend Fruity Metcalfe was turned away for demanding a wider shoulderline.

'I hope you are not going in for those Oxford bags,' said Scholte disapprovingly, when the Prince wore slightly wider trousers.

The master tailor comes into his own when the Prince of Wales dresses for the Ascot race meeting in a pearl grey morning suit.

'Unfortunately I had forgotten something. The Court was in mourning for

LEFT: *The Duke wearing a tweed suit in Sutherland district check – a pinky-grey with blue, black and green overchecks. The cloth was given to him by the Sutherland family when he was Prince of Wales and made up by James and James of London.*

RIGHT: *A checked tweed suit, the unlined jacket by Scholte of Savile Row, with shirt cuffs, covered buttons and a tab at the back of the buttonhole to hold the flower stem. The trousers by H. Harris of New York are made with pleat front and a high waist with satin binding instead of a waistband to give a flat stomach line.*

some distant relative,' says the Duke. 'I called Scholte from the racecourse throwing myself at his mercy.'

Scholte and his tailor sat up all night to make the new black coat, just as Hubert de Givenchy will for the Duchess half a century later.

'It was the only time I ever saw her in bedroom slippers, with no make-up and her hair in a mess,' says Givenchy. 'She called me over to Neuilly and stood in her dressing room with her face completely overwhelmed with grief, and said, "You must make me a black dress and coat for the Duke's funeral. Can you do it?" I replied "Of course" and we worked on it all night. She never forgot. That's when she started to call me Hubert.'

The hats go into dozens of hat boxes. Each floats on a cloud of tissue: straw panamas from Dobbs of Fifth Avenue for the sunbelt holiday at Palm Springs; a Tyrolean country hat in pine forest green velour, with jaunty bristle brush; the British city bowler, made of soft, light felt with a Cavanagh of New York label.

'A soft hat disguised as a hard one,' says the Duke. 'The other day, when the Duchess and I were invited to a wedding in New York, I found I had no bowler. So I went into a shop and bought one.'

The Duke of Windsor is recognized now for his peaked linen golf caps in unexpected colours. In his earlier days, the Prince tried to launch an ink blue bowler and to set a fashion for straw boaters. His efforts were celebrated in doggerel in an advertisement:

Two 'boaters' afloat in Leicester Square,
God Bless the Prince of Wales.

The ink blue dinner jacket, double-breasted and taken from the backs of fashionable dance-band leaders of the 1920s, is his fashion success story.

'My brother and I started to wear it . . . often with a plain dark-red carnation in the lapel,' says the Duke, who had already taken to the wing collar, the soft collar and a comfortable backless waistcoat.

'Fred Astaire happened to notice the lapels of my white waistcoat,' says the Duke. 'Next morning he went to Hawes and Curtis, and asked for a waistcoat to be made in the same style.' The famous haberdasher and shirtmaker in London's Jermyn Street regretfully refused.

Hawes and Curtis take orders from the Duke for ties with thick inner linings that Sydney is rolling deftly into circles and snapping into tie cases. The wadding is designed to make the knot fatter when tied.

'That may be the origin of the myth of the Windsor knot which the Duke does *not* wear,' suggest American *Vogue* in 1967, as the Duke demonstrates to photographer Lord Lichfield – a cousin of the Queen – how he knots his tie.

The Duke tells a favourite anecdote: 'Once in Washington, a reporter . . . asked me what tie I was wearing. I replied "The Guards tie." Misunderstanding my pronunciation, he settled for "Gawd's tie".'

The press reported it 'doubtful as to whether the Almighty had actually ever devised a tie of His own'.

The Duke of Windsor's ties are discreet compared to the clash of checks and tartans that hang in his closets: the Royal Stewart tartan with bottle green velvet jacket, to be worn with Argyll check socks and silver buckled patent slippers, made by Peal of London and marshalled on ram-rod shoe rails at the base of his wardrobe.

Nancy Mitford, fashionably dressed from head to foot in the new Parisian vogue for tartan, comes face-to-face with the Duke of Windsor at dinner.

ABOVE: *The double-breasted dinner jacket, brought to Britain by American dance band leaders, softened men's evening fashion in the 1920s. The Prince of Wales and his brother George started the trend away from stiff shirts and tail coats. The Duke of Windsor's stylish tuxedo is midnight blue with black satin lapels.*

OPPOSITE: *The Duke of Windsor's floor-sweeping fur-lined black coat with astrakhan collar was given to him in the 1930s by his equerry Brigadier-General Trotter.*

ABOVE: *Smoking accessories were part of the Duke's fashionable wardrobe. Gold Cartier cigarette case engraved 'David 29–11–34 George', a present from his brother on the occasion of his wedding to Princess Marina of Greece; pheasant case from Kaiser Wilhelm; flag case engraved HMS Renown, a present from his father in 1921 when the Prince sailed to India; silver match case, a 23rd birthday present in 1917 from his brother Harry, later Duke of Gloucester; silver George V tasselled cigarette case engraved 'For David from his devoted father'.*

TOP: *'Her Royal Highness was always telling him to get it shortened,' says the Duke's valet Sydney Johnson, seen here in the upstairs laundry room with the Duke's coat on the table and the staff uniforms on the rail.*

Lord Lichfield photographed the Duke at the Mill in the 1960s wearing an audacious mix of checked overshirt and tartan trousers, with paisley cravat and argyll socks – an eccentric but stylish golfing outfit.

'It seems I was togged up in Royal Stewart tartan,' she wailed. 'How can one tell?'

'My father's tartan suit . . . began to influence fashions . . . half a century after it was made in the 1890s,' says the Duke. 'I happened to wear it one evening for dinner at La Croë . . . Within a few months tartan had become a popular material for . . . dinner jackets and cummerbunds, to swimming trunks and beach shorts.'

George V's suit lies at rest in the Metropolitan Museum in New York, its muted checks still jaunty and its matching cummerbund scarcely long enough to swaddle a grown man.

'The Duke was very small,' says Lady Mosley. 'He had exactly the same slight figure as his father.'

'Unique and zesty' is how American *Vogue* describes the Duke's 'audacious mixture of check, and texture and pattern' which he stirs together at the Mill. In the dry, bright heat of La Croë, the plaids look out of place.

'We went to the Riviera in July,' says Laura, Duchess of Marlborough. 'It was fiendishly hot and I was wearing the thinnest of dresses and when we arrived at the villa, the Duke was in full Scottish rig. The first thing I said to him was "Oh Sir, aren't you terribly hot?" But he didn't seem to notice.'

'His appearance was magnificent – if indeed a little strange considering the almost tropical heat,' says Fruity Metcalfe, as the ex-King made a theatrical progress down the green lawns of La Croë in the summer of 1939. 'He was

The Duke's bumble-bee striped socks and co-respondent shoes were both fashions of the 1930s that he first wore with plus-fours and check suits at Fort Belvedere. With a natural sense of style, he updated them for resort wear.

ABOVE: *The 1950s were a difficult fashion period for the compact Duchess of Windsor. She shows her style in Balenciaga's black broadtail suit set off by a white ermine bonnet and white kid gloves. On her lapel she wears the Prince of Wales feather diamond brooch that the Duke wanted to give back to the royal family. It was sold at auction to the Hollywood film star Elizabeth Taylor.*

OPPOSITE: *Dior's girlish New Look did not suit the Duchess. But Cecil Beaton did his best to glamorize the heavily embroidered strapless dress with its tiny waist and romantic full skirt.*

completely turned out as a Scotch laird about to go stalking. Beautiful kilt, swords and all the aids. It staggered me a bit.'

The Duchess of Windsor sits on the gilt salon chair, her legs folded to one side. In front of her, the red plush seat of another chair forms a table. She spreads a cloth napkin embroidered WE, and starts to eat her lunch.

'She always brought chicken sandwiches in a little picnic hamper,' says Dior's *haute couture* vendeuse Agnès Bertrand. 'And sometimes she would share her lunch with me.'

'Her day was quite extraordinary,' says Laura, Duchess of Marlborough. 'She would book five or six fittings with couturiers. Her life's work was shopping.'

'I adore to shop,' says the Duchess. 'All my friends know I'd rather shop than eat.'

Lunch with her dressers is fun, because the Duchess is enjoying this little fashion conspiracy. She rolls her eyes and pulls droll faces, and the couture staff begin to feel quite intimate and almost *friends*.

'One day she saw me when she was driving down the Avenue Montaigne, and she made her chauffeur stop the car and all the traffic just to say *bonjour*,' says Dior's tailor Claude Laurent. 'She was a great lady.'

When an outfit is a particular success, there will be a telephone call, or a little note on one of her cards with the entwined ww initials or the Wallis blue writing paper with ducal insignia and crown.

'I kept all those little notes,' says Hubert de Givenchy. 'She was so very nice to all the staff. It was somehow always an event when she came to the salon. But not a solemn occasion, because she was always smiling and joking.'

'She arrived with a smile, and she teased me and she wanted it all to be fun. She couldn't stand having a miserable vendeuse,' says Danielle Porthault of Yves Saint Laurent, whom the Duchess had followed from Dior to the new couture house in 1962.

'Oh, Duchess, now *you* can tell me all about this young Saint Laurent at Dior's,' James Pope-Hennessy begged her in 1958. 'I do so much want to know.'

'The Duchess understood about having the best fitter,' says Erik Mortensen of Balmain. 'I remember how twenty years ago, when she had always been to Madame Marthe at Dior, I saw her wearing a Pierre Cardin dress. And she said to me "Cardin is not really my style, but Marthe has gone there and she is the best fitter in Paris."'

Fleur Cowles asks the Duchess: 'If you could choose only one couturier, who would it be?'

'The one who lets me play with the clothes – not only lets me change the models a bit, but is charming about it when I do,' Wallis replies. 'And he'd have to have the best fitter in Paris.'

The Duchess has finished pecking at her lunch and is standing, toes turned slightly in, balanced like one of the pigeons that roost under the eaves down at the Mill.

'Our white fantail pigeons love to sit for hours on the sills, peering into the windows,' she says.

Wallis, such a quick, busy person, can stand like this, quite, quite still.

'She could stand immobile for half an hour at a time,' said Hollywood designer Jason Lindsey who dressed the Duchess in Nassau. 'But she was not idle . . . she could dictate and give orders to as many as eight or nine people without once moving her body or turning her head.'

The professionals flutter round her pinning and draping, easing the precious fabrics as tight as they dare round her tiny body.

'She would look at the general line of an outfit. If she liked it, but it was too broad for her, she had the model altered and adapted to her. That's why she was so tied to her tailor and fitter,' says Erik Mortensen.

'If I make the skirt any smaller, you won't be able to sit down,' Mainbocher told the Duchess during a fitting.

'Then I won't sit down in it,' she replied.

Upstairs on a shelf in the workrooms is a line-up of the couture mannequins on which the first *toiles* or patterns are cut. Between Lady Diana Cooper, thick-waisted and stooped slightly at the shoulders, and a tiny sparrow-like dummy marked 'Edith Piaf', is a mannequin with 'S.A.R. La Duchesse de Windsor' stencilled on to the cloth torso. The Duchess's measurements from collar-bone to breast-bone, nape to waist, waist to hips, shoulder to elbow, elbow to wrist, have all been precisely charted. Her basic shape – 34, 25, 34 in the inches she understands – has not changed since she was first measured. Other high-society clients show evidence of expanding girths in torsos that are stuffed and re-made until the dummies are scarred with stitches.

Through the grey silk curtains in her dressing *cabine* Wallis can see seam-stresses in their white hospital overalls hurrying up and down stairs, carrying pieces of cloth or parcelled up dresses for delivery.

'The Duchess always arrived at the salon looking as though she had just stepped out of one of our boxes,' says Claude Laurent. 'She had a funny way of sitting down, crossing her legs just before she sat. And she never had a single crease on her clothes.'

'She was *soignée*,' says Agnès Bertrand.

'Being immaculate was the hallmark of her personal style,' says the Countess of Romanones.

At the fashion show, Wallis will perch, her ankles crossed, on a chair just at the top of the staircase.

'She had a magnetism,' says Agnès Bertrand. 'Ever since the first Dior show in 1947, the photographers would flock to her. Even if there was some young star there, they would photograph her, and in the end she didn't like it and asked for a seat at the back.'

The couture showing gives Wallis the story-line of the new season's clothes.

'She knew exactly what she wanted,' says Marc Bohan, designer and artistic director of Dior. 'And I knew more or less what she would choose – always the lead pieces from each collection.'

'Well, I'll *buy* that dress; but I won't *wear* it,' is the Duchess of Windsor's way of turning down, tactfully, a suggested ensemble.

'My favourite couturier simply can't start with a blank board each time. The individuals he dresses regularly must inspire his first ideas,' says Wallis. 'I nearly always recognize the dress designed with me in mind.'

'She chose very well,' says Givenchy. 'She picked clean lines, and then often had things altered to take away anything superfluous.'

'She knew herself by heart,' says Danielle Porthault.

The couturiers and vendeuses can reel off the list of preferences:

'Short evening dresses,' says Marc Bohan. 'She liked light fabrics: black pleated chiffon, faille, *gazar*. I especially remember the navy blue *gazar* dress wrapping across the body that I made for the visit of the Queen to the Duke just before he died.

'She liked blue and all the beige tones, not apricot, never grey. For day it was suits with fitted jackets and slightly flared skirts, dresses and coats, but never wool dresses because she found them too hot.'

'The Duchess felt the heat and the Duke was always cold,' says her coiffeur Alexandre. 'She would go round the house flinging open windows, and the Duke would be shivering in his tweed suits.'

For a brief period, the Duchess turns couturier, creating designs for a paper pattern company in America.

'I've done two or three hundred patterns so far, and I love doing them,' says the Duchess. 'I usually take my ideas from the clothes I wish I *could* wear – so as not to put every other woman in round high necks and the severe lines I insist on for myself.'

For her own person, she contents herself with adapting couture models, or mixing clothes together.

'It is the blouse of one dress I found in Venet's collection, over a little skirt he made to go with it – something all of my own,' she tells Fleur Cowles.

In 1939, she had taken a favourite Mainbocher blouse – high necked and severe, but with a false button at its neck to give the illusion of *deshabillé*. She had it stitched on to a pleated shantung skirt in the same bright blue and sat for a striking portrait by society painter Gerald Brockhurst.

'This will be my jewel for the year,' said the
Duchess of Windsor when she ordered the
fuchsia faille dress with a fur-trimmed stole
encrusted with bead embroidery. Designer
Marc Bohan at Christian Dior drew his
design for her. The Duke told her that the
couture gown was too expensive.

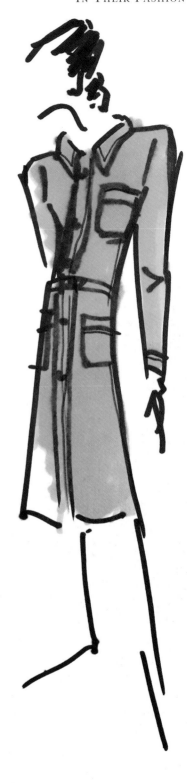

A strictly tailored coat in 'Wallis blue' wool
was the favourite line for the Duchess,
photographed here on the steps of her Paris
home with her pugs. The sketch by Dior's
Marc Bohan shows the outfit as he designed
it for her in 1974 after the Duke's death.

The Duchess of Windsor at Lucien Lelong's couture show in 1940. To her left is her friend and mentor Elsie Mendl, wife of Sir Charles Mendl, Press Attaché to the British Embassy in Paris.

'I am not in the habit of complimenting my rivals,' the great Christian Dior said to the Duchess. 'But your dress is really something special.'

'But it's one of yours,' replied the Duchess. 'You made it for me in velvet, and I had the workroom copy it in a lighter fabric, because I thought that was simpler.'

The Duke is standing in a velvet smoking jacket watching his wife having the final fitting for a blue satin theatre suit. She is standing in front of the triple mirrors in her eau-de-nil dressing room, two of the pugs snuffling at her feet. The mirror reflects her furrowed frown of concentration and the Duke's quizzical smile.

'The Duke used to compliment her publicly. He would say "Something new. I like it." He was full of charm,' says Madame Schlumberger.

'Oh, so this is the great dress? Well, it's lovely, very pretty,' the Duke said to his bride on their wedding day.

A make-up artist overheard Wallis respond to the Duke's dogged gallantry. When he complimented her, she replied, 'Shut up!'

The Duke is anxious about the cost of the Duchess's ever-changing wardrobe.

'Givenchy, your clothes are very beautiful,' says the Duke to the designer when they are ambling round the garden of the Moulin. 'But they are damned expensive.'

'They are not expensive if I wear them a lot,' responds the Duchess. 'They are a good investment.'

'She wanted to have a fuchsia *faille* evening dress with a cape trimmed with mink and worked all over in beads,' says Marc Bohan. 'The Duke said it was so expensive, it would be like buying a piece of jewellery. "Well then, it will be my jewel for this year," the Duchess said.'

'I once asked her what she did with all those clothes,' says Laura, Duchess of Marlborough. 'But she just smiled and said it was a secret.'

'She was very generous,' says her maid. 'She just gave away everything and got rid of it each season.'

Twice a year, she will invest in her couture wardrobe – spending $50,000 (£35,000) a year, claimed the American press.

'I shouldn't think those fashion people charged her much,' says Lady Diana Cooper. 'You don't pay if you are a celebrity. I never paid for a thing in Paris.'

'Everybody was crazy to design for the Duchess,' says Erik Mortensen. 'She was the most chic woman of our time. Of course you didn't ask her the same price as you would some blind Arab. But she did not bargain herself. It was the couture houses who fought to offer her discounts.'

Photographers' flash bulbs record the parade of couture gowns: in ivory Dior at the Bal des Petits Lits Blancs; in yellow Balenciaga for Alexis de Redé's ball; in pale blue Dior with a floor-length coat at Versailles; in pink satin with Ghislaine de Polignac. And it is still only half way through the spring season.

'She didn't have so many clothes,' says the Princesse de Polignac. 'She bought just the right number and only what suited her.'

'She would take from Saint Laurent each season, two suits, one day dress and one evening dress. That's all,' says Danielle Porthault.

'I remember arriving to see the Windsors at the Ritz,' says Laura Marlborough. 'And even that hotel did not have enough cupboard space for all her clothes, so there were all these trunks lined up in the corridor outside.'

'She had a position and she dressed to it,' says Diana Vreeland.

The Duchess of Windsor's secretary is telling the couture house to deliver the dress by noon the following day. *Son Altesse Royale le veult.* She is demanding of herself, of her maids who clean and wash and press every single item at home; she is extremely demanding of the professionals who serve her. They receive tiny royal stick pins or cuff links each Christmas.

'And she once brought me a watch you could use under water,' says Claude Laurent.

The Duchess of Windsor also demands impeccable chic and grooming from other people.

'It upset her if other people were not groomed,' says Alexandre.

Cecil Beaton recalls a nightmare when 'the Duchess of Windsor was present while I was being humiliated wearing a toupé that would not behave itself.'

The Duchess herself is not easily embarrassed.

'I think it's a great compliment to me that you've bought it,' she will say when coming face to face with her dress on another woman.

'She had a striped Givenchy dress at a party given by the Baron de Redé,' says Alexandre. 'There were eight women in the same dress and any other woman would have been furious. The Duchess was clever enough to laugh about it, but Givenchy was very embarrassed.'

'That fisherman's jersey stripe was the dress of the season,' says Givenchy. 'But what I didn't know was that other women were going to have it copied by their little dressmakers. The Duchess made a joke of it and got all the ladies to dance a conga in line.'

In 1951, Wallis came face to face with her strapless, ballerina-length dress, full-skirted and *jeune fille*, on the mother of Jimmy Donahue. An American guest noted the contrast: 'The Duchess very dark, very thin, in pale blue; and Mrs Donahue, golden blonde, rosy-cheeked, and plumpish in pale pink.'

'The only time she did not look good was in the New Look period of big skirts,' says Givenchy. 'It was not her style and she knew it.'

Fifteen years later, the Duchess of Windsor gave a New Year party in Paris.

'I decided to wear a new Yves Saint Laurent dress called Opium, very short, red and encrusted with jewels,' says Jacqueline de Ribes. 'When I saw that the Duchess was wearing the identical dress, I said "Oh Duchess, but the difference is that you are wearing those wonderful Roger Vivier shoes to match, and I'm wearing these awful gold shoes."'

It was said to save face, and the Vicomtesse de Ribes' face was forty years younger.

'The Duchess was never a slave to fashion,' Marc Bohan claims.

'She was above fashion,' says Erik Mortensen of Balmain. 'You couldn't influence her. She understood what was new and what was right for her.'

The Duchess is lying dormant. In her closet is a coral tweed Dior suit, unworn, still in its tissue wrappings, delivered in the autumn that she faded into the twilight. In the large closet on the landing outside, in a plastic hanging wardrobe, is a row of quilted housecoats, so much more practical in her present state than the *mille-feuilles* of silken negligées and nightgowns layered in the dressing room drawers.

'I went to look at the flowers at the funeral,' says Laura, Duchess of Marlborough. 'It was tragic. They were all from dressmakers, jewellers, Dior, Van Cleef, Alexandre. Those people were her life.'

In his bathroom mirror, as he knots his tie, the Duke sees in front of him a rumpled face, the skin slack, except when the smile lifts the flesh up his cheeks into the corners of his pale blue eyes.

The Duchess photographed at a Dior couture show. She attended the collections twice a year in January and July and had a professional eye for spotting the outfits designed with her in mind by her regular designers.

Wallis laughed off the fashion faux pas when eight ladies turned up at Baron de Redés party in Paris in an identical striped dress. Hubert de Givenchy's drawing shows the blue and white matelot sheath he made for the Duchess, whose style was much copied.

'Bing Crosby eyes,' says Anne Slater. 'They both had blue eyes, but hers were a much deeper, penetrating blue.'

'He has his father's eyes, and some, I fancy, of his mannerisms,' says James Pope-Hennessy.

'The eye of Windsor blue surrounded by jaundice,' said Harold Nicolson of the Prince a week before his father's death in January 1936.

The Duke's hair is still thick and strong – hardly changed, except from its newly-minted colour – since he was the golden-haired Prince of Wales.

'He was charming as the boy King,' says Lady Diana Cooper. 'I saw him walk through 400,000 people in France after the First War to celebrate Canada's victory. You could watch this tiny yellow head going through this enormous crowd, no guards, no detectives and smiling.'

The tow-coloured hair darkens with the years.

'He used to put iodine on his hair to keep it yellow,' says Nicholas Lawford.

'The hair is nicotine-coloured,' says James Pope-Hennessy.

His barber in London, as Prince and King, is Charles Topper of Mayfair, who will continue to shave and trim the greying locks of Fruity

Metcalfe and tell him any number of a barber's risqué and ribald jokes.

The Duke keeps for the rest of his life the same parting on the left of his head, the hair smoothed across the crown.

'He had very good proportions and the perfect head,' says Diana Vreeland. 'The Windsor head.'

'He was always combing his hair,' says Horst. 'I remember him taking out that comb all the time before I photographed him.'

Without the comb and the valet to keep him spruce, or the caps on the windy golf course at St-Germain-en-Laye, his hair springs out of control.

'His hair was blown out in tufts on either side of his head,' says James Pope-Hennessy. 'He was looking crumple-faced and wild, like Shaw's Dauphin.'

There is a jaunty glamour about Windsor, even in old age.

'*Un personnage historique*,' says the Baron de Cabrol.

'Here comes my romance,' the Duchess will say, as he walks off the golf course towards her.

Her hair is also relatively unchanged by the years. While her clothes alter

Stylish to the end, the 73-year-old Duchess chose Yves Saint Laurent's vibrantly coloured patchwork skirt and flowered organza blouse at the height of the hippie era in 1969. Yves Saint Laurent's drawing captures the neat elegance of his royal client.

radically with time and fashion seasons, the madonna divide down her crown persists.

'You've changed your hair, Duchess,' Givenchy exclaims when he arrives at Neuilly for dinner in the early 1960s and the Duchess has gone *bouffant*.

'That wasn't a parting,' says the Duchess. 'It was a freeway.'

Cecil Beaton is quick to grasp the chic severity of Mrs Simpson's hairstyle with its 'almost dowdily ladylike, but well-controlled bun of hair'.

'The wide jaw, the smoothly-parted hair, the strong, enamel-less hands give her the appearance of an early Flemish master,' he says while sketching her in 1936. 'But her eyes, incredibly bright, could only be painted today.'

'Like a Japanese lady's hair,' he describes her lacquer-smooth *coiffure*.

Her hairdresser, Alexandre de Paris, is a faithful servant who will accompany her on the sad visit to England for the Duke's funeral.

'We were staying in Buckingham Palace,' says Alexandre. 'And the Duchess said to me in a little, little voice, "I wish David could see me now." When I replied, "But he can!" she looked at me as though I was crazy.'

'I had never stayed in Buckingham Palace before,' the Duchess told Aline de Romanones. 'My rooms were nice; even the bathroom had details like perfumes and bath oils. As soon as I got settled, I sent word to the Queen that Alexandre was there and at her disposal, but she did not accept.'

The dapper, moustachioed coiffeur was introduced to her in Cannes. 'Her Royal Highness gave me very precise instruction the first time I did her hair,' Alexandre says. 'But I followed my own ideas. She called me up, and as she came out of her bathroom, pointing a finger at me, with her blue eyes quite cold, I thought I was finished. But she said, "You did the opposite of what I told you and it was very good. We'll do it again."'

He is her hairdresser for the next thirty-five years, although it will be Edouard from the salon who comes to the Bois for her daily appointment, and finally sets up on his own.

'I went to do her hair even when the Duke and Duchess were just dining in on their own, tête-à-tête,' says Edouard. 'It was part of her ethic of living: never to neglect anything. She was a computer of elegance.'

The Duchess makes Alexandre's career, taking him with her to New York, and introducing him to Elsa Maxwell, who calls him 'Butcher Dartagnan' when he chops off her hair, while with the Duchess he works with her to change her hair within her own image of chic sobriety.

'She has done her hair in a different way. It is smoothed off the brow and falls down the back of her neck in ringlets,' noted Harold Nicolson at La Croë in the summer of 1937. 'It gives her a placid and less strained look.'

'In the period of the puffed out hair, she had hers *bouffant*, but still quite strict with a centre parting,' says Marc Bohan.

'She was always unhappy with her hair,' says Alexandre. 'It was very fine and wouldn't hold, and she could not bear a hair out of place.'

A visitor to Government House, Nassau, had the opposite impression: 'I think she is the only woman whom the Bahamian winds cannot dishevel. Her smooth dark head looks as if it has come out of a Persian miniature, where the Princesses are impervious to time and weather.'

'She learned about her hair from her days in China,' says Alexandre. 'She always had a very defined head.'

'She had such a wonderful shape,' says Nicholas Haslam, 'with that enormous head and tiny body.'

The Duke looks, in middle and later age, ridiculously boyish. It is partly the slender figure, bestowed by nature rather than won by conscious abstention.

ABOVE: *Coiffeur Alexandre was 'discovered' by the Duchess of Windsor in the South of France. She brought him to Paris, introduced him to New York, and he was her loyal servant for 30 years. He even accompanied her to Buckingham Palace for the Duke's funeral in May 1972.*

OPPOSITE: *Because she could not bear to have a hair out of place, Alexandre covered the Duchess's band-box neat chignon in a fine hair net for this late study by Patrick Lichfield. 'Her jawbone is alarming,' said James Pope-Hennessy. 'From the back you can see it jutting beyond the neck.'*

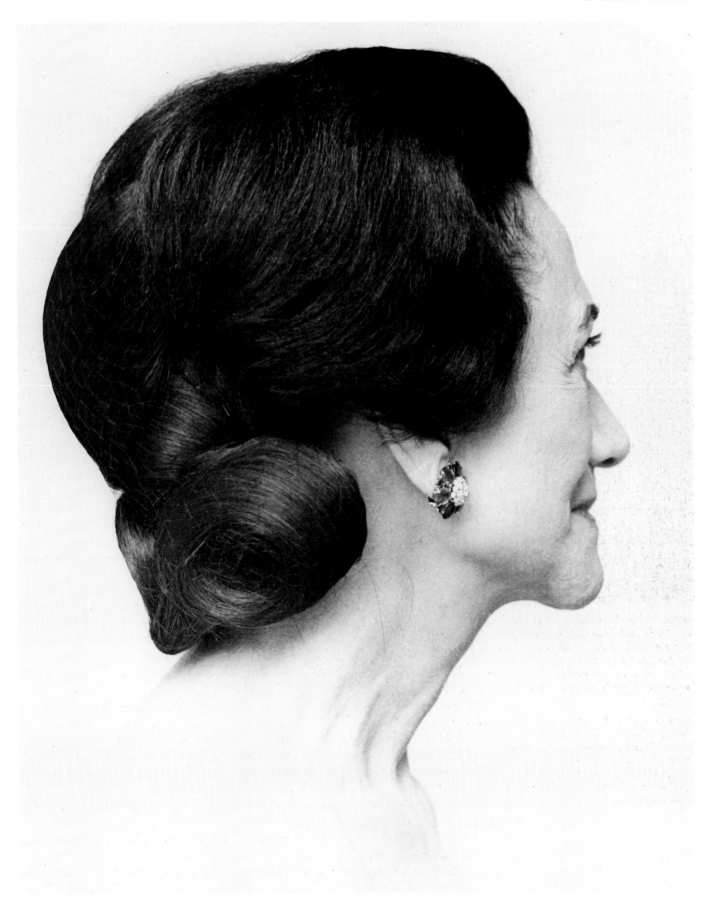

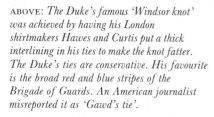

ABOVE: *The Duke's famous 'Windsor knot' was achieved by having his London shirtmakers Hawes and Curtis put a thick interlining in his ties to make the knot fatter. The Duke's ties are conservative. His favourite is the broad red and blue stripes of the Brigade of Guards. An American journalist misreported it as 'Gawd's tie'.*

OPPOSITE: *The Duke ties his silk cravat in his dressing room at the Moulin.*

'We turned towards the boyish young King, so young and seemingly frail. Actually he is forty-two, but one can never believe it,' recorded Chips Channon at George V's funeral.

'He gave one an intensely youthful impression. He had the capacity to spread around him immediately an atmosphere of gaiety and zest for life,' said Sir James Marjoribanks, the British consul in Florida in 1940, when the Duke was forty-six. 'There was . . . an insistence on physical fitness. He was like a young, quickly intelligent naval officer . . . with a boyish vocabulary and a strong sense of fun.'

'It was like being Wallis in Wonderland,' Mrs Simpson said to her husband when she came back from holiday with the Prince. 'It sounds to me,' said Ernest, 'like . . . Peter Pan's Never-Never-Land.' To Ernest, the Prince is always 'Peter Pan'.

'He is not at all a mannikin, but a well-proportioned human being,' claims Pope-Hennessy.

'He like a balloon, she like the skeleton of some tiny bird, hopping in her hobble skirt,' says Nancy Mitford cruelly.

'They were both tiny – a perfect pair,' says Diana Mosley.

Wallis struggles, with a recurrent ulcer and with herself, to keep her slender figure. 'Mrs Simpson . . . looking very well, as she has been on a fish diet for four days,' noted Chips Channon in 1936.

She reports progress to her aunt: 'Four pounds in weight have improved my disposition if not my "behind";' 'I am feeling well but am quite thin not in the face but in the figure;' 'I weigh eight stone undressed but eat and drink as usual.'

'Two old people, very bent, but full of spirit and still both dandies,' said Cecil Beaton. The Duke, in double-breasted blazer and two-tone shoes retained the dapper style of a boulevardier. The Duchess is up-to-the-moment in a 1960s trouser suit with open-work embroidery down the outside legs. Round her neck, the gold chains with bunches of sapphires and rubies that the Duke had given her 20 years before.

'I was weighed this morning and reached eight stones,' the Prince of Wales, at sixteen, wrote to his father, who kept a record of his son's poundage.

'My thinness and lightness of weight were a constant source of worry to him – as, indeed, they are to my wife,' says the Duke, who will weigh a fragile six and a half stone when his nurse helps him to dress for the visit of his niece, the Queen, ten days before he dies.

The Duchess ('you can never be too rich or too thin') had what her couturiers call the 'discipline' not to put on weight.

'It made her a certain kind of woman. She didn't eat much. She disciplined herself not to get fat,' says Eric Mortensen.

'She dreaded putting on weight,' says Agnès Bertrand from Dior. 'She would pat an imaginary stomach and say "That dress makes me look fat."'

'She was fixated on being thin,' says Alexandre. 'One day she said to me "I am devastated. I've put on 100 grammes. I'm going to punish myself with one boiled egg for the day."'

The Duchess tries to use her iron discipline to keep age at bay. Her birthdays are millstones round a wrinkled neck.

'I can't bear them,' she writes from holiday in Sicily in June 1957. 'Each one means that I really must begin to actually age – no more rock and roll so to speak.'

Her dressing-table mirror, surrounded by toys and trinkets and lotions and jars of hope, reflects back a forehead as wrinkled and big-eyed as the pug cushion on the chair beside her.

'Please tell me the name of that face woman in Paris,' she begs her friend 'Foxy' Gwynne from exile in Cannes after the traumatic abdication.

'What a lot WE have to do, Wallis,' writes the ex-King lovingly a month later. 'My first job will be to fill in that "trench" between your eyes.'

At first it is only the photographers who will paint out the lines, smoothing the Windsors' brows and presenting to the world a quite different visage than they have shown the camera.

But Wallis is looking for more permanent 'retouching'.

'The conversation was largely devoted to whether or not the Duchess should have her face lifted,' wrote Noël Coward in 1959. 'Wallis brought this subject up herself with a sort of calculated defiance . . . She is a curiously honest woman and her sense of humour, particularly about herself, is either profound or brilliantly simulated.'

'She had three face lifts, two in London and the last one in Paris,' says Jacqueline de Ribes. 'By the third one, the skin was drawn up and her eyes looked odd.'

Cecil Beaton, who set up his camera in an improvised studio at the Rothschild ball in 1971, described the Duchess of Windsor as 'like a mad Goya . . . Her face so pulled up that the mouth stretches from ear to ear'.

'She wasn't so much frightened of getting old,' says Jacqueline de Ribes. 'It was an aesthetic thing.'

Wallis depends on her team of maquilleur, manicurist, coiffeur, and on her visits to Elizabeth Arden's beauty salon in the Place Vendôme.

'I got up and spent the entire day on hair and nails, etc,' she wrote back in 1931, when she knew that she was to meet the Prince of Wales.

'From the feminine side it will be difficult about hair, face, nails, etc.' fussed Wallis about her wedding in Candé.

'Fuss, fuss, fuss. That's what I remember about photographing her,' says Horst. 'I went to the Hôtel Meurice, and first she was fussing about a blue dress that the maid brought in. She had been getting ready all morning, her

Patrick Lichfield photographed Wallis at the Mill in a graphic PVC short mac, patterned and cut in geometric 1960s style.

hairdresser in at six a.m. She was wearing emeralds, tight round her neck like pearls, and she kept saying "watch my hands".'

'She hated her hands,' says Alexandre. 'She always sat with her hands between her knees, trying to hide them.'

'I remember when there was someone at a dinner party who could read palms,' says the Vicomtesse de Ribes. 'We all stretched out our hands. When the Duke went to have his palm read, there was an awkward silence, and the Duchess suddenly said, "I hope she has the good sense to tell the Duke that his life started when he met me."'

The Duchess controls, as much as she is able, the public image of gentle happiness. A parade of fashionable photographers – Beaton, Dorothy Wilding, Horst, Lichfield – shed kindly light on the Windsors' ageing faces.

The mirror cracks when Richard Avedon publishes, in 1957, a bleak view of the Duke and Duchess in New York: she with ugly painted-in eyebrows and lips, face furrowed with harsh lines; he hang-dog and despairing, the 'blue-eyed charmer' with bags beneath the eyes. Photographic facilities are withdrawn from the world's press by the Windsors to punish him for punishing them.

'She was a coquette,' says coiffeur Edouard. 'And she stayed a coquette to the end, even when she was losing her lucidity. She would look at herself reflected in the mirror, and she seemed to see the face of a young girl.'

OPPOSITE: *Portraitist Dorothy Wilding ironed out the creases on the ageing faces of the Duke and Duchess of Windsor as the retouched and original studio portraits show. Wallis soon demanded more than the photographer's skills and had her face lifted three times.*
'Spent the entire day on hair and nails,' said Wallis the very first time she met the Prince of Wales. As Duchess of Windsor she was meticulous about grooming and had a manicurist do her nails every day.

CHAPTER
— 4 —

OBJECTS OF DESIRE

*'How very beautiful these gems are!' said Dorothea, under a new current of feeling, as sudden as
the gleam. 'It is strange how deeply colours seem to penetrate one, like scent . . . They look like
fragments of heaven. I think that emerald is more beautiful than any of them.'*

GEORGE ELIOT, Middlemarch

THE PANTHER bracelet lies in a puddle of grey November light
beside the window of Cartier in Paris. Outside the jewellery store,
where the Rue de la Paix meets the Place Vendôme, the Duchess of
Windsor's car waits, its engine purring, on 22 November 1952.

Inside, the jungle cat is stirring on its black velvet tray, as Wallis tilts the
head and the sloe-shaped emerald eyes glitter. Now the articulated body is
springing to life. The onyx and diamond-encrusted pelt laps the Duchess's
skinny wrist; slender haunches and outstretched paws reflect myriad points
of light; the stripey tail swishes and snaps shut.

This predatory, gem-set panther is a powerful object of desire. But it is not
a rounded sensual jewel, like the spotted panther sitting cockily on a bauble
of smooth sapphire that the Duke has already bought his wife for a present.

Wallis has other naturalistic trinkets: a pug's head enamel pin with soulful
citrine eyes; a delicate diamond butterfly alighting on a rounded coral flower
bought in 1947; in the early days, she is given a charm in the shape of a
crouching frog.

'I love the new frog and so does "she" – the diamond nearly put her eye
out!!' writes Wallis in 1937.

The Duchess will receive a *jolie-laide* enamel frog bracelet as a tender surprise
present from the Duke a decade ahead, when the fires of passion are dying
down to a warm glow.

'The two old people' Cecil Beaton will call them when he visits the Windsors
for the last time in 1970. 'Had it not been for the sex urges of their youth,' he
reflects, 'these two would not be here together today.'

The panther, rampant on the wrist, is proud, fiery, passionate – a triumph
of the art of high jewellery. Cartier's archives record its sale to the Duchess
of Windsor not – as is usually the case – to their very good client S. A. R. Le
Duc de Windsor.

'The Prince Charming of the Rue de la Paix,' the French cartoonist Sem
calls the boyish Prince of Wales in the 1920s, sketching him as he slips
discreetly into Cartier – as his grandfather Edward VII had done before him
– to buy a bauble for his lady love.

But His Royal Highness has not been buying any jewels for his best beloved
from Cartier this season. For the first time – apart from the war years – since
Mrs Simpson became reigning favourite with Prince and King nearly 20 years
ago, there has been a sudden *interruptus* in the flow of gifts. There was not
even, the salesmen of Cartier or the Windsors' good friend design director

OPPOSITE: *The jewelled cross bracelet was the
most intimate link between Wallis Simpson and
her King. Each represented a stepping stone in
their love story, and a cross they had to bear. A
bracelet of inscribed gold hearts marked happier
moments. Right to left from the diamond clasp:
Cartier's crosses with inscriptions in the royal
handwriting: PLATINUM: 'WE are too 25–
xi–34'. SAPPHIRE: 'Wallis – David
23.6.35' for the Prince's 41st birthday.
YELLOW SAPPHIRE: '"Get Well" Cross
Wallis September 1944 David'. RUBY:
'Wallis – David St Wolfgang 22.9.35', after a
romantic holiday in Austria. BAGUETTE
DIAMOND: 'The Kings Cross God Bless
WE 1.3.36'. EMERALD: 'X Ray Cross
Wallis – David 19.7.36'. The hospital found a
healed ulcer scar. AMETHYST:
'Appendectomy Cross Wallis 31.viii.44
David'. AQUAMARINE: 'God save the
King for Wallis 16.vii.36', when a deranged
man took a pot-shot at Edward VIII. RUBY,
SAPPHIRE, EMERALD: 'Our marriage
Cross Wallis 3.vi.37'.*

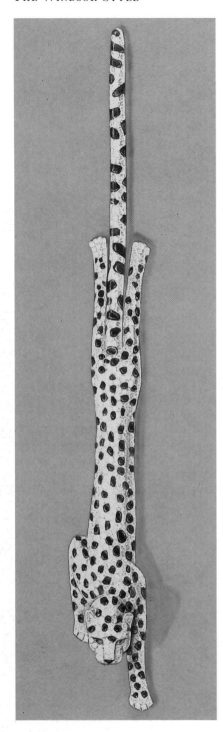

Cartier's Great Cats expressed the Windsors' passion in jewels. OPPOSITE: *The proud head and glittering emerald eyes of the panther bracelet. The articulated body and limbs are of pavé-set diamonds flecked with onyx. The Duchess bought it in December 1952.*

INSET: *Diamond and sapphire panther rampant on a sapphire bauble of 152 carats. The Duke bought it from Cartier in 1949.*

ABOVE: *Cartier's studio drawing of the elongated panther bracelet.*

Jeanne Toussaint might have noted, a specially designed present for Wallis on her 56th birthday this June.

The summer months have been ripe fruit for the jewellers, ever since the Prince of Wales pressed an emerald and diamond charm into Mrs Simpson's hand on a Mediterranean holiday in 1934, or presented her with a diamond hair ornament for her birthday on 19 June 1935.

'Oh! So many happy returns my sweetheart and God bless WE for ever . . . HE is terribly excited about new hair pin and HE hopes SHE is too,' says the note, written in the couple's private language of love, that went with the exotic 'presy'.

When his love is burning hot, the Duke walks into Cartier in the summer of 1938 and buys a bracelet of two fiery rubies cooled by a frame of diamond chips and set in a bold hinged bangle. It marks the first anniversary of their June wedding.

Wallis's midsummer birth date is carved on to her jewels.

'My Wallis from her David 19.VI.36' reads the inscription on the flamboyant ruby and diamond necklace for Wallis's landmark 40th birthday. That comes from another Paris jeweller Van Cleef & Arpels, a few steps away across the Place Vendôme from where Wallis is rotating her wrist and its panther towards the dying daylight.

'There is nothing a man in love can refuse to the woman who makes him happy,' claim Van Cleef & Arpels.

In that tense summer before the abdication in 1936, society had gasped and gossiped at the outward and visible symbols of their King's private passion.

'Mrs Simpson was glittering, and dripped in new jewels and clothes,' reported Diana Cooper after an autumn weekend at the Fort in 1935.

The witty society observer Sir Henry 'Chips' Channon charts the new jewels: 'Mrs Simpson . . . dripping with emeralds – her collection of jewels is the talk of London,' he said on 7 November 1936; and on 26 November 1936: 'She was wearing new jewels – the King must give her new ones every day.'

The obsessive love that reaches its frenzy in the abdication is expressed not only in the King's banal and childish letters, but also in the imaginative and sophisticated jewels, themselves often inscribed with secret messages.

'Hold Tight' says the clasp of the bracelet of rubies flowing through diamond links that the King buys from Van Cleef & Arpels in the spring of 1936, along with a ruby necklace.

'Mrs Simpson was literally smothered in rubies,' reports Chips Channon in mid-summer. 'More and more my beloved,' the King writes to Wallis in June 1936.

More and more jewelled crosses, each engraved with an intimate message, are added to the charm bracelet that is the King's most personal and private link with Mrs Simpson.

'The bracelet of little crosses is a surprise,' says Cecil Beaton, when his sharp eyes picked it out.

Necklaces and hair clips, bracelets and rings, follow as the ex-King in exile, and Wallis awaiting her divorce, communicate in wild, frustrating, shouting matches on inter-continental telephones.

'Of course he's on the line for hours and hours to Cannes every day,' says Fruity Metcalfe. 'I somehow don't think these talks go so well . . . It's only after one of them he ever seems a bit worried and nervous.'

'Oh! darling,' writes the Duke to Wallis, 'one really does wake up some mornings wondering whether one will keep one's sanity if this separation goes on much longer.'

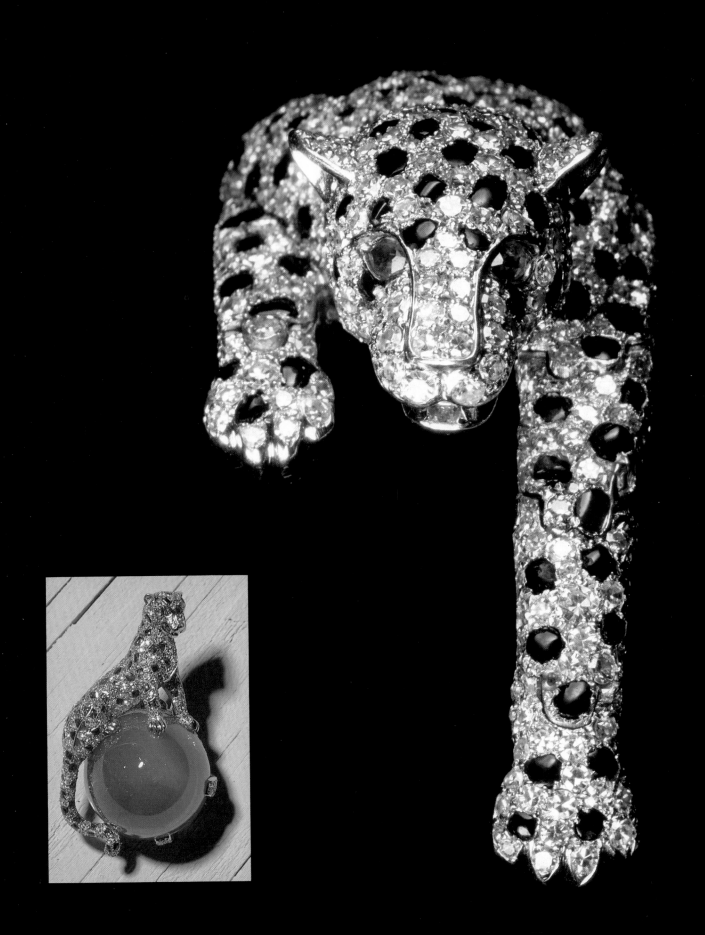

ABOVE: *'For our first anniversary of June third' reads the inscription on the twin ruby hinged bangle the Duke gave Wallis in the summer of 1938 when they were staying at La Croë on the Riviera. He bought the bracelet, set with cushion-shaped Burmese rubies framed in pavé diamonds, from stock at Cartier.*

OPPOSITE: *For Cecil Beaton's romantic picture, the Duchess wore her new ruby bracelet with a dramatic 1939 Mainbocher dress encrusted with red, gold and green bead embroidery lit with mirror sequins and pearls. On her left hand is the emerald and diamond-set engagement ring.*

All the pent-up love and longing, all the words that cannot be said and all the poetic phrases the Duke is unable to express during their enforced separation, go into jewels – especially the erect jewelled plumes, in blood red rubies and glistening diamonds, that Van Cleef make in the maelstrom of the abdication.

'They were ordered on Armistice day 1936 and then delivered one month sooner than expected,' says Jacques Arpels. 'The King was in a hurry.'

'I'm giving . . . you . . . an eanum New Year present,' the Duke explains to Wallis, using the couple's private word for 'small' or 'tiny'. 'The two feathers were for *Christmas*.'

'The women had dressed to the nines, all in red,' noted Cecil Beaton when he photographed Wallis at Candé before her wedding. 'Wallis sported a new jewel in the form of two huge quills, one set with diamonds, the other with rubies. Her dress showed to advantage an incredibly narrow figure . . . The atmosphere was one of suppressed excitement.'

To celebrate their reunion on the day Wallis's divorce becomes absolute in May, there is a rounded ruby and sapphire ring, as succulent as a strawberry. An earlier mix of sapphires and rubies, in a Cartier brooch of 1935, entwines their initials of W and E into a word that becomes part of the private language of love.

'God bless WE Wallis,' says the King. 'He will be missing Her as much as WE will be each other.'

'That brooch meant so much to them both,' says Laura, Duchess of Marlborough, who was married to Lord Dudley when the Duchess's jewels were stolen from the Dudleys' home in 1947.

ABOVE: 'Mrs Simpson was literally smothered in rubies,' reported society diarist 'Chips' Channon in 1936. Inscriptions inside the jewels – all from Van Cleef & Arpels in Paris – tell the King's love story:

RIGHT: 'Hold Tight 27–III–36' reads the diamond and ruby bracelet. Centre: 'My Wallis from her David 19.VI.36' says the clasp of the tassel necklace, given to Wallis for her 40th birthday but redesigned in this form in 1939.

FAR RIGHT: Van Cleef's feathers, 'invisibly' set in a crazy paving of gems, were a Christmas present from the ex-King for Christmas 1936. Right: Matching ivy leaf earrings from Van Cleef in New York.

ABOVE: The Duchess wore all her fine feathers on a white crêpe Dior dress to the Baron de Redé's party in Paris.

'She had been wearing the brooch in London when our butler telephoned the news about the robbery. When we got back, the Duke put the brooch in a safe place and then forgot where he hid it. We stayed up until 5 a.m. searching among all the papers from Windsor he had been sorting. He looked so frail and tired and distraught. When he finally found it under a candlestick on the mantelpiece, he couldn't even speak to me. He just rushed up to the Duchess's bedroom with it.'

To consummate their marriage, the Duke designs an exceptional jewel: a plump cushion of invisibly set sapphires, through which a flexible band of hard, white diamonds slots to fasten the bracelet on his new wife's wrist.

'For our Contract 18-v-37,' its message reads.

Nothing in their 35 years together will match this orgasm of jewels, although the Duke of Windsor strews his wife's bosom with exotic jewelled flowers: a turquoise fleur-de-lys with curling petals and sapphire stamens in March 1938; a bouquet of sapphire and emerald flowers the next month; a blossoming branch of coral and pearls in June. Ten years later he gives his wife the loop and swags of sapphires that Wallis will wear for the Queen's 1972 visit to Neuilly, when the Duke is at the last gasp of his life.

Then he will use a flower pin to woo nurse Oonagh Shanley away from her staff job at the American hospital in Paris to his bedside in Neuilly.

'I had only been with him for five days,' said Oonagh Shanley. 'And he suddenly presented me with this beautiful brooch, begging me to stay. I was with him to the end.'

The flower pin, with its sapphire stem and centre and pinked ivory petals of the Duke's favourite carnation, had been designed by him especially for Wallis.

The Duke is buying his wife an important jewel from New York's Harry Winston in May 1950 – the spring that Jessie Donahue, the daughter of billionaire Frank W. Woolworth, invites the Windsors to stay in Palm Beach, introduces them to her son Jimmy, and provokes a new emotional tornado in the Duke's life.

'The Duchess of Windsor was an admirer of great jewellery and . . . the Duke shared this passion,' says Harry Winston, explaining that his desk was 'literally covered' with the many fine jewels he showed them: 'diamonds, rubies, emeralds, sapphires and pearls'.

'It is often men, even more than women, who appreciate the beauty of a special stone, and will thrill to hold a Kashmir sapphire, a Burmese ruby or a Colombian emerald,' says Joseph Allgood, who joined Cartier at the time of the abdication. 'Of course the Duke knew a lot about stones from his tours of the Empire as Prince of Wales.'

The Duke of Windsor's taste in gems is strong. Pearls – symbols of innocence and purity – are conspicuously absent from his fervid choice of coloured gems, and the Duchess herself prefers exotic canary yellow diamonds to pure white.

'She no longer cares for pearls and never wears them,' Edwina Wilson says.

'I can't think of anything I would rather have than these two diamonds,' Wallis tells Harry Winston in February 1948, when he shows her two luscious pear-shaped diamonds, a ripe golden yellow, suspended in a gold corded wire setting and weighing in at 92.48 carats.

'Mrs Simpson was a great one for collecting yellow diamonds,' says Lady Diana Cooper. 'She would go with Loel Guinness to Cartier or Bulgari and buy several double, treble thousand figure jewels.'

Just before the Windsors sail for France in 1950 with Jimmy Donahue dancing attendance, the Duke buys Wallis a magnificent ring – a glacier white diamond as big as a postage stamp, 31.26 carats and as clear and unfathomable as the limpid deep green emerald he purchased from Cartier in October 1936 on the day Mrs Simpson's decree *nisi* was granted.

'We are ours now 27.x.36' reads the inscription on the inside of the emerald ring.

'The Duchess of Windsor . . . had . . . an engagement ring given to her by King Edward VIII which is one of the greatest emeralds in the world and belonged to the Grand Mogul,' says diarist Marie Belloc Lowndes, relating the story about its purchase in Baghdad ('in those days it was as large as a bird's egg') told to her by Jacques Cartier.

In a private room in his elegant Fifth Avenue store, where the hexagonal show-cases, set like windows into the walls, glow with fine gems, Harry Winston tells the Duke and Duchess of Windsor the story of the 'McLean' diamond.

'When I neglect to wear jewels, astute members of my family call in doctors because it is a sign I'm becoming ill,' said Evalyn Walsh McLean, the Washington hostess from whom Winston had bought the flawless stone.

'Wallis had a love affair with her jewels,' says Laura, Duchess of Marlborough. 'She would play with them like a child with toys, laying them out on a table and touching them. The only other woman I have ever known who felt like that about jewels was Barbara Hutton.'

Now, in these first years of the 1950s, the Duchess of Windsor is amusing herself with Barbara Hutton's cousin Jimmy Donahue. And she is indulging herself in a new orgy of jewels.

She greeted passionately the rubies, sapphires and emeralds poured over her in 1936.

'I can't believe anything so lovely could be given to a girl,' she writes to the King at Fort Belvedere in 1936. 'I can't ever make you know how spoiled I feel. I only hope that I can make you feel that I am always loving you . . .'

Now that she and the Duke – and Jimmy – are back from the United States, Cartier's archives record, almost for the first time, special orders commissioned by S. A. R. La Duchesse de Windsor. These will carry on into the 1960s, as the Duchess busies herself by re-setting her jewels when the Duke's health is failing and they feel financially constrained.

'Those were better days,' the Duke will murmur to costume jewellery designer Ken Lane who admires the Duchess's emeralds.

Wallis's first commission on 1 June 1950 is for re-setting: an oval ruby that she buries in a deep frame of diamonds as a fancy dress ring. A week later, there is a pearl pendant; on 22 June an exuberant diamond palm tree pin, its fruit heavy with a large square diamond.

Two gifts from the Duke punctuate her own list of commissions: a turquoise and amethyst turban brooch and ring, both designed to match the flamboyant lattice work necklace he had made for her in 1947.

On 15 November 1950, just before she sails to New York to the warm attentions of Jimmy Donahue – without the Duke who is completing his memoirs in Paris – the Duchess commissions Cartier to strike a gold medallion, showing a gem-studded engraving of the Statue of Liberty against New York's skyline. The legend round the medal reads: *J'ai deux amours*: I have two loves.

'The Duke and Duchess of Windsor are phfft!' writes the New York *Daily Mirror* columnist Walter Winchell.

Over the next three years, society in Paris and New York seethes with gossip over the nature of the relationship between the overtly homosexual Donahue and the Duchess of Windsor.

OVERLEAF RIGHT: *'For our contract 18–v–37' says the clasp of the bracelet that Wallis wore on her right wrist on her wedding day. Van Cleef & Arpels made the broad band of diamonds that slots through the 'buckle' of cushion-set sapphires surrounded by a sunburst of baguette diamonds and fringed with more circular-cut sapphires.*

OVERLEAF LEFT: *The Duchess was photographed wearing the 'contract' sapphire bracelet by Paris-based photographer George Hoyningen-Huene in 1937. The diamond clips were bought by the Prince of Wales from Cartier in London on 12 June 1935. The delicate diamond diadem was bought from Van Cleef in Paris on 30 December 1936.*

'Why they're in *love*!' gasps a Spanish *Marquesa*, as she watches Wallis and Jimmy flirting together in a Paris nightclub.

'She was mesmerized by him,' says Laura Marlborough. 'Just as the Duke couldn't keep his eyes off her, she couldn't keep her eyes off Jimmy Donahue.'

'She gave herself willingly to the charms of Jimmy Donahue,' says Grace, Countess of Dudley. 'It is easy to see why. He was very amusing.'

Walter Winchell witnesses the Windsors' public reunion at the quayside in New York in December 1950. 'The Duke is a very sad person these days,' he says.

The Duke's brother, King George VI, dies in February 1952; his beloved mother in March 1953; his niece Lilibet is crowned Elizabeth II in June 1953, with the Windsors watching on television at a coronation party given in Paris by their friend Margaret Biddle.

'They've not improved. They never learned to drill,' mutters the Duke as he watches the march past of guards from his Bahamas days.

In earlier years, all the historic royal events would have been commemorated for Wallis in gold and jewels.

'I have lovely diamond clips as a Jubilee present,' she tells her aunt during

ABOVE: *The flawless emerald was cut from a stone the size of a bird's egg that belonged to a Moghul Emperor. The King bought it from Cartier in October 1936 for £10,000 and gave it to Wallis the day her divorce proceedings started. The ring was re-set by Cartier in Paris in 1958 in yellow gold with diamonds.*

INSET: *'We are ours now 27 x 36' the King inscribed the original platinum mount that Wallis kept with her jewels.*

OPPOSITE: *Wallis always considered the emerald as her engagement ring and wore it on the fourth finger of her left hand when she was photographed by Cecil Beaton in 1937. The spiky hair clip set with rubies was bought from Van Cleef & Arpels in Paris in May 1937.*

the celebrations of 1935, when she first borrows a tiara for the royal Court Ball.

'Well, anyway, a tiara is one of the things I shall never have . . .' Mrs Simpson claims just before the abdication. The ex-King buys her a diadem crowned with diamonds from Van Cleef in the dying days of 1936.

The Duchess reigns supreme at Cartier from June 1950 to July 1953. Almost every single entry is on her own account, including the fantastic panther bracelet, which is bought outright in December 1952, not traded in for other jewels or made up from existing loose stones.

An enormous 200 carat sapphire is re-set from an existing brooch, mounted in a border of diamonds on to a diamond necklace in August 1951; in September there is an emerald and ruby cross – in the style of the emotive bracelet of engraved crosses, but not on it at the time of the Duchess's death. A necklace of gold baubles follows in 1952, and a suite of gold sunburst brooch and earrings set with a pearl in July 1953, shortly before Jimmy Donahue is banished by the Duke of Windsor.

'We've had enough of you, Jimmy. Get out!' says the Duke when the inseparable threesome are on holiday together and Donahue's upstart insolence goes too far.

The Donahue years leave a positive legacy.

Seven items in the 1987 Windsor jewel sale in Geneva can be traced back, via the archives of Van Cleef & Arpels, to the account of Mrs James Donahue, mother of Jimmy and the Windsors' friend. Two gold mesh purses, one set with sapphires and diamonds and the other with turquoise and rubies, were originally bought by Mrs Donahue in 1943.

A mosaic of sapphires invisibly set in a rounded dress ring, bought at Christmas 1950 from Van Cleef New York, is an echo of that blood red ruby and sapphire blue ring the Duke bought from Cartier to celebrate his reunion with Wallis after five months' separation.

'The Orient Express passes through Salzburg in the afternoon. I shall be at Candé in the morning . . .' the Duke tells Wallis. 'Our reunion in Candé' reads the inscription inside the ring.

For Christmas 1953, Mrs Donahue, or her son, gives the Duchess a diamond-studded gold handbag mirror in the shape of a heart.

Just as the wild torrent of jewels bought by the Duke in the abdication years flows on as calmer, milder gems, so the Duchess's own frenzy of jewel buying dies down. By 1954, the Duke again takes over the commissioning at Cartier: an amethyst and turquoise bracelet to complete the Duchess's colourful suite of jewels.

The Duchess orders a new Great Cat bracelet in 1956 – a yellow diamond and onyx striped tiger with thick, friendly paws and the head of a gentle, domestic pet. It is a tame partner to the savage, feline panther bracelet that remains king of her jungle jewels.

The summer of 1957 marks the Windsors' twentieth wedding anniversary. The Duke commissions from Cartier a conventionally romantic diamond encrusted heart, entwined with W and E, surmounted by a royal crown and the Roman numerals XX.

In widowhood, all passion spent, the panther jewels locked fast away, the Duchess will wear the heart pinned above her own.

The Duchess of Windsor is dining out in Paris at the wild end of the 1960s.

'We talked of the current trends in clothes, hippies, nudity, pornography . . .' says Cecil Beaton.

The Duke commemorated their twentieth wedding anniversary with this diamond-encrusted heart, surmounted by a ruby crown, with the W and E monogram set in emeralds above a ruby xx in Roman numerals. It was made by Cartier in May 1957 from the Duke's gems. Wallis wore it constantly.

Wallis is wearing a hippie caftan – but in silky black velvet, its high neck and long sleeves severely plain.

Round her neck, in tune with the inchoate times, is a wild flower power necklace – a garland of spiky gold sunflowers set with citrines and quartz, bursting with vitality and scattered with pearls.

'I remember the Duchess at the Moulin wearing a wonderful pale yellow caftan and that necklace with pearls and stones just thrown in,' says Joanne Cummings.

'When I knew her in America in that period of patterned palazzo pyjamas, her necklaces got bigger and rather barbaric,' says society decorator Nicholas Haslam.

'She had chic jewels,' says the Vicomtesse de Ribes. 'She looked much more stylish than those American women with their big stones.'

The garland necklace – like so many of the Duchess's jewels – is ahead of its time. For Wallis had first spotted it at the Paris exhibition of craft jeweller Tony Duquette in early 1951.

All her life, the Duchess of Windsor will be drawn towards the *avant garde* – and especially towards jewellery designers who are linked to fashion design and taken up in society.

The first is Suzanne Belperron, who worked for ten years for René Boivin – a jeweller so much under the spell of the exotic that even his letter heading was decorated with Egyptian hieroglyphics. Boivin's brother-in-law was the couturier Paul Poiret, whose fantastical oriental creations, inspired by the colourful Ballets Russes, swept Paris in the 1920s.

Colour and its use in translucent rock crystal and quartz is the theme of Suzanne Belperron's work when she leaves Boivin to set up on her own in the 1930s. She makes then for Wallis a suite of stained chalcedony beads – the necklace twisted into a flower head and set with sapphires and diamonds, the bracelets shaped like Indian amulets. Another Belperron gold bangle is set with a swarming cluster of pearls to form a sensuous wrist-piece.

This mix of the elegant and the exotic, the shock of colour and a dash of wit, is the Duchess of Windsor's taste in jewellery.

'I saw the Duchess wearing a wonderful choker of rough emeralds and coral,' says Jacqueline de Ribes. 'I said "Isn't it uncomfortable so tight round your neck?"'

'It is a bit tight,' replied Wallis. 'But then it was made to go round the ankle of a Maharajah.'

'Those emeralds used to be one of my anklets,' admits the Maharani of Baroda as she watches the Duchess make a grand entrance at a Paris Ball in 1957.

Jewels are chosen precisely to work with clothes, just as the decoration of the Duchess's homes has an overall scheme.

'My approach to art, whether modern or traditional, is decorative,' says Wallis. 'When I look at a picture I never see it by itself, I see it as part of a room.'

Her ultimate luxury is to wear real gems set as though they were costume jewellery.

'I had been surprised, considering that she dressed so simply, to see that she wore such a mass of dressmakers' jewels,' Marie Belloc Lowndes says of Mrs Simpson to friends of the Prince of Wales. 'At that they all screamed with laughter explaining that all the jewels were real.'

'I sketched her at a ball in the Orangerie at Versailles,' says the Italian artist Nino Caprioglio. 'She was wearing Dior – a short pale blue sheath dress,

ABOVE: *The heart-shaped handbag mirror, framed in corded gold set with diamonds, was made by Van Cleef & Arpels New York and bought in 1953 on the account of Mrs James Donahue – mother of the outrageous Jimmy who became a constant companion of the Duchess.*

TOP: *A heart-shaped cabochon aquamarine in a gold frame made a powder compact by Fulco di Verdura, the eccentric Sicilian Duke who designed shell and animal jewellery for the Duchess in the 1950s.*

RIGHT: *'Her necklaces were big and rather barbaric,' says a society friend. This gilded bib splattered with rubies, emeralds and tiny diamonds was made by Cartier in October 1945, breaking up existing jewels from the Duke's royal inheritance.*

OPPOSITE: *Horst photographed the Duchess in 1947 wearing the bib necklace on a severe oyster silk Mainbocher dress braided in red and gold. On her wrists, a pair of gilt and silver Cartier bangles inscribed: 'For a happier New Year NASSAU 1–1–41 WE.'*

shimmering with embroidery. Over it was a floor length coat in aquamarine organza. And round her neck were those fantastic amethysts and turquoises.'

Wallis's lattice necklace with its lilac and turquoise stones is as big as a baby's bib; another breastplate is in bright gold embedded with cabochon rubies and emeralds. She chooses for herself pieces with small gemstones: rounded beads hanging in swags and clusters; fecund pearl and diamond clusters for earclips by another pioneer of colourful and sculptural jewellery – New York's Seamen Schepps.

Before she has access to fine jewellery, Wallis is obliged to fake it.

'I am buying an aquamarine & crystal ornament and large aquamarine cross to wear around the neck which hangs center front of bust – really lovely on a white dress,' Wallis tells her Aunt Bessie when she is preparing her court presentation outfit in 1931. 'These I need not add are imitations, but effective.'

She fools her biographer Edwina Wilson, who claims: 'She . . . saw a beautiful aquamarine cross . . . made of gorgeous stones. Wallis has a weakness for aquamarines. She bought it, spending more than she might have on an entire court costume.'

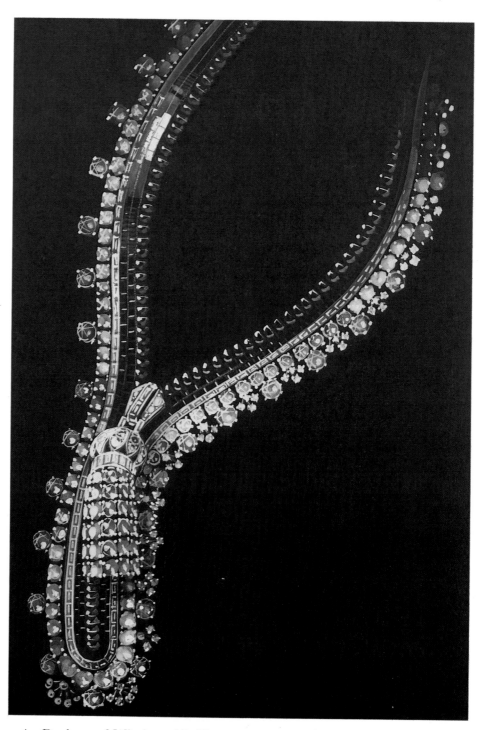

The Duchess of Windsor's most extraordinary fantasy in jewels was the platinum zip edged with diamond 'teeth' and jewelled tassel that Van Cleef designed for the ultimate exit line on a little black dress. 'A fool would know that with tweeds or other daytime clothes one wears gold, and that with evening clothes one wears platinum,' Wallis told bomb-blitzed Britain in 1946, when many of her finest jewels had been stolen in the robbery at Ednam Lodge.

As Duchess of Windsor, Wallis wears costume jewellery only when it is high fashion.

'I hate to admit it,' she tells Fleur Cowles in 1966, 'but I am absolutely fascinated by fake jewellery at the moment. It is so good.'

The closets in her Paris home are filled with boxes of 1960s chains. 'She wore a lot of chains, real and fake, twisted up together,' says Grace, Lady Dudley. There are *faux bijoux* by the jewellery designer Kenneth J. Lane.

'She bought a lot of my things and had fun with them,' says Ken Lane. 'She was very experimental. She was the first person to have one of my "diamond" belts that she wore on a plain black dress.'

Round the Duchess of Windsor's tiny waist goes the broad band of glittering gem-set paste, in the style of the historic Buccleuch diamond girdle.

At Van Cleef in the 1950s, Wallis designs a similar high fashion frivolity – but in real jewels. It is a working zip fastener fashioned out of silver-white platinum and set with diamonds.

'A fool would know that with tweeds or other daytime clothes one wears gold, and that with evening clothes one wears platinum,' a sarcastic Duchess of Windsor tells the press after the theft of her jewels in England in 1946.

But the Duchess collaborates with the *avant garde* jeweller Fulco di Verdura to bring yellow gold back as high style.

In July 1960, the Duchess of Windsor took five cloudy, pear-shaped emeralds into Cartier – the last of the royal inheritance. The stones were set in spiky 1960s style, in radiating baguette diamonds on a link chain. The pendant pear-shaped emerald, which had once belonged to King Alphonso XIII of Spain, was bought by the Windsors from Harry Winston in 1960, trading in two of the Duchess's emerald and diamond necklaces.

Fulco Santostefano della Cerda, Duke of Verdura, must be included in 'the most perfect dinner party imaginable' – according to the Duchess's friend, the society hostess Elsa Maxwell.

Fashionable wardrobes of the 1930s and '40s also have to include Fulco di Verdura's inventive and colourful jewellery. His style is a heady mix of the naturalistic and the fantastic – sea shells scattered with gems; shell earrings fashioned out of bevelled gold; fish and flower pins; sea urchin earclips or a whorl of gold whipped into a ring.

Liz Whitney has, on her bin of manure a
Clip designed by the Duke of Verdura,

writes Cole Porter, immortalizing his favourite designer in a lyric for the show *Let's Face It*. Verdura is commissioned by Cole's wife Linda to make a fantastical gem-set cigarette case to celebrate the theme of each Cole Porter musical on Broadway.

The element of fantasy, wit and the surreal that attracts Wallis to Schiaparelli's clothes, draws her to Fulco's jewellery.

'Mineralogy isn't jewellery,' claims the elegant Sicilian Count, dismissing the most fabulous solitaire diamonds as 'swimming pools'. Fulco's first jewellery designs are in Paris in the 1920s for Coco Chanel, who, although she has a fabulous personal collection of gems given to her by her aristocratic lovers, makes fakes fashionable.

'With my jewellery, women can wear fortunes worth nothing,' she says.

'Everything was very modern and up-to-the-minute, but I never saw Wallis wear costume jewellery,' says Diana Vreeland. 'She wouldn't wear Chanel. And Wallis in *bijoux de théâtre*. That I don't think!'

Among the pieces that the Duchess of Windsor buys from Fulco di Verdura's Fifth Avenue boutique is a heart-shaped cabochon aquamarine embedded in yellow gold made in 1950 as a powder compact; and pearl earclips with dewdrop diamonds set in rope twists of gold.

'I remember the Duchess wearing a marvellous Verdura necklace of angel skin coral and pearls,' says Nicky Haslam. 'You couldn't see the gold for this beautiful blushing pink.'

As well as re-launching yellow gold as high fashion, Verdura rescues from obscurity the pink topaz, making it into a rose pin, its petals shaded from pink to green, which the Duchess of Windsor tells her friends she has designed.

'I'm so sorry I can't exchange it,' says Fulco di Verdura when the Duchess asks to change it for a topaz thistle. 'I'd love to, but alas I can't. Everything here is designed by me, and I understand that this rose is your design.'

The Duchess's taste and style develop as she patronizes the Duke di Verdura. From his sea shell jewellery, she draws inspiration for earclips, taking to New York jeweller David Webb in 1965 bright conker brown and saffron yellow shells that he studs and winds with gold.

'She wasn't just dressed by haute couture,' says Nicky Haslam. 'She was the sort of fashion person who picked up things on her travels and worked them into her wardrobe.'

More snail shells are mounted by Darde & Fils, a Paris jeweller which carries out commissions for the Duchess.

'I went there with her when she was buying a rope pearl choker to replace one that had been stolen,' says Laura, Duchess of Marlborough. Wallis wears the choker with its banded gold and diamond clasp to the Paris *première* of the Duke's memoirs *A King's Story*.

ABOVE: *The Duchess matched her colourful snail-shell earrings to a yellow dress and wore them with a gold and enamel tiger-head pin.*

OPPOSITE: *The Duchess of Windsor's fantastic collection of snail-shell earclips. She first took the yellow and brown Cuban tree-snail shells* bottom left *to David Webb of New York in 1964. He decorated these and similar rust* above left *and white* below right *shells with gold lozenge motifs. Other snail earclips are the mottled grey and white shells* centre top *capped in turquoise; pearly white shells* centre bottom *tipped with cabochon coral; and striped conical shells* centre, *decorated with spirals of gold saw-teeth, made by Darde & Fils of Paris in 1965.*

*The Duchess picked out unusual jewellers.
Suzanne Belperron, an avant-garde designer in
Paris in the 1930s, made this flower necklace of
stained blue chalcedony, sapphires and
diamonds, with matching earrings and bracelets
shaped like Indian amulets.*

Wallis will have other jewels copied – for security, or just for fun.
'Madame Belperron made the Duchess a complete reproduction of the necklace with the drop pearl she wore to the Duke's funeral,' says Diana Vreeland. 'Apart from the lustre, it was hard to tell them apart.'

'She wanted me to copy earrings she had of triple hoops of sapphire beads,' says Ken Lane. 'In the end I couldn't do it, because it was just too labour intensive.'

Fulco di Verdura may plant the seed of the Duchess of Windsor's bunches of ripe gold heavy with ruby and sapphire beads; he may inspire her to be bold with colour and choose animal-shaped jewels. But it is Jeanne Toussaint of Cartier, 'the panther' as her very good friend Louis Cartier calls her, who realizes Wallis's most extravagant jewels.

'We have both been tarts,' Coco Chanel said to Jeanne Toussaint. 'I am the world's greatest fashion designer. You will become an internationally renowned jeweller.'

'In her jewellery creations . . . Madame Toussaint shows voluptuous sensuality,' claims Cecil Beaton, describing Jeanne's exquisite flat, with 'rare and

marvellous sixteenth-century pieces' and its 'fabulous four-poster bed draped with a heavy satin'.

'Her flat is like a secret which few people are privileged to share with her,' says Beaton. The Duke and Duchess of Windsor are part of the élite who dine with Jeanne.

Her early creations for the Windsors in 1940 are a wintry wreath of clustered sapphire beads dripping with diamond icicles and the flamboyant flamingo clip, its tail feathers ruffled with ruby, sapphires and emeralds.

'I like birds,' Jeanne will claim to a German officer when he questions the symbolism of the jewelled birds, trapped inside gold cages, that she puts in Cartier's windows during the Occupation.

For the Windsors, she makes a brooch with two jewelled love birds sitting on a gold nest filled with pearl eggs. An even more exotic bird of paradise, its breast a plump cabochon sapphire and its plumage a fan tail of diamonds, is made for Wallis just after the war in 1946, but stolen that autumn in the robbery at Ednam Lodge, the country home of the Earl of Dudley.

As well as birds there are Cartier's flowers.

The Duchess wore the chalcedony suite for a photograph with the Duke by Karsh of Ottawa. Her Wallis blue safari dress was designed by Yves Saint Laurent. The central flower was detachable and the Duchess often wore it on its own as a flower pin.

173

'My favourite jewel is the one Madame Toussaint wears in her buttonhole,' says the French writer Violet Leduc. 'A bunch of tiny coral bells, faintly wilting, with diamonds at once hidden and showing.'

'She appeared holding a bunch of wisteria,' says Princess Bibesco, a client of Jeanne Toussaint. 'The delicate spring flower of French villages . . . had been transformed . . . into a bunch of diamonds.'

For Wallis, Jeanne Toussaint works her magic on a bunch of grapes, suspending clusters of ripe ruby and emerald beads at either end of a long gold chain.

The Duchess of Windsor's first flower bouquet brooch is by Van Cleef & Arpels – ruby and sapphire gems flowering on leaves and stems of corn yellow gold. Wallis wears it in 1939 for the powerful portrait by Gerald Brockhurst that the Duke will hang in Government House in the Bahamas.

'But I never saw that brooch,' says Ofélia, the wife of the Windsors' butler Georges Sanègre. 'I often used to stand in the *petit salon* looking at the portrait and wondering what became of the clip.'

Cartier's flowers, insects and animals start as representations of nature, but grow more extraordinary and exotic through the 1940s. In 1946, the Duchess has a jewel encrusted bangle patterned as a peacock plume, with ruby and sapphire beads radiating round the feather's eye – which is a sapphire carved into a female head.

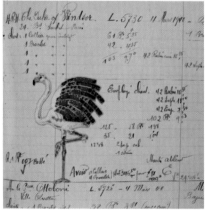

Cartier's ledger sheet shows that the Duke broke up a necklace and four bracelets to make the jewelled flamingo for Wallis in March 1940.

'The Duchess wore those heavy bracelets on her tiny arms,' says Sarah Schlumberger, who dined with the Windsors in Paris. 'It was because she was so fragile that the big ruby and sapphire bracelet looked so chic.'

In the following November of 1947, the Duke buys for Wallis a hinged chimaera bangle carved thickly out of coral. The two bellicose dragon heads with glaring emerald eyes are forerunners of the Great Cat jewels.

These are bred when Jeanne Toussaint – Louis Cartier's passionate and feline 'panther' – meets her namesake in the hall of a pink palazzo belonging to the exotic Marchioness Casati. The stuffed panther is mechanically operated to make it spring forward, claws out, eyes fiery with electric power.

'To discourage thieves,' claims the Marchesa, who drives round in an ink blue Rolls Royce, naked under her sable coat, with a coal black chauffeur whom gossips claim is her lover.

'The sight of the stuffed panther has confirmed me in my desire to create a panther-jewel,' Jeanne wrote to Louis in 1928.

Twenty years later she sculpts a gold and enamel panther, crouching on a cabochon emerald, for a brooch commissioned by the Duke of Windsor. It is the first of Wallis's collection of jungle jewels that are to be the summit of Jeanne Toussaint's naturalistic style.

'I wasn't so sure about the taste of those animal jewels,' says Eric Mortensen of Balmain. 'It was the one thing about the Duchess of Windsor's style with which I was not absolutely in accord.'

'Her jewels were all larger than life,' says Lady Mosley. 'The Duchess always overdid things. Think of all those pugs.'

A fashion for animal skins has influenced Wallis's taste long before Jeanne Toussaint makes panther spots in sapphire or lays tiger stripes in onyx on

The flamboyant flamingo brooch with articulated diamond leg and glittering pavé-set body. The beak is citrine and sapphire, the bird's eye sapphire blue, and the plump feathers are made of emeralds, rubies and diamonds. The pin was big enough to cover the Duchess's left shoulder front.

177

ABOVE: *The double clip which Van Cleef made for Wallis in 1936 was set in Art Deco geometric style with oval sapphires and radiating baguette diamonds. She wore it at the throat of her blue crêpe wedding dress.*

ABOVE RIGHT: *Cecil Beaton captured the quintessentially 1930s elegance of a plain dress with the curving clip in this pensive study of Mrs Simpson in 1936.*

yellow diamonds. Elsie Mendl's house at Versailles was decorated with leopard patterned velvet, which the Duchess takes up for exotic pouffes and cushions to scatter among the Louis Seize furnishings at Neuilly. In the days of the first panther jewels, the Windsors are leasing a house in the Rue de la Faisanderie from Paul-Louis Weiller, who has installed a zebra-patterned staircase.

Wallis is a creature of fashion, and to the rhythm of changing style, she shortens, transforms and re-sets her jewels.

The archives of Van Cleef & Arpels show the necklace of ruby and diamond scallops made for the King to give Mrs Simpson in March 1936, and its transformation into flaunting tassels of ruby by designer Renée-Sim Lacaze in 1939.

'The second necklace – the famous *torsade*, was manufactured using most of the rubies from the first necklace,' admits Jacques Arpels.

The Duke claims to design jewels for his wife. Yet Cartier's archives show that the jeweller tends rather to respond to the ideas and tastes of a good client. Some of the jewels apparently personal to the Duchess – the pug's head pin or the sapphire bauble panther brooch – are bought over the counter from stock. The Duke is a patron of, rather than a collaborator in the design of his wife's collection.

The Duchess of Windsor's contribution is in the way she wears the jewels, using her superbly simple couture dresses as a backcloth for the gems.

ABOVE LEFT: *Beaton drew the bejewelled Wallis Simpson in the ruby and diamond necklace the King gave her for her fortieth birthday in 1936. Three years later she had it re-designed by Van Cleef as the ruby tassel necklace (pp. 156–7).*

ABOVE: *The new Duchess wore the necklace with her ruby and diamond feathers (pp. 156–7) at the Bal des Petits Lits Blancs in France in the summer of 1938.*

'I know women who do put the most fabulous jewels on over all those beads,' says the Duchess. 'To me, the jewels are finished.'

She mixes her colourful gems and high fashion outfits with an artist's eye.

'The slim, trim Duchess . . . wearing purple velvet, square-cut at the neck and tiny in the waist, with a magnificent choker of amethysts and turquoises and matching earrings,' says the Windsors' biographer Joe Bryan.

'I saw her at a ball in an exquisitely simple daffodil yellow Balenciaga sheath dress,' says Hubert de Givenchy. 'She was wearing two fantastic yellow diamond clips, exactly the same colour but one tone deeper. She stood framed by the window waving to me. It was as perfect as a picture.'

The Duke is listening, moist-eyed, to the songs of his childhood. 'All very nice and sad, about "the dear old Kaiser" and *Wiener Mädels*,' says Nicholas Lawford, watching the Duke at Elsie Mendl's party.

'I can't begin to tell you how touched the Duke and I were with the Christmas carols you brought to us – I had tears in my eyes at times,' writes Wallis to Walter Lees, an English friend in Paris, after he takes carol singers to their Neuilly home as a Christmas Eve surprise.

'A rather hard brilliance is often associated with her,' says Lady Mosley. 'But she had a sentimental side.'

The charm bracelets are especially touching, with their childish tokens, engravings and messages.

Italian artist Nino Caprioglio sketched the Duchess of Windsor wearing her flamboyant lattice necklace with a bead-embroidered Dior sheath dress and coat at a ball at the Orangerie in Versailles in the 1950s. To the Duchess's right is her friend the American society hostess Margaret Biddle. In the centre, Woolworth heiress Barbara Hutton.

'One was a heart with a tiny ruby in the centre,' says Aline de Romanones. 'The Duchess told me that was in remembrance of the time they met Ataturk in Turkey.'

'On the right wrist are Hearts (all the nice things that have happened). On the left all the Crosses she has had to bear,' says Nancy Spain. 'I reckoned seven of each.'

By the time the wedding in Candé is celebrated with 'Our Marriage Cross' glowing with emerald, sapphire and ruby, there are seven delicate jewelled crucifixes on the diamond-studded chain.

The first and plainest platinum cross, inscribed 'We are too', is bought for Wallis from Cartier by the Prince of Wales on 3 December 1934 – just after his friend, companion and brother George marries Princess Marina of Greece.

'As I watched the Prince during the weeks preceding it, it seemed to me that a sadness began to envelop him,' says Wallis. 'He and his younger brother were very close.'

'It's full of the most *dreadful* birds,' the Prince would joke to guests at the

Fort, as he opened the door of Prince George's room on a pelican-patterned wallpaper.

'The Prince and his brother George were always coming in buying presents for their girl friends,' says Joseph Allgood, Vice-Chairman of Cartier, London. 'The Prince of Wales would come in through the rear entrance in Albemarle Street, past the leather goods and writing paper, and be shown into a private room.'

It is here, in the inner sanctum of Cartier's London branch in Bond Street – set up with the help of Edward VII's last mistress Alice Keppel – that the Prince buys the jewelled Latin crosses that will look so brazen against bare suntanned flesh on the *Nählin* cruise in abdication year.

'They both wore crucifixes,' says Lady Diana Cooper. 'He had two round a chain on his neck and she had a bracelet.' Mrs Simpson's bejewelled hand reaching out to touch the King, sends shock waves across the world.

His crosses carry simple dedications: 'Wallis–David', the date of the Prince's 41st birthday; the place name of St Wolfgang, a small town in Austria – the

The Duchess favoured bold mixes of coloured stones. This amethyst and turquoise lattice necklace sprinkled with diamonds was made by Cartier in September 1947 using stones believed to have been given to the Duke by his grandmother Queen Alexandra. The Duchess later had earrings, a dress ring and two pins in matching colours.

The gem menagerie. TOP: *Frog bangle in green enamel with gold spiral spots and ruby eyes. The Duke bought it from New York jeweller David Webb in 1964.*

ABOVE: *Diamond butterfly on a succulent cabochon coral flower with emerald petals. The Duke bought it from Cartier in July 1947.*

land of the Prince's childhood songs – which the couple visit in the autumn of 1935.

The cruise down the Dalmatian coast in 1936 is one of the couple's sentimental journeys marked with jewelled souvenirs.

'One evening . . . the Prince took from his pocket a tiny velvet case and put it into my hand. It contained a little emerald charm for my bracelet,' says Wallis in the summer of 1934 as her relationship with the Prince of Wales crosses 'the indefinable boundary between friendship and love'.

She will soon give him a gem-set gold cigarette case from Cartier with an enamelled map of their romantic holidays – the sea cruises in green, journeys by land in red. 'David from Wallis Christmas 1935', it reads. On 23 November the next year – as the abdication starts to breach the wall of press silence – the King adds the fateful *Näh) in* cruise to his cigarette case and copies the idea for a jewelled half-moon compact and matching lipstick case for Wallis.

'I could not get the King situation out of my mind,' Chips Channon is writing. 'This morning the *Daily Mail* publishes a leader of praise for the King, so fulsome and exaggerated as to be almost dangerous.'

The crosses on Wallis's bracelet are stepping stones in the royal love affair. They also record illness, anxiety and intimations of death. 'God save the King for Wallis' on a watery blue aquamarine cross marks escape from a would-be assassin's bullet, as an Irishman takes a pot shot at the King in July 1936. 'X Ray Cross Wallis – David 10.7.36' the King inscribes another emerald-set crucifix one week earlier.

'I had myself X-rayed from head to toes,' Wallis tells Mrs Merryman. 'They found a *healed* ulcer scar.'

Eight years later, the Duchess is in hospital in New York after an appendix operation and two more crucifixes are added to her bracelet: 'Appendectomy Cross Wallis' is picked out on the back of an amethyst cross; and '"Get Well" Cross Wallis Sept. 1944' inscribes a cross of golden yellow sapphires.

Mrs Ernest Simpson's personal choice of charms is breezy, rather than sentimental. From early April 1934 – two weeks after the Prince's earlier favourite Thelma, Lady Furness, returns from America to find her place usurped – Wallis is buying trinkets from Cartier.

'Oh Thelma, the little man is going to be so lonely,' Wallis says on the eve of her friend's departure.

'Well, dear,' Thelma replies. 'You look after him for me while I'm away.'

'OK' are the defiant letters in gold that Wallis adds to her chain of charms that summer. 'I doo Too' is its inscription. There are plaques inscribed 'Run Along', 'Hello', a gold hair pin and a ladybird.

'No account to be sent,' notes the Cartier salesman discreetly at the top of the ledger. 'Client will call.'

The presents that Wallis gives are practical and their messages straightforward.

'Many Happy Returns of the day,' she says on the Prince's thirty-ninth birthday. 'This small "presy" is to conceal Bryant & May's [match] books on your dining table at the Fort.'

Wallis's most intimate birthday message to the Prince is 'Hold Tight' inscribed on a diamond waistcoat button – the initial E picked out in pavé-set gems. It is part of a dress suite of cufflinks and buttons made by Cartier for his father's Jubilee celebrations and for the Prince's birthday on 23 June 1935.

'Family birthdays were festive occasions, and the ritual was always the same,' explains the Duke. 'Our presents were always displayed on a square table covered with a white tablecloth, from which hung the initial . . . in wired

The first panther, in gold and enamel, crouching on a 116-carat emerald. It was designed by Cartier for the Duke, using his own emeralds, in 1948. Matching emerald panther earrings were given to Princess Michael of Kent.

The Duchess wearing the panther clip sitting with the Duke in their garden in Paris.

ABOVE: *The palm tree medallion was a memory of the war years when the Duke was Governor of the Bahamas.*

TOP: *'J'ai deux amours' – 'I have two loves' – reads the gold medal of the Statue of Liberty and 'mon pays' – 'my country'. The Duchess ordered it just before she sailed to see Jimmy Donahue.*

OPPOSITE: *Wallis spelled out her love story in charms. Left to right:* Gold heart with 'David Thumb 1944' on the back. Ladybird inscribed 'David 4/12/36'. A locket dated April '35, interior inscribed 'Wallis-David' with a lock of the Prince's fair hair. Run Along medallion dated 11/9/34. Gold OK inscribed 'I doo too July'. Hello plaque dated May 1934. Gold hairpin and hinged notebook with initial D and W and dated June 1934. Plaque with figure 3 dated March 1934. Frog charm. Entwined WE inscribed 'October'. Hinged envelope engraved telegram E.P. *(for Edward Prince).*

flowers. Dominating the grouped gifts . . . was a tiered birthday cake.'

The King's inscriptions on Wallis's jewels are all passionate, emotional, intimate. He writes – often in his own hand – the secret words and messages of their private world, where their dogs are fussed over like children and the King of England becomes a child again.

'THEY say that THEY liked this bracelet and that THEY want you to wear it always in the evening,' writes His Majesty Edward VIII, as he gives Wallis the ruby and diamond bracelet inscribed 'Hold Tight'. 'THEY have told Mr Van Cleef but are very sad THEY can't make christen or write tonight. A boy loves a girl more and more and more.'

'Wallis! Hello eanum pig 1934' are the words that the Prince engraves on a geometric emerald and diamond pin.

'Please – please! "Everybody" – all of "Us" here – send all of "YOU" oohs enormous oohs for Christmas,' writes the ex-King from Cannes two weeks after the abdication. 'HE (I hide face) Eanum and Pig (I hide face again) and all the toys miss YOU ALL . . . more than they can say.'

In the Windsors' boudoir in their Paris home are a pair of stuffed toy pigs; in the Duchess's bedroom, the pug cushions; by the Duke's bed more pugs and the raggedy chimney-sweep doll.

The cairn terrier, Wallis's pugs and the toys all become sentimental talismans of the romance. A medallion records the anguish and despair at the death of Slipper, the Cairn terrier that the Prince had given Wallis for Christmas 1934 along with jewelled tokens of his love.

'I have a cairn puppy – adorable . . .' Wallis tells Aunt Bessie. 'I have 2 more bracelets and a small diamond that sticks into my hair.'

'Our Mr Loo 7.VII.34 6.IV.37' the Duke scratches on the sole of the slipper embedded with an emerald Indian charm in the gold medal struck by Cartier.

Other inscriptions also express pain and anxiety rather than joy.

'For a happier New Year Nassau 1.3.41' the Duke writes inside a barbaric gold bangle, when the Windsors are struggling to make something of his appointment as Governor General of the Bahamas.

'Is there scope here for his great gifts, his inspiration, his long training?' asks Wallis. 'I am only a woman, but I am his wife, and I do not believe that in Nassau he is serving the Empire as importantly as he might.'

All the love the Duke feels for his enduring romance is also carved on precious metal.

On the gold heart he gives his wife for her charm bracelet on their return to Paris from the Bahamas in 1944, his love is inscribed in symbols and words: '+ qu'hier et – que demain; more than yesterday and less than tomorrow'. On the back is an echo of the child's tale of Tom Thumb in the inscription 'David Thumb'.

'It was, overwhelmingly, a mother–son relationship,' says the Windsor historian Michael Bloch. 'His letters to her are infantile, adoring, trusting, full of baby talk; they plead for affection and protection. Hers to him are sensible, affectionate, admonishing, possessive.'

'Sometimes I think you haven't grown up where love is concerned,' says Wallis to her 'Peter Pan' Prince.

'King's Cross,' goes the child's nursery rhyme. Edward VIII engraves the words 'The Kings Cross God bless WE' on a diamond crucifix which he buys from Cartier on 3 March 1936, when Wallis is taking a week's break in Paris with her friend 'Foxy' Gwynne.

'That little King insists I return and I might as well with the telephone about 4 times daily,' an angry Wallis writes to Aunt Bessie.

The next month she inscribes in her own hand inside a solid gold notebook cover the prophetic words of Eleanor Farjeon's nursery rhyme:

King's Cross, what shall we do?
His purple robe is rent in two.
Out of his crown he's torn the gems.
He's thrown his sceptre into the Thames . . .

'King's Cross,' Mrs Simpson will order her taxi cab five months later as she flees London and the lowering crisis to catch the train for Balmoral.

'I'm sorry, lady,' the driver replies.

March 1953: Queen Mary, England's dowager Queen, is in bed in the last month of her life, gazing out at the green gardens of St James's Park and down The Mall to her former home at Buckingham Palace.

Next door in her private sitting room at Marlborough House, a parlour maid is dusting the 90 precious objects gathered on the rosewood writing table, where Queen Mary would sit gloating over her latest acquisitions.

'All the beautiful objects, are ever a constant joy to me,' she writes to a collector friend. 'It always seems strange to me that there can be people to whom these things mean and say nothing to them. They miss much in life.'

In her upstairs drawing room, with its blue grey silk walls and family portraits and flower prints, are all her most treasured *bibelots*.

'Tables were laden with Royal seals cut in topaz mounted in gold,' says James Pope-Hennessy. 'Miniatures and photographs of the Queen's children, cameos and Fabergé animals of platinum, diamonds and gold . . . the series of gold boxes . . . into which precious materials have been fitted.'

'I am caressing it with my eyes,' Queen Mary will announce to the owner of some covetable *objet* as her hobby turns into a private passion.

Among Wallis's souvenirs was the Cartier medallion commemorating the death of their cairn terrier 'Slipper'. It shows a diamond-studded slipper and a carved emerald Indian token. On the reverse the dog's pet name is inscribed: '"Our Mr Loo" 7.VII.34 6.IV.37'.

This gold and enamel pug pin with soulful citrine eyes was bought by the Duke from Cartier in January 1952.

The Duke was himself a collector of beautiful objects. ABOVE RIGHT: *Solid gold eighteenth century tabatière engraved with a classical scene of a warrior crowned with a laurel wreath, flanked by Justice, Prudence and a triumphal archway studded with diamonds. It was given to the Louvre in Paris in 1973 after the Duke's death, the only one of the Windsors' fabulous collection of gold boxes to go into a museum collection.*

ABOVE: *'No excuse for going in the wrong direction Easter 1939' says Cartier's gold pocket watch. On the reverse is a compass engraved with a sundial.*

The fruits of her collecting – Chinese vases and fine French porcelain – are displayed in glass-fronted cabinets. Scattered on tables, beside vases filled with Queen Mary's favourite white lilies, are diamond-encrusted boxes, and a more exotic rose-quartz clockwork Buddah set with gems along with miniature agate elephants supporting jewelled howdahs.

Queen Mary has a precise position for each little treasure.

'It was impossible to remove for cleaning or repair the smallest coral object from some obscure *vitrine* without the Queen noticing its absence,' says James Pope-Hennessy.

'May I go back and say goodbye to that dear little cabinet?' the Queen will say, as she hovers expectantly on the doorstep of her host's home.

Over in Paris, at No 4 Route du Champ d'Entraînement, the Duke and Duchess of Windsor are setting up home in that same year of 1953. The two housemaids are in the salon dusting a strikingly similar collection of precious objects: gold boxes – a *tabatière*, diamonds embedded round its engraved classical columns; an exquisite eighteenth-century box with pastoral scenes enamelled in sugar sweet colours with cherubs cavorting across puffs of white cloud; the Duke's seals glowing with citrine, marbled blue lapis or facets of deep green bloodstone veined in red; the Duchess's porcelain animals *couchant* on each commode.

'A small, overcrowded drawing room,' says Cecil Beaton. 'Masses of royal souvenirs, gold boxes, sealing wax, stamps and seals.'

There is even a collection of decorative elephants.

'In China . . . Wallis began her collection of "lucky" elephants – tiny figures carved of ivory and jade and turquoise,' says Edwina Wilson.

The Duke has been surrounded by things of beauty ever since his childhood in York Cottage on the Sandringham estate, when his mother, 'in négligée resting on the sofa', would call her five children into her boudoir before dinner.

'I am sure that my cultural interests began at my mother's knee,' he says.

The Duke's collection of historic royal seals. In the foreground: *George IV's bust on a seal dated 1823.* Right foreground: *Gold fob seal 1825, set with citrine, engraved 'Needs must when the devil drives'.* Far right: *Lapis lazuli ball on gold and hardstone 1885 seal engraved M.V. – the monogram of Queen Mary.* Centre table: *1905 lapis seal with bust of Roman emperor and Edward VII's cypher. Lying flat, left to right: Lapis seal, Edward VII cypher; bloodstone seal, George IV cypher; bloodstone seal, cypher future Edward VII; chalcedony seal, Prince of Wales feathers; faceted bloodstone seal, armorials Prince Albert; citrine seal, cypher Edward VIII.*

'Her soft voice, her cultivated mind, the cosy room overflowing with personal treasures were all inseparable ingredients of the happiness associated with this last hour of a child's day.'

As with his mother, his wife has a home for everything.

'She sets the ornament in place, outlines it with chalk, then removes the piece and melts candle wax round the outline,' explains Margaret Biddle. 'The ornament, replaced while the wax is still soft, is then secured against accidental jostling.'

'We are both terrific collectors by nature,' says the Duchess. 'And collections need a place to stay.'

Like her mother-in-law, who has refused to the end to receive her, Wallis spends happy afternoons scouring the antique shops.

'The old shops of the Left Bank in Paris have an endless appeal for me,' she says. 'They know me pretty well by now . . . so I don't have much chance of picking up a bargain.'

'I used to be sent off antique-spotting for Aunt May,' says the Marchioness of Cambridge. 'She would say "He's asking £350, but offer him £250 and see what he says."'

'I find it difficult to pick up anything of historical interest except by paying huge sums and then the things are not worth it,' Queen Mary complains to a collector friend.

The Duke shares the urge for acquisition with his mother and Wallis.

'They were always going off to Christies to buy those gold boxes,' says Laura, Duchess of Marlborough. 'The Duke and Duchess were both mad about collecting.'

The Duke of Windsor brought to his marriage some favourite treasures – Fabergé boxes from Queen Alexandra's collection and cigarette cases galore. The tobacco that seeps into his weakening lungs is stored in silver boxes of exquisite elegance, their round lids framing the engraved royal coat of arms.

Every member of his family presses on him a splendid cigarette case.

'David from Mama, Xmas 1919' is inscribed inside a sleek ridged silver case when the Prince is 19. 'Xmas 1925, David from Bertie' reads his brother's message on a similar ridged case decorated with the Prince of Wales feathers in gold. 'David 29-11-34 George' is the inscription on an 18 carat gold cigarette case from his favourite brother, the Duke of Kent, who was to die so tragically in Scotland in an air crash while the Duke of Windsor was serving in the Bahamas.

'The Duke broke down at the beginning and wept like a child all the way through,' said a mourner at Prince George's memorial service. 'It was the only time I saw him lose his self-control like that.'

'David' engraved Wallis in her own handwriting on the outside of a silver cigarette case. 'From Wallis, Nassau 1941'.

The Duke's personal trinkets – his gold Cartier pill boxes and cigar piercers, pocket magnifying glass and card cases, are far outshone by the elegant accessories – the *Nécessaires du Soir* as the French jewellers describe them – that he gives to Wallis as love tokens. They will also be inscribed in the family tradition and sometimes converted from royal heirlooms.

'The Duchess had a silver box with cabochon stones sunk into it that were all taken off George V's and Edward VII's tie pins,' says her *coiffeur* Alexandre.

'Since I hardly ever wear a pin in my tie, I had the tops of them mounted on the Duchess's various gold accessories which she carries in her handbag,' says the Duke. 'A jewelled horseshoe, for example, on a compact; King Edward's monogram on a case for her comb.'

ABOVE: *The Duke had the tops of his historic royal tie pins mounted on a gold basketweave handbag suite designed by Van Cleef & Arpels in 1950. The central motif on this notebook holder is a diamond framed medallion of the Duke's parents, George V and Queen Mary.*

OPPOSITE: *The ultimate frivolity: Cartier designed a tiger lorgnette in October 1954 for the Duke to give Wallis. The handle was in striped gold and enamel with emerald tiger eyes. Artist René Bouché drew the Duchess using the lorgnette for American 'Vogue' in May 1955. The Duchess had the picture framed for her dressing table. In it she is wearing the gold sunburst earrings set with a pearl that she gave to Princess Michael of Kent.*

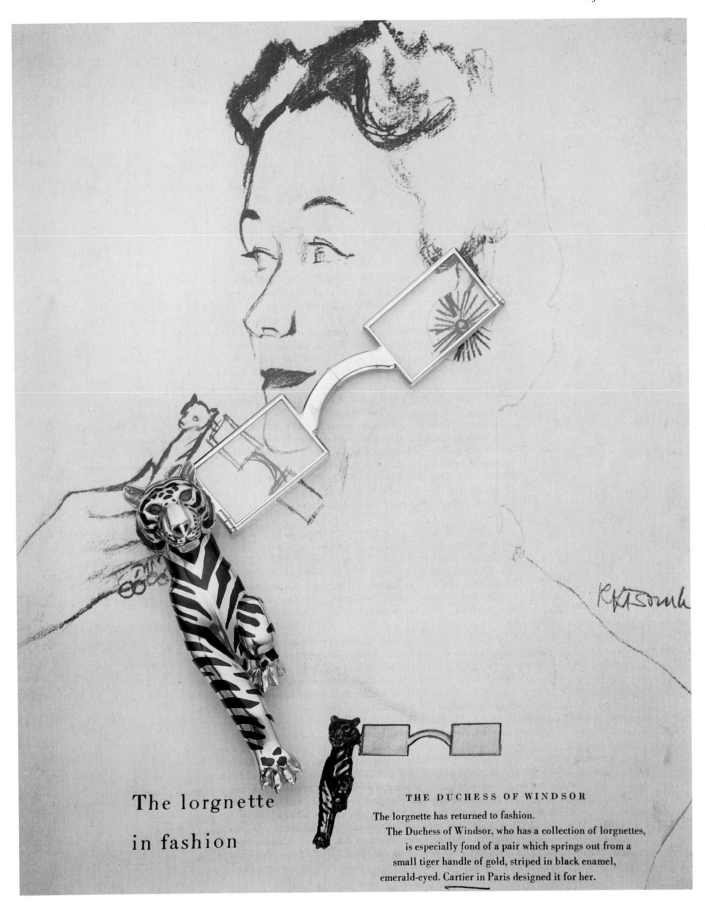

The lorgnette in fashion

THE DUCHESS OF WINDSOR

The lorgnette has returned to fashion.

The Duchess of Windsor, who has a collection of lorgnettes, is especially fond of a pair which springs out from a small tiger handle of gold, striped in black enamel, emerald-eyed. Cartier in Paris designed it for her.

The 18 carat gold handbag suite by Van Cleef & Arpels is a riot of frivolity, with Kaiser Wilhelm's crowned cypher making a flamboyant W for Wallis on her basket weave gold comb case, and the proud Royal Navy anchor sunk in the top of her lipstick holder.

The most emotive trinket is the jewelled powder compact, set with a crazy paving of gems and its engraved map of the love cruise.

'The Duchess was always making up at table which of course is very sexy,' says Nicky Haslam. 'And she had these wonderful little tortoiseshell boxes with that chic 1940s sophistication that nobody has any more.'

'Wallis was fastidious about bags,' says Diana Vreeland. 'She had all these wonderful *minaudières* and witty things from Cartier in the shape of a pug and an egg.'

The pug nestles in the palm of the hand. The egg is an object of regal beauty – a tactile gold and diamond powder case, hung from a gold ropework

LEFT: *Mrs Simpson photographed by Horst in 1935 reclining on a chaise longue among exotic lilies. Her clinging lamé dress was by Mainbocher. In her hair: ruby and diamond clips. On her left wrist: the tell-tale jewelled crosses with their private messages.*

OPPOSITE: *The half-moon powder compact with a mosaic of precious stones and matching lipstick case was a present from the King in December 1936. On the back, Cartier engraved an enamelled map of the romantic holidays the couple took together. A year earlier, Wallis had given the Prince a jewelled cigarette case with maps, inscribed 'David from Wallis Christmas 1935'. For map on reverse see page 58.*

border like a gleaming Easter egg, and engraved with the royal coat of arms and the Duchess's WW monogram.

'Wallis from Edward 1947' writes the Duke inside the miniature barrel of gold fluttering with diamond butterflies, that he buys for his wife from Cartier ten years after their wedding.

Wallis's wit and dash gleam in her fashionable accessories.

'The Duchess of Windsor, who has a collection of lorgnettes . . . is especially fond of a pair which springs out from a small tiger handle of gold striped on black enamel, emerald-eyed. Cartier in Paris made it for her,' reports American *Vogue* in May 1955. René Bouché's elegant sketch of the Duchess, wearing her new sunburst gold and diamond earrings and grasping the tiger handle, is framed on her dressing table.

'Wallis needed glasses to read a menu,' says Diana Vreeland. 'She had a wonderful gold lorgnette on a chain with tiny diamonds set between the links, and the gold chain would hang in straps over her shoulders.'

Queen Mary with her fetish for family history, would have relished more the engraved pieces recording rites of passage.

'The charming . . . frame with the commemoration of the Pce and Pcss of Wales' marriage I shall give to my eldest son as I am doing all I can to encourage his collecting family things,' she writes.

Although her son is never crowned King, he takes with him into exile a King's ransom of jewels and gems. Cartier's meticulous archives record an apparently inexhaustible supply of brooches, necklaces and rings to unmount and re-set, and loose stones brought in '*sur papier*' as the French phrase goes, to set in some of the Duchess's more important pieces.

The Duchess of Windsor's most flamboyant jewels are 'made over', including the flamingo brooch of 1940, created from a necklace and four bracelets that produce 42 rubies, the same number of sapphires and emeralds and 102 diamonds. The first Toussaint panther of 1948 – and its matching earrings which the Duchess is to bestow on Princess Michael of Kent – uses emeralds supplied by the Duke. This is after all the Windsor gems have supposedly been lost in the robbery of 1946.

One year after the theft, Cartier records an enormous deposit of loose stones: quantities of amethysts and emeralds, diamonds, sapphires and rubies that make up first the showy amethyst and turquoise lattice necklace, then Jeanne Toussaint's clusters of ruby and emerald grapes; an emerald and diamond clasp for the necklace of coral ropes; an emerald ball and diamond necklace converting to a diadem – all produced in the autumn of 1949.

Eleven years later, Wallis will walk into Cartier with five cloudy deep green emeralds and fistfuls of diamonds, which are turned into a spiky 1960s necklace, with explosions of baguette diamonds round the central stones and links of diamonds forming a chain. On to the necklace clips the fine 50 carat pear-shaped emerald, a historic stone from the collection of King Alphonso of Spain, that the Windsors have just bought in New York.

'One of Winston's little efforts,' the Duchess will say to Grace Dudley.

'His Royal Highness tells me that . . . you would accept the Duchess's two Emerald and Diamond necklaces in exchange for the Pear-shaped Emerald pendant which you delivered to the Duke and Duchess aboard SS *United States*,' writes the Duke's private secretary to Harry Winston on 27 May 1960.

The legend of the 'Alexandra emeralds' that courtiers claim to recognize on Mrs Simpson and identify as Queen Alexandra's inheritance, persists throughout the Duke's life, although he and the Windsors' legal adviser Maître Suzanne Blum constantly refute the claim.

Egg-shaped gold and diamond powder case, with rope border and diamond ring handle, designed by Cartier in 1950. This surface is engraved with the arms of the Duke of Windsor. The reverse has the WW Wallis Windsor monogram below a royal coronet.

'The Duke of Windsor formally denied that he ever had any jewels from the British royal family,' says Maître Blum. 'Everything was divided up very strictly.'

'I never wore and I never had any jewels from my husband's family,' the Duchess confirmed.

The robbery in 1946 at Ednam Lodge, the home of the Earl of Dudley, fuels speculation about the Duchess of Windsor's collection, which the distraught Duke claimed was under-insured at £20,000.

'Are you sure they haven't touched my guns or fishing rods?' Eric Dudley asks his butler when he rings to tell his master of the break-in.

'The Duchess's jewel case was like a small trunk,' says the former Lady Dudley. 'At the bottom were all the Fabergé boxes that the Duke had inherited from Queen Alexandra. We found them on their tray abandoned on one of the upstairs window sills.'

The bell that summons the servants to their hall for tea, serves as an all-clear to the thief who shins up a white rope which is left dangling from a hook on the window frame. By the time the Duchess's maid returns from tea, the bird has flown – in particular the spectacular jewelled bird of paradise, its swelling breast a large sapphire, which had arrived from Cartier that morning.

'The Duke kept saying "I told you they shouldn't have sent it." And it is the only time I saw the Duchess as anything but charming,' says Laura Marlborough, then Lady Dudley. 'She was absolutely distraught and demanded to put my servants – all of them had been with me for ages – through the third degree. And when I wouldn't have it, she was most unpleasant.'

The angry Duchess does nothing to discourage the public rumour that the robbery has been master-minded by the British royal family.

'Nothing has ever been heard of any of the jewels again,' says Laura, Duchess of Marlborough.

In fact, the mystery is solved in 1960 when Richard 'Tiptoe' Dunphie confesses in court to the Windsor jewel theft and is gaoled at Suffolk Assize for seven years for a series of robberies. Three days later, his dramatic escape from Norwich prison and eventual recapture make headline news. Police investigations suggest that while the Windsor jewels were 'hot' they were kept on a boat near Kings Lynn, and that later the major gems were taken out of their distinctive settings. Dunphie will admit only to an involvement with three accomplices and to selling the jewels to a 'fence' in London.

The stolen gems – ten good pieces – are only the diamond-studded tip of the Duchess's heap of pre and post abdication jewels, and of the loose stones and re-set pieces on which her collection will be built up in the late 1940s and '50s.

The sources of the well-spring of gems that feeds the Duchess of Windsor's *rivières* of jewels are private family heirlooms and gifts of empire to the future King Edward VIII – especially on his tour of India in 1921–22.

'The King would come here with pockets full of gems from all over the empire,' say Van Cleef & Arpels, whose ruby tasselled necklace for Wallis was made from loose stones.

'When the Duchess was wearing her marvellous daffodil yellow clips on a Givenchy dress, she told me that the Duke had been given the stones by a maharajah in India when he was Prince of Wales,' says Alexandre.

Queen Mary is the recipient of majestic Maharajahs' gifts at the Delhi Durbar of 1911; she glories in the fabulous collection of royal heirlooms; she acquires ever more gems from relatives exiled after the Russian revolution.

'Ropes of the most wonderful pearls were taken out, all graduated, the

RIGHT: *'I can't think of anything I would rather have than these two diamonds,' Wallis told the jeweller Harry Winston when she saw the perfect pear-shaped yellow diamonds. The Windsors bought the lapel clips centre in 1948. The pear-shaped yellow diamonds top with circular diamonds, were re-mounted as earclips by Cartier in January 1969. The Duchess told her hairdresser Alexandre that the diamonds had been given to the Prince of Wales by an Indian maharajah on his tour of 1921.*

OPPOSITE: *Cecil Beaton photographed the Duchess wearing her yellow diamonds at the Rothschild Ball. 'Her face so pulled up that the mouth stretches from ear to ear,' he said. Guests were asked to dress in the Rothschild colours of yellow and blue. Wallis's friend Ghislaine de Polignac sketched her inset as the picture of elegance.*

largest being the size of a big cherry,' says royal Equerry Sir Frederick Ponsonby as he watches Romanov treasures laid out before Queen Mary.

'I know that May was passionately fond of jewellery,' says the owner of those jewels, the Romanov Grand-Duchess Olga.

The graduated milky white pearls which the Duchess of Windsor wears with a lustrous pendant tear drop to the Duke's funeral, are a final forgiving gesture from Queen Mary to her dearest David.

Photographs of Wallis wearing the globular pearl necklace, set with its diamond Cartier clasp and detachable pearl pendant, can be dated from 1953 – the year Queen Mary dies peacefully in her sleep, just four months before the coronation of her granddaughter Elizabeth II.

'We were sitting after dinner in the house at Neuilly,' says the Princess de Polignac, 'and one of the guests said "Oh Duchess, what fabulous pearls."'

The priceless central string of 28 graduated natural pearls with oval diamond clasp was a gift from Queen Mary above – a final gesture of reconciliation to her beloved son and his wife she never knew. The second outside string of 29 cultured pearls came from Van Cleef & Arpels in Paris in 1964; its attached baroque pearl pendant was re-set by Cartier in 1950. Wallis wore to the Duke's funeral the dramatic earrings, one black pearl, the other white, set in diamonds, made by Van Cleef in 1957. The pearl ring was re-set by Cartier in 1964.

OPPOSITE: *Wallis photographed by Dorothy Wilding wearing Queen Mary's pearls. On her left wrist, the bracelet of engraved gold hearts that balanced the jewelled crosses. The brilliant white diamond ring the size of a postage stamp was bought by the Windsors from Harry Winston of New York in May 1950.*

'The Duke inherited them from his mother,' replied Wallis.

'I feel so sorry for your great anxiety about your wife,' Queen Mary had written to the Duke when Wallis had an emergency operation in America in February 1951 and old age had thawed her frosty spirit. Yet the majestic Queen was unbending in her refusal to receive the Duchess.

'The fluids in her veins must always have been as icy-cold as they now are in death,' the Duke says sadly to Wallis when his mother dies.

May 1972. The Duke is in bed gathering his dying strength for the first visit of his niece and Queen to his home. Downstairs in the long salon, the Duchess pours China tea, wearing a discreet dark blue Dior dress, sapphires at her ears and pinned to the left shoulder. Around her are 35 years of accumulated treasures. Queen Mary's formal portrait is on the wall.

In her love of beautiful possessions, in her passion for jewels, in her *bibelots* and *bijoux*, the Duke of Windsor found his mother in Wallis.

'Just before His Royal Highness died, I heard him say four words,' says Sydney Johnson. 'Mama, Mama, Mama, Mama.'

EPILOGUE
THE DISPERSAL

IN the early summer of 1972, ten days after the death of the Duke of Windsor, Lord Louis Mountbatten, who had been created Earl Mountbatten of Burma in 1947, and who was 'Uncle Dickie' to the royal family, paid a visit to the grieving Duchess in Paris.

'More than my best man, he was my best friend all my life,' Mountbatten had said at the funeral of his second cousin. In fact, the ex-King had been hurt that Dickie had not been present when he married Wallis and that had broken the bond between them. But because of the long-standing friendship, Mountbatten had been charged with the task of ensuring that the most vital objects and papers were returned to the royal archive at Windsor.

'It was awful,' Wallis told Aline de Romanones after Lord Mountbatten's visit. 'He wanted me to make out a will right there and then, giving everything to David's family and, of course, some to himself. He had it all worked out, just where everything should go. Well, I did my best to stick up for my rights. After all, I do want to be fair, and what should go to the royal family should go . . .'

The Duchess had inherited outright her late husband's estate and she was to live on for another 14 years in an increasingly twilight world. Although plagued by lapses of memory and paranoia, the 76-year-old Wallis was in possession of all her faculties in 1972, but it seems that she did not sign at that point any legally binding agreement to return the royal inheritance. Lord Mountbatten certainly got some of the Duke's papers (but not the private letters), his uniforms, robes, orders and decorations (but not his swords). These were all handed over to the Duke's niece, the Queen.

The Duchess also discussed with Mountbatten the possibility of setting up a Windsor trust in memory of the Duke and under the patronage of Prince Charles, but this was never realized.

On 30 March 1973, two months after she had been operated on for a broken hip, the Duchess did sign a major legal document. She made over to the French state and its Minister of Cultural Affairs all the Louis XVI furniture she had collected, along with a quantity of porcelain and a few paintings. The settlement was in lieu of death duties and in gratitude to France for playing host to the Windsors for a quarter of a century.

The furniture (Appendix I) was conservatively valued at six and a half million francs (three-quarters of a million pounds). The Stubbs painting, destined for the Louvre, was valued at one million NF (£100,000).

Various precious objects were presented at that time to the museums, although not yet put on display, notably some of the Duchess's fine collection of porcelain (but not any of the major dinner services) at the National Ceramic Museum at Sèvres, and two of the gold boxes (valued at 250,000 NF, £25,000 each) which went to the Musée du Louvre.

It is one of the paradoxes of Wallis Windsor, that she was in many ways the dominant partner in the relationship and a supreme housekeeper, yet she retained a Southern Belle's view of money as something that a man looks after. Financial affairs were a preoccupation and hobby for the Duke, and after his death Wallis appears to have left everything in the hands of her lawyer, executor and professional adviser Maître Suzanne Blum and, in the earlier part of her widowhood, to her Swiss secretary Johanna Schütz and to her Swiss banker Monsieur Amiguet.

Maître Blum, one of France's most distinguished lawyers, and only two years younger than the Duchess, had been introduced to the Windsors by her first husband, Paul Weill, the Duke's Paris attorney. Until his death, the Duke was represented by the British law firm of Allen and Overy, and he relied also on the advice of his Private Secretary John Utter, a former banker and American diplomat. Utter stayed on until he retired through ill health and apparent differences with the Duchess in 1975; he died in 1980.

In November 1975, the Duchess of Windsor, who was by then very frail and had turned to neat vodka for solace, was taken into the American hospital in Paris with a stomach ulcer. She returned to her home in May 1976 and from then until her death in May 1986 was a reclusive invalid. Miss Schütz left in April 1978, and Maître Blum was for the next eight years not only *executeur testamentaire* but, in her own words 'defender of the moral rights and interests of the Duchess of Windsor'.

After the Duke's death, the Duchess was convinced that she had been left penniless, and told friends that she would find it hard to manage. It seems probable that the Duke and Duchess had been living beyond their means. The Duke's death coincided with the international oil price rise and subsequent period of escalating inflation. Yet the Duke's estate was supposedly valued at three million pounds at the time of his death; the Duchess owned a quantity of valuable jewellery; and in June 1973 the Moulin de la Tuilerie was sold for £350,000.

Wallis had also accumulated treasures of her own: Lady Diana Cooper remembers her buying canary diamonds; Laura, Duchess of Marlborough recalls being taken to a warehouse stacked with Aubusson carpets which the Duchess described as 'an investment'.

For whatever reasons, financial or in a 'tidying up' operation by the Duchess's three joint executors during her failing years, a number of the Windsor possessions were sold, most of them privately, and many in the United States in the late 1970s and early 1980s. The Duchess herself was apparently overwhelmed by deteriorating arteriosclerosis in 1978–9 – the last time that most of her Paris friends were able to see her.

According to his divorced widow, Nathan Cummings of Consolidated Foods bought the Meissen Flying Tiger dinner service, a quantity of silver and other goods, offered directly to him for sale around 1979. Twelve major pieces of jewellery, all rubies set with diamonds, were on the market well before the Duchess's death. They included a necklace of 18 rubies set in a frame of diamonds (bought by a friend of the Duchess's in Paris) and a ring set with such a fine Burmese ruby that although it was only eight carats the asking price was £250,000. Most of this jewellery was sold in New York. Dealers in Paris claim to know of other pieces of jewellery that were supposedly sold or offered during the Duchess's declining years, but such stories cannot be substantiated.

What is certain is that at the time of the Duchess's death, the magnificent collection of silver which the Duke had brought from England, many of the gold boxes, the historic porcelain dinner services, the collection of china pugs and various other *objets d'art*, and the Duke's cellar of rare wines had already been disposed of. Sources in Paris speak of a 'garage sale' of the Louis Vuitton travelling trunks and the Duke's jade-handled guns and daggers.

The shell of the house remained, with its furniture promised to the French state, but with royal and historical mementoes and personal effects still intact.

These are the contents that Mohamed Al-Fayed bought from the executors of the Duchess of Windsor's estate in 1986, in order to preserve the royal heritage and as a memorial to the Windsors' Paris years. From the French government, Mr Al-Fayed received the lease of the house in return for a commitment to restore and conserve it.

Many of the remaining objects, in particular the personal clothes and effects, the spongebags, medicines, underclothes and make-up, are normally a relative's sad duty to sift and dispose of. Although the Duchess of Windsor still had a number of Baltimore relations, she had distanced herself from her family, and signed a document in 1973 declaring that she had no descendant or heir who might have any claim on her property.

The Duke, at the time of his death, had his brother Harry still living, his niece Elizabeth on the throne of England and a safety net of relatives to prevent the relics of his brief Kingship being sold, exploited, or used to embarrass his family.

Prince Charles, who had paid a surprise visit to the Windsors when he was staying in Paris in October 1970, was a very early visitor to the Windsor mansion after it had been taken over by Mr Al-Fayed, who had offered to return to the Queen any piece of royal heritage. A Dutch painting, believed by the Duke of Windsor to be the infant Queen Victoria, has already been returned to Hampton Court.

From 1972 until the death of the Duchess in 1986, the royal family seems to have been under the misapprehension that 'Uncle Dickie' (who was murdered by the Irish Republican Army in 1979) had successfully negotiated the return of the royal heritage and particularly the most emotive of the royal jewels. It is unlikely that Lord Mountbatten or the Queen had any inkling that many of the jewels were inscribed and therefore of both historic and personal interest.

The decision announced by Maître Blum soon after the Duchess's death to sell her collection of jewels in favour of the Institut Louis Pasteur for medical research in Paris took the royal family by surprise. It also astounded the Duchess's friends who had never known her or the Duke take any interest whatsoever in charity.

It had been expected that the jewels with a royal connection – notably Queen Mary's lustrous pearls and the diamond Prince of Wales feather brooch, as well as other pieces delineated by the Duke before his death – would be returned to the British royal family for Prince Charles and his future Queen. In fact, the Prince of Wales feathers were offered to Princess Michael of Kent as a wedding present in 1978, supposedly at the suggestion of the Duchess, although she was at that stage only partially lucid.

According to royal sources, Prince Michael was advised that although his wife Marie-Christine might accept the Duchess's gift, it would not be acceptable for her to be seen wearing it, as it was appropriate only to the Princess of Wales. After some discussion, the feather brooch was 'exchanged' for a pair of Cartier emerald panther earrings.

A request was made to Sotheby's, who auctioned the jewels in Geneva, not to photograph the Prince of Wales feather brooch in the sale catalogue. In the event, it was purchased by the Hollywood film actress Elizabeth Taylor.

The rest of the jewels were more interesting to the connoisseur of 1940s jewellery than to royal archivists, although many of the stones originally came from the Duke's family. In spite of the attempts by French museums to negotiate for the collection, it has been thoroughly dispersed, with most of the inscribed and personal pieces going to a jewellery collector of Syrian origin.

The only members of the royal family to receive a memento from the Duchess were the other Kents – Princess Alexandra and the Duke of Kent – the children of the Duke of Windsor's favourite brother George who was killed in a wartime aeroplane crash in 1942. That suggestion was made in 1976 by Lady Monckton of Brenchley, widow of Walter Monckton who had steered King Edward VIII through the abdication crisis.

Other loyal friends of Wallis to receive mementoes were Aline de Roman-ones and the Baronne de Cabrol. These bequests, like the token gifts to the British Embassy in Paris and to Prince Charles himself, are likely to have been made by the executors of the Duchess of Windsor, rather than at her personal behest.

The Duke of Windsor supposedly wrote a clause in his will stipulating that the jewelled love tokens he had bought his wife should never be worn by another woman. He might well have been shocked and hurt to discover that no one of his family stepped in to claim his Garter banner, the royal despatch box, the historic tomes signed personally by Queen Victoria, the family albums of snapshots or the ten volumes on the drawings of Windsor Castle given as birthday presents from his mother until her death.

The Duchess of Windsor would perhaps have been proud to find that the furniture she had selected to make a regal home for her ex-King should have found a final resting place in the private apartments at Versailles – the sumptuous palace of a King on whom the sun never set.

THE DUCHESS OF WINDSOR'S COOKBOOK

The Duchess of Windsor was renowned for her table – and for the imaginative dishes she served. She collected recipes from her own family in Baltimore, from the Prince of Wales's English cook at Fort Belvedere, from her time in China and later in the Bahamas, and from the finest French chefs. Here is a small selection of recipes – many of them scribbled down in the Duchess's own generous handwriting – to give a taste of the Windsor style at table. All recipes have been drawn directly from the Windsor papers and none of them has been tested.

 **Cocktail Delicacies**

GLAZED BACON

Halve some good slices of bacon. Lay out on baking sheet, cover with brown sugar, cook in high oven until the top is caramelized and the underneath crisp. Shake and serve very hot.

SHRIMP COCKTAIL CABBAGE

Take a nice green cabbage and two pounds of small cooked shrimps. Cut cabbage top, dig out about two inches deep. Arrange the shrimps on the cabbage, holding them with tooth picks. Pour mayonnaise in the centre. Put the cabbage on a dish and decorate with green cabbage leaves. Serve very cold.

STUFFED GRAPES

Choose good sized grapes. Wash thoroughly and peel. Halve with sharp knife and remove pips. Place slices of Gruyère cheese between halves and hold together with small sticks.

RADISHES WITH CREAM CHEESE AND CHIVES

Slit radishes, slice off rounded side so that it will lie flat. Mash cream cheese with chopped chives and spread generously on flat side of radishes. Serve chilled.

 **Royal Salads**

SALADE VICTORIA

Take equal parts of (1) Shredded flesh of rock lobster (2) Truffles and cucumbers cut into dice (3) Asparagus tips. Season with mayonnaise sauce with the addition of the soft parts of the lobster and coral pepper.

SALADE WINDSOR

Take equal parts of (1) Celery (2) Truffles (3) White meat of chicken (4) Ox tongue (5) Cooked mushrooms. All cut into thin strips, dressed with mayonnaise sauce and sharpened with Derby sauce. Pile up, and surround with a border of rampions stuck into the salad.

Salade Prince de Galles

Take (1) Several sardines; wipe off oil, remove the bones and divide into small pieces. (2) Lettuce, endive, cress and chervil. Put all in a salad bowl and add: chopped capers, two hard-boiled eggs of which the yolks are grated and seasoned with salt, pepper, mustard and cayenne. Add gradually three spoonfuls of oil and two of lemon juice. Stir well and garnish with slices of lemon and conserved nasturtiums.

Baltimore Favourites

Wallis's mother Alice Montague Warfield was a splendid – if extravagant – cook. Her daughter kept the file of Southern recipes she had brought with her to Europe from Baltimore.

Shrimp and Corn Pie

2 cups uncooked corn, 2 well-beaten eggs, 2 tbs melted fat, 2/3 cup milk, 1 cup cooked shrimps. 1 tsp salt, 1/2 tsp pepper, 1/8 tsp mace, 1 tbs onion juice, baking powder biscuits. Place corn, eggs, fat, milk, shrimps and seasonings in a bowl and mix well. Pour into a greased baking dish. Cover with biscuit dough and bake in hot oven for ten minutes. Reduce heat and bake an additional 25 minutes.

Oyster Loaf

2 cups chopped oysters, 1 tbs minced green pepper, 1 tsp chopped onion, 2 well-beaten eggs, 1/2 tsp salt, 1/8 tsp pepper, 1/2 cup each breadcrumbs and oyster liquor, 2 tsp butter. Combine all ingredients. Mix well. Pour into buttered baking dish. Dot with butter. Set dish in pan of hot water and bake in moderate oven for 30 minutes.

Sweet Potatoes with Sherry

Pare and slice 6 medium sweet potatoes lengthwise into sticks 1/2 inch thick. Pack them closely into a greased baking dish. Sprinkle with quarter cup sugar, a dash of powdered cloves and 1 tsp grated lemon peel and dot with 3 tbs butter. Add 1/4 cup boiling water. Cover and bake in a hot oven for about 30 minutes. Add sherry or sweet cider just before serving.

Montague Egg Bread

Beat 2 eggs and add 3 cups of milk, 1/2 cup corn meal and 1 tsp salt which have been sifted together. Add 1 tsp melted butter. Bake in greased pudding dish set in a pan of water in medium oven for 45 minutes.

Bahamas Delights

Working with her French chef, Daniel Pinaudier, at Government House in the Bahamas, the Duchess was able to take ideas from the local cuisine.

Avocados Tahiti

Cut the avocados in half, allowing one half per person. Remove pits. Fill center with rum slightly flavoured with brown sugar. Serve on ice.

Glace aux Mangoes (ou Glace Bahamiane)

1 quart mangoes purée, 10 ounces powder sugar. Juice of 2 lemons, 1 cup water. Peel mangoes, force through strainer, add sugar, lemon juice, water and mix carefully. Freeze with two parts ice and 1 part salt. When frozen remove. Pour the ice into a mould, line top with wax paper, then place cover on mould. Seal the mould with butter and pack in mixture of two parts chopped ice to one part of salt. Let remain for one hour. Serve this ice with the following mangoes: peel and slice mangoes, place them in a bowl, spread on powder sugar and pour over a generous amount of very good rum and chill in refrigerator about 3 hours.

♛ French Chef's Specials

The *haute cuisine* served for dinner at the Windsors', especially by chef Lucien Massey, was classic. But the Duchess also encouraged unusual dishes.

SOUFFLÉ DE BOEUF À LA MOILLA

As Mrs Ernest Simpson, Wallis had given the Prince of Wales 'a savoury of marrow bones' the very first time she entertained him on 30 January 1934.
Take about 1 lb beef marrow, cut in pieces about 1 inch square. Soak some time in salt water then blanch in boiling water with a little salt, strain and put in a little glaze and about half fill soufflé case. Have a nice cream forcemeat made from fillet of beef and fill up the case and steam. Serve brown sauce.

FILET D'AGNEAU GRILLÉ DIJONNAISE

3 boned loins of lamb, 4 ounces butter, 3 egg plants, 1 egg, watercress. Salt, pepper, French mustard, breadcrumbs, gravy. Cut the boned lamb in two in the length, season, spread well with French mustard and baste with melted butter. Place the fillets on broiler, well greased, and broil about 10 to 12 minutes. Sear each side. In a dish, make a bed with fried eggplants, put in the broiled fillets, pour some gravy round, decorate with watercress and serve very hot, good gravy separately. Serves 6.

POMMES DE TERRES RITZ

Bake one medium sized potato per person, scoop from skin, mix with salt, pepper and 1 egg yolk per potato. Shape mixture into small ovals, brown in mixture of oil and butter and serve immediately.

♛ Sundays at The Mill

The Duchess based the meals at the Mill – and especially Sunday supper – on a sophisticated version of English country house cooking.

OEUFS ST MALO

One and a half pounds cooked, boned and flaked white fish, 6 cold poached eggs. Three-quarter cup mayonnaise, 6 tbs olive oil, 3 tbs vinegar and 1 tbs chopped parsley. 1 tsp chopped chives, salt, pepper. Make a sauce with salt, pepper, vinegar and olive oil. Put in the fish and chives, mix well. Let cool about two hours in refrigerator. Then add chopped parsley. Place this fish salad in a center of a dish. Put round the poached eggs, pour the mayonnaise over the eggs, sprinkle with parsley and serve very cold.

CHICKEN DUCHESS OF WINDSOR

Have a large chicken cut for frying. Season with salt, pepper and dash of paprika. Roll lightly in flour and fry quickly in fat. Remove from skillet to large baking dish with a tight cover. Add quarter cup sliced carrot, three-quarter cup milk, 1 teaspoon chopped parsley, a little sage and a few drops of onion juice. Cover. Bake for 3 to 4 hours until chicken is fork tender. Bake 10 minutes uncovered to brown top. Add additional milk during cooking if necessary.

PAIN PERDU VIENNOISE

Cut day-old French bread into ¾ inch slices. Beat 2 egg yolks with 2 tsp granulated sugar. Add ⅓ cup cream with ⅔ cup milk. Soak bread in egg-milk mixture and remove. Melt 1½ tbs butter in a pan and brown bread on both sides. Serve with hot fruit jam or custard.

Sweets

The Duchess of Windsor's chefs were all superb pastry cooks. Yet the Duke preferred Viennese pastries from his childhood, English puddings and, above all, fruit desserts like the stewed peaches he ate the day he died.

RØD-GRØD

(Danish recipe from the Duke's grandmother Queen Alexandra.)
Half pound red currants, quarter pound raspberries. 6 oz loaf sugar, 2 pints water, 1 stick cinnamon, 1 vanilla pod.
Boil together for a few minutes. Strain through hair sieve. Return to pan and thicken with 2 oz Danish sago flour, 1 oz potato flour, quarter bottle claret. Boil for minute or two and pour into china moulds or basins watered and sugared. Keep in cool place 24 hours or more. Turn on to a glass or silver dish. Serve milk and cream separately.

BREAD AND BUTTER PUDDING

(Wallis swapped this recipe with her friend Elsie Mendl.)
Boil together one quart of milk with eight ounces of sugar and one teaspoon of vanilla. Pour over the yolks of twelve eggs and stir together. Pour into a deep earthenware pie dish. Cut square slices of bread (as for sandwiches) then into triangles. Butter them and place on the cream mixture. Put the dish in a pan filled with boiling water and bake in a very slow oven for one hour.

The Famous Windsor Savouries

French guests were charmed by the mouthwatering savouries which the Duchess had first learned from the cook at Fort Belvedere.

WELSH RAREBIT SAVOURY

Put into a pan 1 oz butter, tbs Parmesan cheese, tbs breadcrumbs, tbs cream, pinch of pepper, salt, mustard and a very little chutney.
Melt and pour over Romary's Wheaten biscuits or some other biscuit. Put on baking sheet and brown in oven.

DOIGTS AU FROMAGE

Take a fairly ripe Camembert and one portion of St Ivel's cream cheese. Pass together through a hair sieve. Mix well with whipped cream, season to taste and freeze in biscuit mould. Turn out and cut in fingers. Dust in grated Parmesan cheese.

SAVOURY 'SOUS CLOCHE'

Place on a Pyrex plate a round of fried toast, then some chopped ham cooked with a pinch of curry powder. Place on top a slice of tomato (which has previously been soaked in French salad dressing). Cover with Hollandaise sauce, then place a fried mushroom on top. Cover with 'bell glass' and place in oven to warm up. Serve at table with bell glass on.

The Duchess of Windsor's Diet

All her life, Wallis struggled to keep her pin-thin figure. Among her papers, in her own handwriting, is the sparse regime she wrote out in French for her chef to follow if she had gained one single pound.

BREAKFAST: Orange juice. Coffee without sugar.
LUNCH: Grilled meat 190 to 200 grammes, tomato salad with lemon juice and one hard boiled egg. Coffee.
DINNER: Grilled meat 190 to 200 grammes, grilled tomatoes.

DONATIONS TO VERSAILLES

GRAND SALON

Louis XV commode in red lacquer with marble top and gilded bronze

Small Louis XVI ebony writing table with gilded bronze and copper

A pair of Louis XV cabriolet chairs, decorated with garlands, leaves, flowers, shells, covered in pale blue and silver silk

A lacquered and gilded Louis XV cabriolet leg chair, decorated flowers

A pair of Louis XVI bergère chairs, blue velvet, medallion back

Two cabriolet chairs transition period, lacquered wood, flowered silk

A pair of Louis XVI footstools, gilded, petit-point tapestry

A pair of Louis XVI chairs, medallion back, Chinese embroidered silk

Four Louis XVI medallion chairs, lacquered wood, mustard striped velvet

Louis XVI two-tier cake table, signed A. Weisweiller

Louis XV black lacquer corner-piece, marble top, flower decoration

Louis XV commode, red lacquer, gilded bronze and marble top

Marquetry and gilded bronze table, Louis XV to transformation

Two tripod guéridons, early 19 century, ebony and gilded bronze

A bronze tripod guéridon, bronze lion-head feet

A pair Louis XVI medallion chairs, cream flower painted silk

A Louis XV cabriolet lacquered chair, decorated flowers and leaves, blue and silver silk

Pair of Louis XV chairs decorated with shells and flowers, shell-pattern velvet

Two blue and white lacquer *voyeuse*, covered in flower petit-point, Windsor cypher on side

Small Louis XVI sofa, basket of flowers decoration on back

Louis XV crystal chandelier, eight gilded bronze branches

Painting *Port of Antibes* by Eugène Boudin

Vase of Flowers signed Fantini 1873

PETIT SALON

Two trellis jardinières with flower decoration

Two Louis XVI ebony corner-pieces, marble top, red lacquered doors

George Stubbs painting of Ashton, Viscount Curzon

Louis XV marquetry coiffeuse

Small bureau with marquetry flowers, Louis XV transformation

Pair of Louis XV grey flower lacquer chairs, flame velvet

Pair of cabriolet Louis XV armchairs, flower decoration, pink flower embroidery

Louis XV gilded chair, scarlet leather upholstery

Two Louis XV bergère chairs, yellow velvet

Louis XV gilded bronze elephant clock, signed Jean Baptiste Baillon

Louis XV chimney-piece, with dog, duck, lion and eagle

Pair of Louis XV candelabras, in cockerel porcelain

Pair of Louis XVI candelabras, bronze lily design

Glassed lamp with Japanese porcelain base

DINING ROOM

Two gilded wood standing lamps, style Louis XIV

Two gilded bronze chandeliers with flower decoration

Two ostrich egg wall candelabras in gilded bronze

Louis XV console table in red lacquer, clock signed Vigier, Paris

Two Saxe porcelain pots, flower and chimaera decoration, pot lid as artichoke

BOUDOIR
Four Louis XVI lacquered chairs, dusky pink velvet
Two Louis XVI lacquered wood chairs, yellow moiré silk
Two gilded bronze candlesticks with Saxe porcelain flowers and monkey musicians
Two Louis XV gilded bronze wall-lights, Saxe flowers and trellis nest
A six-branch chandelier with white Saxe flowers and foliage

DUKE OF WINDSOR'S STUDY
A gilded bronze mantelpiece clock with French flags and soldiers

ENTRANCE HALL
A pair of Louis XV stools, gilded wood, yellow and silver silk
Red leather chest with arms of Marie-Leczinska
Pair glassed lamps with gilded bronze base, style Louis XVI
Two crystal chandeliers, gilded bronze, style Louis XV
Six 18th-century Saxe porcelain candlesticks, four flower, two fruit
Meissen porcelain service of 27 pieces (Sèvres museum)

GOLD BOXES AT MUSEE DU LOUVRE
Gold tabatière, décor engraved in bas-relief with garlanded warrior, with figures of Justice and Prudence,
diamond decoration, signed Thomas-Pierre Breton (1739–1767)
Gold rectangular tabatière, each of six faces enamelled with Venus in chariot with cherubs, pastoral scenes, love birds and white dog on red cushion, signed Jean Ducrollay (1734–1761)

MUSEE NATIONAL DE SEVRES
Meissen 18-century group of three birds in white basket
Late 18/early 19 century pair of white Meissen porcelain baskets
Mid 18 century faience pot in shape of cabbage with dog on lid, Holitisch (Hungary)
Trompe-l'oeil cabbage pot, porcelain Jacob Petit, 19 century
Meissen flower-painted leaf-shaped plate, 1730
Barrel-shaped mustard pot, porcelain made by Locre
Mid 19 century pair of Meissen bowls with painted fruit
Mustard pot with flower decoration, porcelain Boisette, 18 century
Pair of Meissen pugs, 1774–1815
Pair of oval terrines with dishes and fancy decoration, Meissen 1730
Pair of chandeliers, Meissen 18 century, with painted flower decoration
Pair of Meissen terrines, 17 century, décor in relief, child with horn of plenty on lid

THE DUCHESS OF WINDSOR'S JEWELS
SOTHEBY'S SALE AT GENEVA

2 and 3 April, 1987

THURSDAY, 2 APRIL 1987

1. A gold, ruby and sapphire clip by Cartier, Paris, 1946
SF71,500 ....$47,667 .... £29,424

2. A pair of 18-carat gold and sapphire earclips by Cartier, Paris, 1949
SF30,800 ....$20,533 .... £12,675

3. A pair of 18-carat white gold, sapphire and diamond earclips by Cartier, Paris, *circa* 1950
SF71,500 ....$47,667 .... £29,424

4. A pair of 18-carat gold, ruby and diamond earclips, mounted by Cartier, Paris, *circa* 1950
SF82,500 ....$55,000 .... £33,951

5. A pair of 18-carat gold and shell earclips by David Webb, New York 1964–5
SF30,800 ....$20,533 .... £12,675

6. A pair of 18-carat gold and shell earclips, by David Webb, New York, 1964–5
SF28,600 ....$19,067 .... £11,770

7. A pair of 18-carat gold and shell earclips by David Webb, New York, 1964–5
SF28,600 ....$19,067 .... £11,770

8. A pair of gold, shell and turquoise earclips, *circa* 1965
SF15,400 ....$10,267 .... £ 6,337

9. A pair of gold, shell and coral earclips, *circa* 1965
SF33,000 ....$22,000 .... £13,580

10. A pair of gold and shell earclips by Darde & Fils, Paris, *circa* 1965
SF26,400 ....$17,600 .... £10,864

11. A pair of gold and shell earclips by Darde & Fils, *circa* 1965
SF15,400 ....$10,267 .... £ 6,337

12. A platinum and diamond necklace by Cartier, Paris
SF88,000 ....$58,667 .... £36,214

13. A diamond clip lorgnette by Van Cleef & Arpels, New York, *circa* 1935
SF176,000....................$117,333 .... £72,425

14. A cultured pearl and diamond bar brooch/pendant hanger by Darde & Fils, *circa* 1960
SF41,800 ....$27,687 .... £17,202

15. A diamond dress suite by Cartier, London, 1935: cufflinks set with W and E, buttons and stud set with E
SF660,000....................$440,000 .... £271,605

16. A suite of three star sapphire and diamond buttons by Van Cleef & Arpels, Paris
SF143,000....................$95,333 .... £58,848

17. A cultured pearl, emerald and diamond bracelet, *circa* 1935
SF275,000....................$183,333 .... £113,169

18. A pair of 18-carat white gold, cultured pearl and diamond earclips by Seaman Schepps
SF71,500 ....$47,667 .... £29,424

19. A pair of 18-carat gold, amethyst, turquoise and diamond earclips by Cartier, Paris, 1947
SF88,000 ....$58,667 .... £36,214

20. An 18-carat gold, turquoise and sapphire dress ring of turban design, Paris, *circa* 1950
SF66,000 ....$44,000 .... £27,160

21. An 18-carat gold, amethyst, turquoise and diamond lapel brooch by Cartier, Paris, 1950
SF52,800 ....$35,200 .... £21,725

22. An 18-carat gold, amethyst and turquoise clip by Cartier, Paris, *circa* 1950
SF61,600 ....$41,067 .... £25,356

23. A pair of cultured pearl and diamond earclips by Verdura, *circa* 1950
SF35,200 ....$23,467 .... £14,486

24. A pair of 18-carat gold and diamond earclips, French, *circa* 1945
SF66,000 ....$44,000 .... £27,160

25. An 18-carat gold and diamond dress ring, French, *circa* 1950
SF48,400 ....$32,267 .... £19,918

26. An emerald, ruby and diamond brooch by Cartier, Paris, 1957, heart-shaped, intials W.E. above Roman numeral XX
SF451,000....................$300,667 .... £185,597

27. A diamond clip, *circa* 1935, designed as plume and crown of Prince of Wales.
Bought by Elizabeth Taylor
SF935,000....................$623,333 .... £384,774

28. A gold and diamond egg-shaped powder case by Cartier, Paris, *circa* 1950
SF444,000....................$293,333 .... £181,070

29. An 18-carat gold, coral, emerald and diamond hinged

bangle by Cartier, Paris, 1947, carved as confronted dragons' heads
SF231,000.................$154,000 ....£95,062

30. An 18-carat gold, coral, emerald and diamond clip, by Cartier, Paris, 1946, designed as a butterfly
SF187,000.................$124,667 ....£76,955

31. Nine gem-set Latin crosses on a diamond bracelet by Cartier, circa 1935, all inscribed
SF572,000.................$381,333 ....£235,391

32. An 18-carat gold and gem-set cigarette case by Cartier, London, 1935, the front decorated with map
SF440,000.................$293,333 ....£181,070

33. An 18-carat gold and gem-set powder compact, French, circa 1936, reverse decorated with a map
SF176,000.................$117,333 ....£72,428

34. A sapphire chain link bracelet by Cartier, circa 1945
SF220,000.................$146,667 ....£90,535

35. An 18-carat gold, sapphire, ruby and diamond hinged bangle by Cartier, Paris, 1946, designed as peacock's feather
SF220,000.................$146,667 ....£90,535

36. A pair of gold and ruby pins by Van Cleef & Arpels, New York
SF33,000 ....$22,000 ....£13,580

37. A pair of gold and ruby earclips by Cartier, Paris, circa 1945
SF52,800 ....$35,200 ....£21,728

38. A gold chain necklace, supporting three gem-set Latin crosses
SF77,000 ....$51,333 ....£31,687

39. An interesting collection of twelve charms
SF198,000.................$132,000 ....£81,481

40. A pair of sapphire and diamond earclips by Van Cleef & Arpels, New York, 1944, designed as flowerhead
SF176,000.................$117,333 ....£72,428

41. An invisibly-set sapphire ring by Van Cleef & Arpels, New York, 1950
SF99,000 ....$66,000 ....£40,741

42. An 18-carat gold, sapphire and diamond pin by Van Cleef & Arpels, New York, 1950
SF55,000 ....$36,667 ....£22,634

43. A ruby and sapphire brooch by Cartier, London, 1936, designed as initials W.E. entwined
SF132,000.................$88,000 ....£54,321

44. An 18-carat yellow gold, platinum, ruby and sapphire dress ring by Cartier, Paris, 1937, inscribed 'Our Reunion in Candé'
SF143,000.................$95,333 ....£58,848

45. A gold, enamel, ruby and diamond demi parure by David Webb, New York, 1964, confronted frog bangle and earclips
SF176,000.................$117,333 ....£72,428

46. A gold, turquoise, amethyst and diamond bib necklace by Cartier, Paris, 1947
SF907,500.................$605,000 ....£373,457

47. A pair of gold and emerald penannular bangles, probably circa 1940
SF220,000.................$146,667 ....£90,535

48. A pair of gold, emerald and rose diamond earrings, mounted by Cartier, Paris, 1957
SF60,500 ....$40,333 ....£24,897

49. A gold, ruby and diamond dress ring, mounted by Cartier, Paris, 1963
SF132,000.................$88,000 ....£54,321

50. A gold, emerald and diamond dress ring by Cartier, Paris, 1963
SF110,000.................$73,333 ....£45,267

51. An 18-carat gold and gem-set bib necklace by Cartier, Paris, 1940
SF605,000.................$403,333 ....£248,971

52. A ruby, sapphire, emerald, citrine and diamond clip, mounted by Cartier, Paris, 1940, designed as a flamingo
SF1,210,000.................$806,667 ....£497,942

53. An 18-carat gold and enamel hinged bangle, French, probably circa 1960
SF99,000 ....$66,000 ....£40,741

54. An 18-carat gold, enamel and diamond clip, Italian, circa 1960
SF71,500 ....$47,667 ....£29,424

55. A gold, enamel and emerald panther clip by Cartier, Paris, 1948
SF154,000.................$102,667 ....£63,374

56. An 18-carat gold and enamel lorgnette by Cartier, Paris, 1954, designed as a tiger. Bought for Cartier archives
SF220,000.................$146,667 ....£90,535

57. An onyx and diamond panther bracelet by Cartier, Paris, 1952
SF2,090,000.................$1,393,333.................£860,082

58. An onyx and diamond panther clip by Cartier, Paris, 1966
SF286,000.................$190,667 ....£117,695

59. A sapphire and diamond panther clip by Cartier, Paris, 1949, panther pavé-set crouched on cabochon sapphire. Bought for Cartier archives
SF1,540,000.................$1,026,667.................£633,745

60. An onyx and diamond tiger clip, by Cartier, Paris, 1959
SF660,000.................$440,000 ....£271,605

61. An onyx and diamond tiger bracelet, by Cartier, Paris, 1956
SF1,430,000.................$953,333 ....£588,477

62. A cultured pearl and diamond sautoir set with heart motif
SF275,000.................$183,333 ....£113,169

63. A single-row cultured pearl necklace by Van Cleef & Arpels, New York, 1964
SF297,000.................$198,000 ....£122,222

64. A pearl and diamond ring by Cartier, Paris, 1964
SF275,000.................$183,333 ....£113,169

65. A single-row pearl necklace by Cartier, Paris
SF1,100,000.................$733,333 ....£452,675

66. A pair of pearl and diamond earclips by Van Cleef & Arpels, New York, 1957
SF231,000.................$154,000 ....£95,062

67. A pearl and diamond pendant by Cartier, Paris, 1950
SF451,000.................$300,667 ....£185,597

68. An 18-carat gold, cultured pearl and diamond choker by Darde & Fils, Paris, circa 1960
SF77,000 ....$51,333 ....£31,687

69. A pair of 18-carat gold, seed pearl and diamond earrings by Cartier, Paris
SF45,100 ....$30,067 ....£18,560

70. A sapphire and diamond jarretière bracelet by Van Cleef & Arpels, 1937, inscribed 'For our Contract'
SF1,540,000.................$1,026,667.................£633,745

71. A sapphire and diamond necklace by Cartier, *circa* 1940, designed as flowerhead wreath
SF1,265,000.................$843,333...................£520,576
72. A sapphire and diamond clip by Cartier, Paris, 1949. Worn for visit of Queen Elizabeth II to Windsors, May 1972
SF440,000.....................$293,333.................£181,070
73. A sapphire and diamond ring by Cartier, Paris, 1949
SF121,000.....................$80,667.....................£49,794
74. A sapphire and diamond pendant by Cartier, Paris, 1951. Bought for Joan Collins
SF561,000.....................$374,000...................£230,874
75. A pair of sapphire and diamond pendant earclips, probably by Cartier
SF660,000.....................$440,000...................£271,605
76. An emerald and diamond bracelet, French, 1935, inscribed. Bought by Garrard, the Crown Jewellers
SF528,000.....................$352,000...................£217,284
77. An emerald and diamond earclip, mounted by Cartier
SF242,000.....................$161,333...................£99,588
78. An emerald and diamond clip, mounted by Cartier, Paris, 1948
SF231,000.....................$154,000...................£95,062
79. An emerald and diamond pendant by Harry Winston, 1960
SF1,320,000.................$880,000...................£543,210
80. An emerald and diamond necklace, mounted by Cartier, Paris, 1960
SF825,000.....................$550,000...................£339,506
81. An emerald and diamond ring, mounted by Cartier, Paris, 1958. Inscribed 'We are ours now' and considered as engagement ring. Bought by Laurence Graff
SF3,190,000.................$2,126,667..............£1,312,757
82. An 18-carat gold and diamond nécessaire du soir by Cartier, Paris, 1947
SF440,000.....................$293,333...................£181,070
83. A pair of invisibly-set ruby and diamond earclips by Van Cleef & Arpels, New York, designed as ivy leaf
SF220,000.....................$146,667...................£90,535
84. An invisibly set ruby and diamond clip by Van Cleef & Arpels, Paris, 1936, designed as two feathers
SF1,650,000.................$1,000,000...................£679,012
85. A pair of ruby and diamond earclips, mounted by Cartier, Paris, 1965
SF275,000.....................$183,333...................£113,169
86. A ruby and diamond hinged penannular bangle by Cartier, Paris, 1938, inscribed 'For our first anniversary of June third'
SF385,000.....................$256,667...................£158,436
87. A ruby and diamond bracelet by Van Cleef & Arpels, Paris, 1936, inscribed 'Hold Tight'
SF968,000.....................$645,333...................£398,354
88. A ruby and diamond tassel necklace by Van Cleef & Arpels, 1939, inscribed 'My Wallis from her David'
SF3,905,000.................$2,603,333..............£1,606,996
89. An enamel, ruby and diamond evening bag, *circa* 1930
SF297,000.....................$198,000...................£122,222
90. A pair of fancy yellow pear-shaped diamond earclips, mounted by Cartier, Paris, 1968. Bought by Laurence Graff
SF1,320,000.................$880,000...................£543,210
91. A pair of yellow diamond lapel clips by Harry Winston, 1948. Bought by Laurence Graff

SF3,410,000.................$2,273,333..............£1,403,392
92. A pair of diamond earclips by Cartier, Paris, 1962
SF506,000.....................$337,333...................£208,230
93. A diamond crossover bangle by Cartier, Paris, 1956
SF429,000.....................$286,000...................£176,543
94. A diamond brooch by Harry Winston, New York, 1956
SF935,000.....................$623,333...................£384,774
95. A diamond ring by Harry Winston, 1950.
SF4,730,000.................$3,153,333..............£1,946,502

HIGHLIGHTS OF SECOND DAY OF SALE, *Friday, 3 April 1987*

96. An 18-carat gold, coral, emerald and diamond choker by Cartier, Paris, 1949
SF170,000.....................$113,333...................£69,959
97. A gold and gem-set ring by Cartier, Paris, 1947, set with cabochon coral
SF88,000.....................$58,667...................£36,214
101. A gold and cultured pearl cuff bangle, Belperron, *circa* 1940
SF66,000.....................$44,000...................£27,160
103. A 14-carat gold and aquamarine heart-shaped compact by Verdura, *circa* 1950
SF220,000.....................$146,667...................£90,535
105. A pair of 18 carat gold and enamel cufflinks, English, *circa* 1915, with cyphers of King George V and Queen Mary
SF154,000.....................$102,667...................£63,374
106. A gold chain bracelet by Cartier, Latin cross inscribed 'God protect My darling David in his Going out & coming In'
SF66,000.....................$44,000...................£27,160
107. An 18 carat gold and diamond handbag mirror by Van Cleef & Arpels, New York, 1953, designed as heart, originally purchased by Mrs James Donahue
SF77,000.....................$51,333...................£31,687
112. A massive parcel-gilt silver penannular bangle by Cartier, *circa* 1940, inscribed 'For a happier New Year NASSAU'
SF60,500.....................$40,333...................£24,897
116. A pair of gold cufflinks, English, 1905, cypher Geo V as Prince of Wales
SF88,000.....................$58,667...................£36,214
117. A pair of gold cufflinks, English, 1915, monogram and crown of Geo V
SF110,000.....................$73,333...................£45,267
120. A pair of 15-carat gold cufflinks, English, 1905, portrait Queen Alexandra, King Edward VII
SF176,000.....................$117,333...................£72,428
121. A pair of 18-carat gold cufflinks, English, 1920, cyphers King George V, Queen Mary
SF132,000.....................$88,000...................£54,321
123. Stained blue chalcedony, sapphire and diamond necklace, probably Belperron, *circa* 1935
SF275,000.....................$183,333...................£113,169
124. Earclips to above
SF132,000.....................$88,000...................£54,321
125. Ridged coronet bangles to above
SF220,000.....................$146,667...................£90,535

127. A two-coloured gold mesh, sapphire and diamond purse by Van Cleef & Arpels, New York, 1954
SF60,500 .... $40,333 .... £24,897

128. A gold mesh, ruby, turquoise and diamond purse by Van Cleef & Arpels, New York, 1942, originally purchased by Mrs James Donahue
SF165,000 .... $110,000 .... £67,901

134. A gold pocket watch by Cartier, Paris, inscribed 'No excuse for going in the Wrong direction, Easter 1939'
SF770,000 .... $513,333 .... £316,872

142. A platinum wedding ring, English, 1937, inscribed 'Wallis 18-10-35 Your David 3-VI-37'
SF198,000 .... $132,000 .... £81,481

146. A two-coloured gold, enamel, cultured pearl, tourmaline and quartz necklace, French, circa 1950, designed as garland
SF165,000 .... $110,000 .... £67,901

152. A gold pipe cleaner, inscribed 'David Xmas 1945, Paris en plein marche noir'
SF33,000 .... $22,000 .... £13,580

154. A diamond eternity ring with heart
SF82,000 .... $55,000 .... £33,951

155. A platinum photograph frame by Cartier, London, 1947, engraved with cypher of Duchess of Windsor, inscribed: 'All the things I said each year in the other locket 1935–1946–1947–More & more & more Wallis from David Easter 1947'
SF308,000 .... $205,333 .... £126,749

161. A three-coloured gold and ruby circular pendant, designed as tropical seascape, circa 1940
SF115,500 .... $47,531 .... £77,000

164. A 14-carat gold, emerald and diamond pendant, circa 1937, medallion applied with diamond slipper, inscribed 'Our Mr Loo'
SF121,000 .... $80,667 .... £49,794

166. A lady's 18-carat gold handbag suite by Van Cleef & Arpels, circa 1950, of basket weave design applied with motifs
SF990,000 .... $660,000 .... £407,407

168. A triple hoop ring in yellow, white and red gold, another ring inscribed 'Darling . . . Wallis'
SF46,200 .... $30,800 .... £19,012

173. A lady's leather and gold belt by Cartier, 1950, studded with gold coins
SF110,000 .... $73,333 .... £45,267

174. A 14-carat two-coloured gold bracelet by Cartier, New York, medallion Edward VIII, inscribed 'More and More'
SF77,000 .... $51,333 .... £31,687

177. Four wedding rings, all inscribed
SF27,500 .... $18,333 .... £11,317

187. A silver cigarette case, 1904, engraved 'From G.R.I. H.M.S. Renown, India, October 26th 1921'
SF38,500 .... $25,667 .... £15,844

191. A silver pocket frame, 1898, engraved 'From Great Grandmama V.R.I. 24th May 1899'
SF550,000 .... $366,667 .... £226,337

192. A silver-mounted photograph frame, 1921, photograph of Queen Alexandra
SF418,000 .... $278,667 .... £172,016

193. A silver frame, photograph Duke and Duchess of Windsor bathing
SF330,000 .... $220,000 .... £135,802

194. A silver frame, photograph HRH The Prince of Wales, later Edward VIII
SF528,000 .... $352,000 .... £217,284

195. A white enamel gem-studded frame, photograph Queen Mary
SF682,000 .... $454,667 .... £280,658

201. A tortoiseshell and gold mounted box, English, 1815, diamond Prince of Wales feathers
SF242,000 .... $161,333 .... £99,588

218. A silver cigarette case, London, 1909, engraved 'David from Mama, Xmas 1913'
SF110,000 .... $73,333 .... £45,268

219. A silver cigarette case, London, 1925, engraved 'Xmas 1925, David from Bertie'
SF143,000 .... $95,333 .... £58,848

226. A silver gilt ink-stand, Garrard & Co Ltd, London, 1910, engraved 'Edward, Prince of Wales from his parents, June 23rd 1911'
SF242,000 .... $161,333 .... £99,588

238. A gold cypher and lapis lazuli desk seal, 1905, cypher Edward VII
SF418,000 .... $278,667 .... £172,016

246. A silver hunter pocket watch, inscribed 'For dear David from his affectionate Papa'
SF55,000 .... $36,667 .... £22,634

254. A Royal Naval officer's sword, dated 1913, inscribed 'To Edward Prince of Wales Lieutenant R.N. from his affectionate father George, March 1913'
SF2,200,000 .... $1,466,667 .... £905,350

260. A fine cased presentation Scottish dress dirk and skean-dhu, mounted with silver and ivory, dated 1925
SF605,000 .... $403,333 .... £248,971

263. A presentation kukri mounted with silver and ivory and with gem-set scabbard, dated 1921, inscribed 'Presented by the Gurkha Officers Association, Darjeeling, to H.R.H. the Prince of Wales 1921'
SF176,000 .... $117,333 .... £72,428

284. A case of gilt livery buttons bearing crest of Prince of Wales
SF110,000 .... $73,333 .... £45,268

288. A sealskin silver-mounted dress sporran, cypher King Geo V
SF27,500 .... $18,333 .... £11,317

299. A set of four George III silver table candlesticks, 1762
SF396,000 .... $264,000 .... £162,963

300. A silver tankard, 1919, engraved 'To dear David "Edward of Wales" from his loving Grand Parents Edward VII and Alexandra for his Confirmation 1910'
SF330,000 .... $220,000 .... £135,802

BIBLIOGRAPHY

BALMAIN, Pierre: *My Years and Seasons*, Cassell, 1964
BEATON, Cecil: *The Wandering Years, Diaries: 1922–39*,
Weidenfeld & Nicolson, 1961
BEATON, Cecil: *The Parting Years, Diaries: 1963–74*,
Weidenfeld & Nicolson, 1978
BEATON, Cecil: *Self-Portrait with Friends* (ed. Richard Buckle),
Weidenfeld & Nicolson, 1979
BIRMINGHAM, Stephen: *Duchess, The Story of Wallis Warfield
Windsor*, Little Brown & Company, USA, 1981
BLOCH, Michael: *The Duke of Windsor's War*, Weidenfeld &
Nicolson, 1982
BLOCH, Michael: *Operation Willi*, Weidenfeld & Nicolson, 1984
BLOCH, Michael: *Wallis & Edward: Letters 1931–1937*,
Weidenfeld & Nicolson, 1986
BRYAN III, Joe, and Charles Murphy: *The Windsor Story*,
Granada, 1979
CHANNON, Sir Henry: *Chips: The Diaries of Sir Henry Channon*
(ed. Robert Rhodes James), Weidenfeld & Nicolson, 1967
CHARLES-ROUX, Edmonde: *Chanel*, Jonathan Cape, 1976
COOPER, Diana: *The Light of Common Day*,
Rupert Hart-Davis, 1959
CORNFORTH, John: *The Inspiration of the Past*, Viking, with
Country Life, 1985
COWARD, Noël: *The Noël Coward Diaries*
(ed. Graham Payn and Sheridan Morley),
Weidenfeld & Nicolson, 1982
CRAWFORD, Marion: *The Little Princesses*, Cassell, 1950
DONALDSON, Frances: *Edward VIII*,
Weidenfeld & Nicolson, 1974
GABARDI, Melissa: *Les Bijoux de l'Art Déco aux Années 40*,
Les Editions de l'Amateur, Paris, n.d.
GAUTIER, Gilberte: *Cartier, The Legend*, Arlington Books, 1983
HASTINGS, Selina: *Nancy Mitford*, Hamish Hamilton, 1985
LAWFORD, Valentine: *Vogue's Book of Houses, Gardens, People*,
Condé Nast Publications, 1963
LOWNDES, Mary Belloc: *Diaries and Letters*,
Chatto & Windus, 1977
MARLBOROUGH, Laura, Duchess of: *Laughter from a Cloud*,
Weidenfeld & Nicolson, 1980
MENKES, Suzy: *The Royal Jewels*, Grafton Books, 1985
MOSLEY, Diana: *The Duchess of Windsor*,
Sidgwick & Jackson, 1980
MOSLEY, Diana: *A Life of Contrasts*, Hamish Hamilton, 1977
NADELHOFFER, Hans: *Cartier, Jewellers Extraordinary*,
Thames & Hudson, 1984
PONSONBY, Sir Frederick: *Recollections of Three Reigns*,
Eyre & Spottiswoode, 1951

POPE-HENNESSY, James: *A Lonely Business* (ed. Peter Quennell),
Weidenfeld and Nicolson, 1981
POPE-HENNESSY, James: *Queen Mary, 1867–1953*,
Allen & Unwin, 1959
RAULET, Sylvie: *Art Deco Jewelry*, Thames & Hudson, 1985
RAULET, Sylvie: *Van Cleef & Arpels*, Editions du Regard,
Paris, 1986
ROSE, Kenneth: *King George V*, Weidenfeld & Nicolson, 1983
ROSE, Kenneth: *Kings, Queens and Courtiers*,
Weidenfeld & Nicolson, 1985
ROSS, Josephine: *Beaton in Vogue*, Thames & Hudson, 1986
SAINT LAURENT, Yves: *Yves Saint Laurent*,
Herscher/Musée des Arts de la Mode, 1986
SOTHEBY: *The Jewels of the Duchess of Windsor*, Sotheby's, 1987
THORNTON, Michael: *Royal Feud*, Michael Joseph, 1985
TOMERLIN LEE, Sarah (ed.): *American Fashion*,
André Deutsch, 1976
VICKERS, Hugo: *Cecil Beaton*, Weidenfeld & Nicolson, 1985
VORRES, Ian: *The Last Grand-Duchess*, Hutchinson, 1964
VREELAND, Diana: *D.V.*, Weidenfeld & Nicolson, 1984
WARWICK, Christopher: *Abdication*, Sidgwick & Jackson, 1986
WHITE, PALMER: *Elsa Schiaparelli*, Aurum Press, 1986
WILSON, Edwina H: *Her Name was Wallis Warfield*, E. P. Dutton,
New York, 1936
WINDSOR, The Duchess of: *The Heart Has its Reasons*,
Michael Joseph, 1956
WINDSOR, The Duke of: *A King's Story, The Memoirs of the Duke of
Windsor*, Putnam, New York, 1947
WINDSOR, The Duke of: *A Family Album*, Cassell, 1960
ZIEGLER, Philip: *Diana Cooper*, Hamish Hamilton, 1981

Major magazine articles
Harpers Bazaar, USA, May 1966:
The Duchess of Windsor Talks Clothes with Fleur Cowles
Life, July 1956: My Garden by HRH The Duke of Windsor
She, March 1956: King in Exile by Nancy Spain
She, December 1956: Talking to the Windsors by Nancy Spain
She, December 1960: Tea with the Duchess by Nancy Spain
Vanity Fair, May 1986: The Dear Romance by the Countess of
Romanones
Vogue, French, June 1964:
Le Duc et la Duchesse de Windsor à Paris by Valentine
Lawford
Vogue, USA, November 1967:
A Weekend with HRH The Duke and the Duchess of Windsor
Woman's Home Companion, October 1954:
Our First Real Home by The Duchess of Windsor

SOURCE NOTES

CHAPTER 1 AT HOME

This chapter is drawn from research at the Windsor home and conversations with staff, especially the Duke's valet Sydney Johnson, and with the Windsors' dinner guests. Dates are given for first quotes and apply to subsequent printed remarks unless otherwise stated. Valentine Lawford is the *nom de plume* of Nicholas Lawford.

Page 11
Quotation: *American Fashion*, p. 187.
'BWAA DE BOOLLONE': Nicholas Lawford, letter to his mother, 6 February 1939.
'DENTIST SMILE': Channon, *Chips: Diaries*, p. 32.
'THE GUESTS CAN WAIT . . .': Princesse de Polignac to the author, 6 November 1986.
CURLY WROUGHT-IRON BANISTERS . . . AND FOLLOWING DESCRIPTIONS: Valentine Lawford, *Vogue's Book of Houses, Gardens, People*.
'VERY SILKEN AND NATTY . . .': Pope-Hennessy, *A Lonely Business*, p. 210.

Page 12
'IT WAS LIKE GOING BACK . . .': Kenneth J. Lane to the author, 13 December 1986.
'THE WINDSORS SPELLED GLAMOUR . . .': Grace, Lady Dudley to the author, 14 November 1986.
'THE DUCHESS WAS NOT . . .': Joanne Cummings to the author, 11 December 1986.
'IT MANAGES TO BE CHIC . . .': Fleur Cowles, *Harper's Bazaar*, May 1966.

Page 13
GLASS OF CHILLED CHAMPAGNE . . .: Baron and Baronne de Cabrol to the author, 19 December 1986.
'POETRY OF FLOWERS': Alexandre to the author, 18 December 1986.
CECIL BEATON HAD DESCRIBED . . .: *Beaton in Vogue*, p. 126.

Page 14
'MANY ORCHIDS AND WHITE ARUMS . . .': Nicolson, *Diaries and Letters*, p. 255.

Page 16
'IT'S TERRIBLY, TERRIBLY ELSIE DE WOLFE': Hugo Vickers to the author, 16 September 1986.
'LADY MENDL TAUGHT THE DUCHESS . . .': Paul-Louis Weiller to the author, 6 November 1986.
'GO ON! BUY IT!': *New York Times*, 25 December 1986.
'ELSIE NATURALLY HAD WONDERFUL TASTE . . .': Vreeland, *DV*, p. 122.
'FRENCH FURNITURE IS MORE ELEGANT': Lawford, *Letters*, 28 November 1938.
'I SEND A KIND MESSAGE': Duchess of Windsor, *The Heart Has its Reasons*, p. 356.
'LOOK, IT STILL FITS ME LIKE A GLOVE': *Sunday Mirror*, 25 May 1986.
CALLED EACH OTHER 'DARLING': Nicolson, *Diaries and Letters*, 1930–39, p. 352.
'SHE DOES NOT CURL UP . . .': Pope-Hennessy, *A Lonely Business*, p. 216.

'SHE INVENTED THE FASHION . . .': Diana Vreeland to the author, 3 February 1987; also earlier conversation, January 1985.

Page 17
'SO VERY LARGE . . .': Pope-Hennessy, *A Lonely Business*, p. 211.
'OIL-DRILLING EYES . . .': Anne Slater to the author, 10 December 1986.
'NOTHING LIKE HER': Bryan and Murphy, *The Windsor Story*, p. 602.
'HER ROYAL HIGHNESS WOULD NEVER THINK . . .': Aline de Romanones, *Vanity Fair*, June 1986.
'I ALWAYS SIT HERE': French *Vogue*, June 1964.
'NAUGHTY BOY': Joanne Cummings to the author.
'THE BABIES SEND YOU . . .': *Wallis & Edward Letters*, paperback, p. 221.
'A PAT TO SLIPPY POO': *Ibid*, p. 254.
'HE SENDS YOU A MILLION . . .': *Ibid*, p. 257.
'HE WAS OUR DOG . . .' *Ibid*, p. 305.

Page 18
'OUR MR LOO': Cartier archives, Paris.
'PREEZIE, A FAITHFUL . . .': Bryan and Murphy, *The Windsor Story*, p. 670.
'WE COULDN'T AFFORD THE BEST . . .': *Wallis & Edward Letters*, p. 52.

Page 19
'GREAT GIGLAMP SMILE': Pope-Hennessy, *A Lonely Business*, p. 211.
'I CAN'T STAND PEOPLE MY AGE': Romanones, *Vanity Fair*, June 1986.
'YOU ARE SO LUCKY': Diana Mosley to the author, 15 April 1987.
'BROAD FIREWORK LAUGHTER': *Beaton in Vogue*, p. 126.

Page 22
PEOPLE FOR KT'S: *Wallis & Edward Letters*, p. 98.
'HE WAS ALWAYS DOING THE WAITING': Lady Diana Cooper to the author, 8 February 1984.
'LIKE A LOTTERY DRUM': Erik Mortensen to the author, 30 January 1987.
COUNT NICHOLAS PALAVICINI: to the author, 11 December 1986.
'FASTIDIOUSLY PRESENTED HORS D'OEUVRES': *Beaton in Vogue*, p. 127.
'PUFFBALLS OF CHEESE': French *Vogue*, June 1964.
'IT WAS NOT AT ALL FRENCH': Vicomtesse de Ribes to the author, 13 April 1987.
'CHEFS ARE CURIOUSLY COLOUR-BLIND': Bryan and Murphy, *The Windsor Story*, p. 614.
'HER (GASP) ROYAL (SHUDDER)': Nicolson, *Diaries and Letters*, p. 352.

Page 23
'I CURTSIED TO THE DUKE . . .': Romanones, *Vanity Fair*, June 1986.
SYDNEY JOHNSON HAS WATCHED: to the author.
'TERRAPIN, SQUAB . . .': The Duchess of Windsor, *The Heart Has its Reasons*, p. 29.
'WHY DOES THE DUCHESS . . .': Sydney Johnson to the author.
'WITH A TILED ROOF': Duchess of Windsor, *The Heart Has its Reasons*, p. 116.
'ENDLESS AFTERNOONS GIVEN TO COMBING . . .': *Ibid*, p. 363.
STEPHANE BOUDIN: John Cornforth, *Country Life*, April 1983.

'IT WILL BE A SYMPHONY . . .': Channon, *Chips: Diaries*, p. 37.
'MY DUCHESS': Grace Dudley to the author.
'BOUDIN WEEKENDS': Cornforth, *Country Life*.

Page 24
'DUKE'S VELVET CLOAK': Nancy Spain, *She*, March 1956.
ORCHESTRA OF MONKEYS: Erik Mortensen to the author.
FRENCH PASTORAL WALLPAPER: Duchess of Windsor, *The Heart Has its Reasons*, p. 158.
'IT CONTRIBUTES TO THE GAIETY . . .': Edwina H. Wilson, *Her Name was Wallis Warfield*, p. 85.
FINE LINEN . . . SEVRES PORCELAIN: research at Windsor house.

Page 25
'AWFUL LOT OF IRONING': to author.
HUMBERT DES LYONS DE FEUCHIN: to the author, 6 November 1986.
COLE PORTER: Diana Mosley, *The Duchess of Windsor*, paperback, p. 192.

Page 26
'HE WANTED ME TO . . .': Romanones, *Vanity Fair*.
'TRULY MAGNIFICENT COLLECTION': Duchess of Windsor, *The Heart Has its Reasons*, p. 312.

Page 28
DINNER SERVICES: Lawford, *Vogue's Book of Houses, Gardens, People*.
'NOT THOSE OLD PEOPLE': Grace Dudley to the author.
TASTE IN PORCELAIN: Musée National de Céramique, Sèvres.
'THEY HAD NOTHING AND NO-ONE': Sydney Johnson to the author.
DINNER MENU: Album of Baron Fred de Cabrol.
'AFTER ALL THOSE COCKTAILS . . .': Joanne Cummings to the author.
'A LITTLE SURPRISE': French *Vogue*.

Page 30
TONIGHT'S DINNER: descriptions of food to author from Parisian guests.
'THE COOKING FROM MARYLAND . . .': French *Vogue*.
'BLACK BEAN SOUP': Duchess of Windsor, *The Heart Has its Reasons*, p. 190
SERVING UP TADPOLES: Duke of Windsor, *A King's Story*, p. 40.
'THE SECRET OF ALL THIS . . .': *Ibid*, p. 185.
SALADE MACHES: James Viane, British Embassy chef, to the author.
'DO ALL AMERICAN WOMEN . . .': Duchess of Windsor, *The Heart Has its Reasons*, p. 148.
'I HAD MY OWN FIXED IDEAS . . .': *Ibid*, p. 147.
'ENTREES AND EGG DISHES . . .': *Wallis & Edward Letters*, p. 39.
'MADAME . . . I CANNOT': Mosley, *The Duchess of Windsor*, p. 197.

Page 31
SHOOT IN THEIR THOUSAND: Duke of Windsor, *A King's Story*, p. 49.
'I MARRIED THE DUKE . . .': Polignac to the author.
REQUEST FOR PEACH: Sydney Johnson to the author.
'IT WAS LIKE A GOOD RALLY': Mosley, *The Duchess of Windsor*, p. 192.
'SHE WAS QUICK . . .': Lady Mosley to author.
'SEEDLESS RAISIN': Bryan and Murphy, *A Windsor Story*, p. 28.
'HEIR CONDITIONED': *Ibid*, p. 550.
'OH SIR . . .': Beaton, *The Wandering Years*, p. 302.
'TWO POSES OF ME . . .': *Wallis & Edward Letters*, p. 54.
'WHAT A PITY': Mme Pierre Schlumberger to the author, 20 November 1986.
'I JUST LOVE YOUR PANSIES': Maggie Nolan to the author, July 1984.
WHEN ANOTHER GUEST: Mosley, *The Duchess of Windsor*, p. 192.
'EXTRAORDINARY GIFT . . .': *Ibid*, p. 192 and Lord Monckton of Brenchley to the author, 16 April 1986.
'INTERESTED IN MY JOB': Duchess of Windsor, *The Heart Has its Reasons*, p. 193.
'SHE WAS VERY TENDER . . .': Hubert de Givenchy to the author, 24 March 1987.

Page 32
'ALWAYS KICKS HIM': Channon, *Chips: Diaries*, p. 76.
THERE ARE 18 INDOOR STAFF: Bryan and Murphy, *The Windsor Story*, p. 607.
FAVOURITE SACHER TORTE: French *Vogue*.
CRUNCHY GINGER BISCUITS: Romanones, *Vanity Fair*.

Page 34
'AM IN SUCH A GALE . . .': *Wallis & Edward Letters*, p. 41.

'KEPT SIXTY SOULS . . .': Kenneth Rose, *King George V*, p. 296.
'NOW DON'T STAY CHATTING . . .': Cummings.
'TIME FOR BED': Horst with Valentine/Nicholas Lawford, to author 11 December 1986.
'LIKE A NANNY/GOVERNESS': *Ibid*.
'IT DOESN'T LOOK VERY PRETTY': Channon, *Chips: Diaries*, p. 35.
'YOU MUST ALWAYS REMEMBER . . .': Duke of Windsor, *A King's Story*, p. 134.
'YOU REALIZE . . .': Pope-Hennessy, *A Lonely Business*, p. 215.
'THAT'S QUITE RIGHT': Lawford, *Letters*, 17 October 1938.
PRIME MINISTER STANLEY BALDWIN: Frances Donaldson, *King Edward VIII*, p. 302.

Page 35
'HRH WAS IN A MARVELLOUS MOOD': Lawford, *Letters*, 17 October 1938.
'IT WAS PILED WITH PAPERS . . .': Vreeland, *DV*, p. 67.
'THE NOOSPAPERS': quoted from Jack le Vien film, *A King's Story*.
'HALLO! IT'S THE DOOK HERE': Bryan and Murphy, *The Windsor Story*, p. 666.
GILDED BATHTUB: *Ibid*, p. 472.
PAPER IN LAVATORY: Sydney Johnson.
'GOD BLESS WE': *Wallis & Edward Letters*, p. 209.
'ON CHRISTMAS DAY': *New York Times*, 25 December 1986.
'THE GAMEKEEPERS, GARDENERS . . .': Duke of Windsor, *A King's Story*, p. 53.
'I HAVE JUST COMPLETED . . .': *Wallis & Edward Letters*, p. 165.
'SHE WAS KIND TO US': Viane to author, July 1984.

Page 36
'I'M SORRY, JOHN': Bryan and Murphy, *The Windsor Story*, p. 671.
'AN OUTSIZE SCENT BOTTLE': Nancy Spain, *She*, December 1956.
'A SENSUOUS EXPERIENCE': Romanones, *Vanity Fair*.
'DULL FRENCH DINNERS . . .': Polignac.
'MORAL ENGAGEMENT': *Ibid*.

Page 38
'NOBODY HAS THE RIGHT': Romanones, *Vanity Fair*.
COMATOSE DUCHESS: Baronne de Cabrol.
'HEARD OF LIBERACE': Mosley, *The Duchess of Windsor*, p. 191.
'TAPPING . . . OUT RATHER PATHETICALLY': Lawford, *Letters*, 17 October 1938.
'THE MUTTERSPRACHE . . .': Duke of Windsor, *A King's Story*, p. 41.
'THE ANCIENT WALLS . . . DISAPPROVAL': *Ibid*, p. 188.
'AN ALMOST CONTINUOUS BALL . . .': *Ibid*, p. 193.
'FOR A BRIEF PERIOD . . .': *Ibid.*, p. 193.
'DON'T MENTION IT . . .': Birmingham, *Duchess*, p. 270.
'A BLONDE LADY (FRENCH)' AND FOLLOWING PARA: Noël Coward, *Diaries*, p. 399.

Page 39
'ALEXANDER'S RAGTIME BAND': Romanones, *Vanity Fair*.
'I'VE ABDICATED': Nicholas Lawford to the author.
'LONGED TO ESCAPE': Laura, Duchess of Marlborough to the author, 18 March 1987.
'ARE YOU FOND OF THE DUCHESS?': Laura, Duchess of Marlborough to the author, 18 March 1987.
'YOUR DREARY ATTIC': Romanones, *Vanity Fair*.
'PASSION FOR LITTLE HELMETS': Lawford, *Letters*, 6 February 1939.
'ANGELIC COFFEE-COLOURED FACE': Bloch, *Duke of Windsor's War*, p. 356.

Page 40
'IT WAS HARD WORK' AND FOLLOWING PARA: Sydney Johnson to the author.

Page 42
'I REMEMBER ARRIVING . . .': Horst to the author, 11 December 1986.
LADY MOSLEY ADMITS: Mosley, *The Duchess of Windsor*, p. 191.
'BEAUTIFUL, BUT I WONDER . . .': Birmingham, *Duchess*, p. 230.
'I MET HER . . .': Lawford to the author.

Page 43
'THE DUKE'S LOVE FOR HER . . .': Thornton, *Royal Feud*, paperback, p. 10.
'AS FAR AS THE PAINTER'S . . .': Duke of Windsor, *A Family Album*, p. 7.
'HE WAS IN ROARS . . .': Donaldson, *Edward VIII*, p. 101.
'SHE SHOULDN'T HAVE DONE IT': Mitford, *Loved Ones*, p. 188.

Page 44
'WHAT DO YOU AND THE WINDSORS' AND FOLLOWING QUOTE: Birmingham, *Duchess*, p. 231.
'I CAN'T HELP FEELING . . .': Lawford, *Letters*, 6 February 1939.
'PICK A FLOWER FROM THE GARDEN': Grace, Lady Dudley to the author.
'THERE MAY BE A HAPPIER COUPLE . . .': Mosley, *The Duchess of Windsor*, p. 187.
'SO THAT A FLY WOULD SLIP OFF IT': *Beaton in Vogue*, p. 127.
'HE SLEEPS IN A ROOM . . .': Channon, *Chips: Diaries*, p. 102.
'JUST LIKE A LITTLE SCHOOLBOY' AND FOLLOWING QUOTE: Vreeland *DV*, p. 75.

Page 45
'I AM BEING PRESENTED . . .': *Wallis & Edward Letters*, p. 50.
'IT WAS THE ONLY THING HE DID . . .': Romanones, *Vanity Fair*.
'IT WAS THE FIRST THING . . .': Sydney Johnson to the author.
'IT'S THE KIND OF ROOM . . .': Lawford, *Vogue's Book of Houses, Gardens, People*.

'SHE USED TO GO IN . . .': Grace, Lady Dudley to the author.
LOOKING AT SOLDIER PRINTS: Sydney Johnson to the author.

Page 46
ARTIST DIMITRI BOUCHENE: Nancy Spain, *She*, March 1956.
'A CHARMING, FEMININE SETTING': *Beaton in Vogue*, p. 126.

Page 47
'YOU CAN WEAR A DRESS . . .': Romanones, *Vanity Fair*.
EVERY SINGLE NIGHT: Grace, Lady Dudley to the author.
'I WAS STAYING AT THE MILL . . .': Philippe du Pasquier to the author, 1 February 1986.

Page 48
'GREEK MASK OF TRAGEDY . . .': Mosley, *The Duchess of Windsor*, p. 211.
'ISN'T THIS A PRETTY PARK': Baronne de Cabrol to the author.
'ONE IN WHITE SATIN . . .': Vreeland, *DV*, p. 69.
'DUKE'S ARRIVAL TONIGHT': Sydney Johnson to the author.
'CROWN OF FLEUR DE LYS': Windsor archive, Paris.

CHAPTER 2   AT PLAY

The Duke of Windsor's own thoughts on his garden are drawn from a major series in *Life* magazine in 1956. I am indebted to James Pope-Hennessy for his acutely observed essay 'The King Over the Millstream' published in his posthumous self-portrait *A Lonely Business*. Quotations from the Windsor friends in Paris and New York are identified in first quote only.

Page 51
Quotation: Vita Sackville-West, *The Garden*, Michael Joseph, p. 14.
AT WAR WITH THE ALGAE AND FOLLOWING DESCRIPTIONS OF GARDEN: *Life*, July 1956.
TINY SILVER ACORNS: Nancy Spain, *She*, December 1960.
'MY MOTHER LOATHED THE COUNTRY': Pope-Hennessy, *A Lonely Business*, p. 213.
FROM THE TOP, YOU CAN SEE: Visit by author to the Moulin de la Tuilerie, 15 April 1987.
'LES CELIBATAIRES': Pope-Hennessy, *A Lonely Business*, p. 212.
'OUR FIRST REAL HOME': Duchess of Windsor, *Woman's Home Companion*, October 1954.
'A SOURCE OF SUPPLY FOR THE VASES': *Life*.

Page 52
GERALD VAN DER KEMP: Princesse de Polignac to author, 16 November 1986.
RUSSELL PAGE: *Life*, July 1956.
AROUND THE STILL LAKE: Duke of Windsor, *A King's Story*, p. 44.
ANTIQUED SUNDIAL: Pope-Hennessy, *A Lonely Business*, p. 212.
'IT WAS A VERY WISE OLD BIRD': Jack le Vien film, *A King's Story*.
CERISE FELT BASEBALL CAP: Pope-Hennessy, *A Lonely Business*, p. 212.
'IN A GRANDIOSE . . . DIRT GARDENING' AND FOLLOWING QUOTATIONS: *Life*.
'THOSE DAMN WEEKENDS': Duke of Windsor, *A King's Story*, p. 237.
'I CREATED A HOME AT THE FORT': *Life*.

Page 53
'DOWN CAME THE . . . YEW TREES': Duke of Windsor, *A King's Story*, p. 237.
'LOVELY MORNING . . .': James Pope-Hennessy, *Queen Mary*, p. 600.
'OUR ARTIST HAS PORTRAYED . . .': *Punch*, October 1934.
'MY MOTHER LIKED FLOWERS . . .': *Life*.
'THE DUCHESS HOPES . . .': *Ibid*.
HOLDING 'WILD CHASES': *Ibid*.
'MEADOW SAGE . . .': *Ibid*.
'AT LAST THAT STINKING . . .': Duchess of Windsor to Major Gray Phillips, sale of letters, Phillips auction house, London, January 1987.

Page 56
GARDENING IS A MOOD: *Life*.
'AS THE DUKE'S GERMAN . . .': Pope-Hennessy, *A Lonely Business*, p. 213.
'SHADOWY, STEEP-SIDED CANYON . . .': Duke of Windsor, *A King's Story*, p. 152.
'THEY PULLED EVERYTHING . . .': Diana Mosley to the author, 15 April 1987.
'FAVOURITE RECREATION': Duke of Windsor, *A Family Album*, p. 8.

'THIS IS THE SHOOTING SEASON': Duchess of Windsor to Major Gray Phillips, Phillips letters auction, 28 January 1987.
'ALL OUR FRIENDS . . . UNKIND': Nancy Spain, *She*.
CHRISTMAS CARD: Album Baron de Cabrol.

Page 57
'I MAY NOT BE THE MILLER'S DAUGHTER . . .': Pope-Hennessy, *A Lonely Business*, p. 209.
'I AM A SUNDIAL . . .': *Ibid*, p. 212.
HALF AN HOUR FAST: Donaldson, *Edward VIII*, p. 177.
'A FEW HOURS LATER . . .': Lady Diana Cooper, *The Light of Common Day*, p. 162.
COUNTRY WRITING PAPER: Phillips letters auction, 28 January 1987.
'NO EXCUSES . . .': *The Jewels of the Duchess of Windsor*, Sotheby's catalogue no. 134.
'REPRESENTS THE DUKE'S LIFE': Pope-Hennessy, *A Lonely Business*, p. 210.
'MY EDUCATION WAS COMPLETED . . .': Duke of Windsor, *A King's Story*, p. 212.
'EVERY BUTTON IN THE BRITISH ARMY . . .': Duke of Windsor, *A Family Album*, p. 138.

Page 60
REVOLVING HUT: Duke of Windsor, *A King's Story*, p. 11.
'I CALL IT MY LAWN': Pope-Hennessy, *A Lonely Business*, p. 210.
'RIDDLED WITH WEEDS': Nancy Spain, *She*.
'CALL IT OUR MUSEUM': Duke of Windsor, *A Family Album*, p. 137.
'MY COMMISSION IN THE ROYAL NAVY': *op. cit.*

Page 62
'THE DEAD LIE OUT UNBURIED . . .': Duke of Windsor, *A King's Story*, p. 118.
'FUSS IN THE NEWSPAPERS . . .': Nancy Spain, *She*.
'THREE ACCIDENTAL OCCASIONS . . .': Duke of Windsor, *A Family Album*, p. 138.
DRUMS ROLLED HOME TO WALES: Kenneth Rose to the author, 6 January 1987.
'THIS IS A CHEERFUL ROOM': Duke of Windsor, *A Family Album*, p. 138.
'THE KING OVER THE MILLSTREAM': Pope-Hennessy, *A Lonely Business*, p. 209.
TROMPE L'OEIL CHINA: Musée National de Céramique, Sèvres.
FANNY FARMER'S COOK BOOK: Duchess of Windsor, *The Heart Has its Reasons*, p. 80.
'MEISSEN: PAIR OF BASKETS . . .': archive Musée National de Céramique, Sèvres.
COOL GREEN DINING ROOM AND FOLLOWING DESCRIPTIONS OF THE MOULIN: *Woman's Home Companion*.
'IT WAS VERY BRIGHT': Diana Mosley to the author, 15 April 1987.
'LIKE AN ENGLISH HOUSE . . .': Grace, Lady Dudley to the author, 14 November 1986.

Page 63
PAVED WITH GRAVESTONES: *Woman's Home Companion*.

'CARPET . . . KIND OF TARTAN . . .': Hubert de Givenchy to the author, 23 March 1987.
'MEDALLIONS ON THE WALLS . . .': Bryan and Murphy, *The Windsor Story*, p. 685.
'THE ONLY THING ABOUT THE MILL . . .': autobiography of Billy Baldwin, published in USA, p. 292.
'I'M GOING TO DO SOMETHING DREADFUL . . .': Alexandre to the author, 18 December 1986.
'ANOTHER SERIOUS PERFECTIONIST MEAL': Pope-Hennessy, *A Lonely Business*, p. 215.
LITTLE GREY SHRIMPS: French *Vogue*, June 1964.
'I'VE STOPPED PUTTING LITTLE TABLES': *Ibid.*
MAITRE D'HOTEL IN NAVY BLUE: Nancy Spain, *She*.
'JUST ONE SLICE OF BREAD': French *Vogue*, June 1964.
BACK IN VIRGINIA WATER: Nancy Spain, *She*.
'YES IT IS VERY ENGLISH': *Ibid.*

Page 66
'THE BATHROOM WAS LOADED . . .': James Pope-Hennessy, *A Lonely Business*, p. 212.
TOOTHPASTE SQUEEZED ON TO THE BRUSH: Philippe du Pasquier to the author, 1 February 1987.
GEORGE IV CORONATION PRINTS: Nancy Spain, *She*.
'LORD DUDLEY WOKE' AND FOLLOWING ANECDOTE: Ghislaine de Polignac to the author, 6 November 1986.
'FURRY TOWELLING BATHROBE': Nancy Spain, *She*.
'YOU LIKED DAIQUIRIS': Anne Slater to the author, 12 December 1986.
'IT'S VERY QUAINT' AND FOLLOWING: Pope-Hennessy, *A Lonely Business*, p. 217.
THE WALLS WERE COVERED . . . RED FABRIC: The Duke of Windsor, *A King's Story*, p. 29.
'HE ALWAYS LIVED IN THE SIMPLEST WAY . . .': Bryan and Murphy, *The Windsor Story*, p. 605.

Page 67
'FOUR MAIDS . . . IN GREEN UNIFORMS': Joanne Cummings to the author, 11 December 1986.
'PRINCE CHARLES SAID . . .': Sydney Johnson to the author.
'I SHALL USE IT AS A TEA GOWN . . .': *Wallis & Edward Letters*, p. 183.
'IT'S A VERY DIFFICULT ONE': Nancy Spain, *She*.
'A VIRGINIA HAM OF TOTAL PERFECTION': Pope-Hennessy, *A Lonely Business*, p. 222.

Page 68
'THE PRINCE . . . DONALD TARTAN . . .': Diana Cooper, *The Light of Common Day*, p. 162.
'WE HAVE BEEN BUZZING LIKE BEES . . .': *Wallis & Edward Letters*, p. 65.
'FILL INSIDE STRAIGHTS': Duchess of Windsor, *The Heart Has its Reasons*, p. 114.

Page 73
DUKE'S LOVE OF COMPETITIVE GAMES: Nancy Spain, *She*.
'AFTER LIVING IN RENTED HOUSES . . .': *Woman's Home Companion*.
'THE RAIN WAS FALLING DOWN' AND FOLLOWING PARAS: Vreeland, *DV*, p. 72.

RIVIERA
Page 75
Quotation: Nicolson, *Diaries and Letters*, p. 351.
'THEY BROUGHT MORE TRUNKS . . .': Birmingham, *Duchess*, p. 215.
'WE'LL MAKE A BOULEVARDIER OF HIM YET': Nancy Spain, *She*.
PART OF AN 'ENCHANTED WORLD': *Wallis & Edward Letters*, p. 121.
'LANGOUSTINES FOR HIM': *Ibid.*, p. 191.
'TRAINS WERE HELD . . .': Duchess of Windsor, *The Heart Has its Reasons*, p. 202.
'IT WAS PATHETIC TO SEE . . .': Donaldson, *Edward VIII*, p. 311.
'WORRIED ABOUT THE WEATHER': Alexandre to the author, 18 December 1986.

Page 76
'RIVIERA HAS CHEAP AIR . . .': *Wallis & Edward Letters*, p. 288.
'MAYBE WE CAN MAKE THE RIVIERA . . .': *Ibid.*, p. 288.
'ENGLISH PEOPLE . . . BEYOND BELIEF': Noël Coward, *Diaries*, p. 61.
'LAWN HAD PRACTICALLY DISAPPEARED': Duchess of Windsor, *The Heart Has its Reasons*, p. 311.

'IMAGINE . . . SENSE OF LUXURY': Baronne de Cabrol to the author.
'I GAVE THEM A DELICIOUS DINNER': Noël Coward, *Diaries*, p. 55.
'PLUMP, PIGEON-SHAPED . . .': Pope-Hennessy, *A Lonely Business*, p. 209.
'NOBLE WHITE VESSEL': Bryan and Murphy, *The Windsor Story*, p. 473.
'A DREAM-LIKE PLACE': *Ibid.*, p. 473.
'I HAVE A TERRIBLE LONGING': *Wallis & Edward Letters*, p. 42.

Page 78
AFFAIR WITH ELSIE MENDL: Mary Lou Luther, *Los Angeles Times*, to the author, October 1986.
'TEMPTED TO CLASSIFY HER': Pope-Hennessy, *A Lonely Business*, p. 211.
'VILLA IN THE WATER': *Wallis & Edward Letters*, p. 152.
'EXISTENCE ON WATER IS VASTLY RESTFUL': *Ibid.*, p. 315.
SKYLIGHT OF VARIEGATED GLASS: Bryan and Murphy, *The Windsor Story*, p. 471.
'MY FATHER . . . NAUTICAL HABIT': Duke of Windsor, *A King's Story*, p. 8.
'WHITE TOWER OUT OF A CALM SEA': *Ibid.*, p. 183.
'THERE'S NOT ONE GOLF COURSE': Bryan and Murphy, *The Windsor Story*, p. 573.

Page 82
A BIT OF AN ADVENTURE: Lady Diana Cooper to the author.
'LOVELY SOFT WARM EVENING': Harold Nicolson, *Diaries and Letters*, p. 351.
'TWO ICE-FILLED SILVER BUCKETS': Birmingham, *Duchess*, p. 223.
'A TINY WHITE TABLE': Bryan and Murphy, *The Windsor Story*, p. 573.
ALL THE CHARM IN THE WORLD: *Ibid.*, p. 626.
'HIS FACE BEGINS TO SHOW . . .': Hugo Vickers, *Cecil Beaton*, p. 340.
'WET SLAB IN A FISHMONGER'S': Donaldson, *Edward VIII*, p. 344.
'HIS GLAMOUR AND HIS CHARM': Noël Coward, *Diaries*, p. 352.

Page 86
'IS IT RAINING IN HERE?': Duke of Windsor, *A King's Story*, p. 83.
'LOOK LIKE A WAITER': Anne Slater to the author, 11 December 1986.
'THE DUCHESS LIKES A MAN TO DRESS UP': Duke of Windsor, *A Family Album*, p. 142.
'WALLIS AND I GAMBLED': Noël Coward, *Diaries*, p. 55.
'BUT I KEPT THE BEST ONE': Birmingham, *Duchess*, p. 227.
'FROM RESORT TO RESORT': Bryan and Murphy, *The Windsor Story*, p. 568.
'A REVOLVING DOOR': Duke of Windsor, *A King's Story*, p. 162.
'GIFT OF A SUNLAMP': Bryan and Murphy, *The Windsor Story*, p. 568.
'STRONG NEW YORK SIDE': Pope-Hennessy, *A Lonely Business*, p. 211.
'PART OF EVERY YEAR': Duchess of Windsor, *The Heart Has its Reasons*, p. 365.
'PANTS ACROSS THE SEA': Duke of Windsor, *A Family Album*, p. 103.

NEW YORK
Page 87
Quotation: Irving Berlin, 'We're a Couple of Swells' from *Easter Parade*.
'I SAW THEM AT LE HAVRE': Diana Neill to the author, 18 December 1986.
'CAPTAIN HAS BEEN VERY NICE': *Wallis & Edward Letters*, p. 86.
CROSSING THE ATLANTIC: Grace Dudley to the author.
'BLASTED A WELCOME': Duke of Windsor, *A King's Story*, p. 149.
AMERICAN VITALITY TANGIBLE: Bloch, *Duke of Windsor's War*, p. 175.

Page 88
'SCARCELY BELIEVE MY EYES': *Wallis & Edward Letters*, p. 70.
'ATROCIOUS DRIVING UP PARK': Joanne Cummings to the author, December 1986.
'A TAILOR NAMED HARRIS': Duke of Windsor, *A Family Album*, p. 103.
'THE MOST SERIOUS CLIENTS': *American Fashion*, p. 164.
'I TOOK MY MOTHER': Kenneth J. Lane to the author, 13 December 1986.
'A LITTLE RESTAURANT': extracted from Billy Baldwin autobiography.

Page 90
'YOUR LITTLE DUCHESS': *Ibid.*
'THEIR ROYAL HIGHNESSES NEVER': Sydney Johnson to the author.
POCKET MONEY: Bryan and Murphy, *The Windsor Story*, p. 209.
'ONLY LIKED AMERICAN WOMEN': Diana Vreeland to the author.
'WHEREVER THE DUKE AND DUCHESS': Bryan and Murphy, *The Windsor Story*, p. 569.
'A FETISHISTIC CONCERN': Beaton, *The Glass of Fashion*, p. 206.

NEGRO SEAMSTRESS: Duchess of Windsor, *The Heart Has its Reasons*, p. 52.
DUCHESS OF WINDSOR BALL: Bryan and Murphy, *The Windsor Story*, p. 594.
'MIDNIGHT OFTEN FOUND ME': Duke of Windsor, *A King's Story*, p. 160.
BRING ONE FOR THE DUKE/CORONATION'S OVER: Birmingham, *Duchess*, p. 242.

Page 91
'THEY BEGAN . . . CAFE SOCIETY': *Ibid*, p. 215.
'MY FATHER . . . NIGHT CLUB': Duke of Windsor, *A King's Story*, p. 193.
'THE WINDSORS WERE CAFE SOCIETY': Billy Baldwin autobiography.
'BAD REPUTATION IN NEW YORK': Jean Amory to the author, 8 December 1986.

'A VALET, A MAID, TWO PUGS': Bryan and Murphy, *The Windsor Story*, p. 571.
'THE WOMAN I MOST ADMIRE': Birmingham, *Duchess*, p. 229.

Page 92
'UNEASY LIES THE HEAD': Vickers, *Cecil Beaton*, p. 453.
'AN ENORMOUS ADMIRATION': Bryan and Murphy, *The Windsor Story*, p. 669.
'TRUE GLAMOUR . . . VULGARITY': Noël Coward, *Diaries*, p. 223.
'YOU KNOW WHAT MY DAY WAS': Bryan and Murphy, *The Windsor Story*, p. 565.
'EVENINGS . . . HAVE BEEN DREADFUL': Donaldson, *Edward VIII*, p. 314.
'BOREDOM IS APPALLING': *Wallis & Edward Letters*, p. 268.
OTHERS ARE TIRED: Birmingham, *Duchess*, p. 226.
'THE GAYEST CHRISTMASES' AND FOLLOWING PARAS: Nancy Spain, *She*.
THEY ARE A HAPPY COUPLE: Beaton, *The Parting Years*, p. 111.

CHAPTER 3 IN THEIR FASHION

The Duke of Windsor's own treatise on fashion, *A Family Album*, published in 1960, was particularly helpful. My gratitude to the fashion houses of Balmain, Dior, Givenchy and Saint Laurent. All quotations from couturiers and friends are detailed in first quote only.

Page 95
Quotations: Duke of Windsor, *A Family Album*, p. 12.
Duchess of Windsor's Commonplace Book, quoted in *Wallis & Edward Letters*, p. 315.
'AARGH, THE COLLECTIONS': Princesse de Polignac to the author, 6 November 1986.
'THE DUCHESS LOVES PARIS': *Ibid*.
TRIM BOUCLE SUIT/OCELOT HAT: Windsor archive, Paris.
'AVENUE PAPA': Princesse de Polignac.
'BON BOULEVARDIER': Baron de Cabrol to the author, 19 December 1986.
'BRIGHT TWEEDED OPULENCE': Duke of Windsor, *A Family Album*, p. 41.
'MEN TEND TO LOOK MORE . . . ALIKE': Lawford, *Vogue's Book of Houses, Gardens, People*.
'ELEVATED SOBRIETY . . .': *Elle*, Paris, May 1986.

Page 96
'THIS REPORTER . . . MRS SIMPSON': Windsor archive, Paris.
'MY OWN PERSONAL IDEAS': *Harper's Bazaar*, America, May 1966.
DRIVING HER OUT TO ORSAY: Lady Mosley to the author, 15 April 1987
S.A.R. LETTERING: Hubert de Givenchy to the author, 2 March 1987.
'THEY ALL WANTED TO KNOW': *Ibid*.
'THE ROYALTY STUFF': *Wallis & Edward Letters*, p. 113.
'SOMETHING SOPHISTICATED': *Ibid*, p. 108.
'ANY CHEAP PALE BLUE': *Ibid*.
'SEND ME THE DRESS': *Ibid*.
'MY EVENING CLOTHES': *Ibid*, p. 148.
'SELLING THE OLD ONES': *Ibid*, p. 181.
'LIKE BLACKBIRDS': *Ibid*.
'YOU HAVE TO WEAR BLACK': *Harper's Bazaar*, May 1966.
'SHE ALWAYS CHOSE FROM DIOR . . .': Agnès Bertrand to the author, 20 November 1986.
CHRISTIAN DIOR MUSEUM: 20 November 1986.
'MY SITTER IS AT HER BEST/POSTERIOR INVITES BUSTLE': *Beaton in Vogue*, p. 126.

Page 98
CHINESE PRINCESS: Wilson, *Her Name was Wallis Warfield*, p. 74.
'SARI OF THIN . . . SILK': Lady Mosley to the author.
'LOOKED TOO BEAUTIFUL': Vreeland, *DV*, p. 68.
'MY WHITE TIE DRESS': *Wallis & Edward Letters*, p. 88.
'ARMOUR-PLATED SHIRTS': Duke of Windsor, *A Family Album*, p. 108.
'NEATEST, NEWEST LUGGAGE': *Beaton in Vogue*, p. 126.
'CHIC AND WORRIED ABOUT IT': Lady Diana Cooper to the author, February 1984.
'SOIGNEE, NOT DEGAGEE': Diana Vreeland to the author, 10 January 1985.
PEACOCK BLUE FEATHER: Bryan and Murphy, *The Windsor Story*, p. 27.
BRIGHT RED SASH: Duchess of Windsor, *The Heart Has its Reasons*, p. 13.

PRINCE PAUL/EVA LUTYENS: *Ibid*, p. 205.
'FASHION PURITY': Marc Bohan to the author, 20 November 1986.
YVES SAINT LAURENT STYLE: Danielle Porthault to the author, 23 October 1986.

Page 99
'DRESSED IN PLUS TWENTIES': Cooper, *Light of Common Day*, p. 161.
'INCONGRUOUS FIGURE': Duchess of Windsor, *The Heart Has its Reasons*, p. 184.
GOLF PLAYER/PERFECTLY SMART: Edmonde Charles-Roux, *Chanel*, p. 232.
'BAGGY KNICKERBOCKER': Duke of Windsor, *A Family Album*, p. 125.
'BUTTONED-UP CHILDHOOD': *Ibid*, p. 24.
'IT WAS MY IMPULSE . . .': *Ibid*, p. 105.
'IMPECCABLY DRESSED': Laura, Duchess of Marlborough to the author, 28 April 1987.
FUSSY ABOUT SUITS: Sydney Johnson to the author, October 1986.
'MY FATHER SET FEW . . .': Duke of Windsor, *A Family Album*, p. 60.
'DUKE SCAMPERED IN': Pope-Hennessy, *A Lonely Business*, p. 218.

Page 102
'HE WAS QUITE LOUD': Lawford to the author, 11 December 1986.
THICK BUTTONED WAISTCOAT: Duke of Windsor, *A Family Album*, p. 125.
'MOST SHOWY OF ALL': *Ibid*, p. 130.
'HE HAS . . . HIS OWN MANNER': *Vogue USA*, November 1967.
'MY AMERICAN FRIENDS': Duke of Windsor, *A Family Album*, p. 85.
PURPLE AND BLACK/CORONET BRAID/HER MAID: Wilson, *Her Name was Wallis Warfield*, p. 90.
SATIN BLOUSE IN JOCKEY COLOURS: *Ibid*, p. 90.
'MESSENGER-BOY'S SUITS': *Beaton in Vogue*, p. 126.
'CLEVER WOMAN': Channon, *Chips: Diaries*, p. 60.
'BEJEWELLED, VIRTUOUS': Nicolson, *Diaries and Letters*, p. 235.
MADEMOISELLE CHANEL: Alexandre to the author, 18 December 1986.
'SHE WORE TWEED SKIRTS': Grace, Countess of Dudley to the author, 14 November 1986.

Page 106
GOVERNESS MARION CRAWFORD: Crawford, Marion, *The Little Princesses*, p. 36.
ROLL-NECK SWEATER: Erik Mortensen to the author.
'WALLIS ADMIRABLY CORRECT': Cooper, *Light of Common Day*, p. 161.
DUCHESS COULD BE LOUD: Vicomtesse de Ribes to the author, 13 April 1987.
'QUEEN CUTIE': Thornton, *Royal Feud*, p. 119.
SPORTS AND PLAY CLOTHES: Windsor archive, Paris.
'WITH A BABY'S BONNET': *Beaton in Vogue*, p. 126.
'HE HAD NO HAT': Cooper, *Light of Common Day*, p. 175.
'GOING NATIVE': Duke of Windsor, *A Family Album*, p. 133.
'PUT HIS SHIRT ON': Duchess of Windsor, *The Heart Has its Reasons*, p. 231.
'I LIKE MY WORK': *Ibid*, p. 198.
'ROBINSON CRUSOE CLOTHES': *Ibid*, p. 202.

Page 108
YVONNE DESLANDRES: *Elle* magazine Paris, May 1986.

LATINS/MEDITERRANEAN FISHERMEN: Duke of Windsor, *A Family Album*, pp. 122/133.
'FLY IN OVER THE TRANSOM': Bryan and Murphy, *The Windsor Story*, p. 580.
HAVE A 'PANSY': Auction of Letters, Phillips, London, 28 January 1987.
'IN FLORIDA . . .': Duke of Windsor, *A Family Album*, p. 122.
'BLUE IS HER COLOUR': Wilson, *Her Name was Wallis Warfield*, p. 89.
DRESSED YOUNG FOR HER AGE: James Viane to the author, July 1984.
'WEARING PALE PINK PIQUE': Nino Caprioglio to the author, 28 April 1987.
'WEARING CRIMSON TROUSERS': Donaldson, *Edward VIII*, p. 44.
GRANDFATHER OVERDID/BRITISH TAILORING PRESS: Duke of Windsor, *A Family Album*, p. 41.

Page 109
'HE IS UTTERLY HIMSELF': Cooper, *Light of Common Day*, p. 178.
'BLUE JEANS . . . NOT . . . FOR ME': Duke of Windsor, *A Family Album*, p. 123.
'BRAWNY GREAT COW . . . SECOND-RATE AMERICAN': Vickers, *Cecil Beaton*, p. 193.

Page 113
'I HAVE BEEN DELIGHTED': *Ibid*, p. 198.
'THE MOST INDEPENDENT WOMAN': Duke of Windsor, *A King's Story*, p. 258.
FOR HER TROUSSEAU: *Life* magazine, May/June 1937, p. 64.
THE MUSIC COLLECTION: Palmer White, *Schiaparelli*, p. 164.

Page 116
ONLY 'FROU-FROU' COSTUME: Wilson, *Her Name was Wallis Warfield*, p. 90.
BERTHA GRANT PARTY: *Wallis & Edward Letters*, p. 44.

Page 117
'MY COSTUME NOT BAD': *Ibid*, p. 99.
COLUMN OF SAPPHIRE CREPE: Archive Costume Institute, Metropolitan Museum, NY.
PLATINUM WEDDING RING: Sotheby's, *The Jewels of the Duchess of Windsor*, p. 142.

Page 120
'DRESS IS INTRICATELY CUT': archive Metropolitan Museum.
'SOMEHOW THE PREPARATIONS . . .': Duchess of Windsor, *The Heart Has its Reasons*, p. 297.
'I DIDN'T LIKE THE DRESS': Diana Cooper to the author.
'WALLIS . . . UNLOVABLE': Vickers, *Cecil Beaton*, p. 199.
MAINBOCHER HAS MADE AND FOLLOWING INFO: *American Fashion*, pp. 111–63.
'MARY'S CLOTHES . . . RATHER NAKED': *Wallis & Edward Letters*, p. 192.
'MAINBOCHER WAS RESPONSIBLE': Vreeland to author.
'PARIS COME TO ME': *Wallis & Edward Letters*, p. 302.
'I WOULD GO TO PARIS': *Ibid*, p. 44.
FOR HER TROUSSEAU: archive Metropolitan Museum.

Page 121
'IRON A CRINOLINE': Pope-Hennessy, *A Lonely Business*, p. 217.
'WOMEN OF THE WORLD': *Life* magazine, May/June 1937.
PRINCE OF WALES FEATHERS/JIMMY DONAHUE ROSES: Laura, Duchess of Marlborough to the author.
STRIPED SHIRTS/MONOGRAM: Windsor archive, Paris.
'HIS FATHER'S COAT': Sydney Johnson to the author.
GENERAL TROTTER/LONDON CABBIES: Duke of Windsor, *A Family Album*, p. 120.

Page 124
'NOW THIS, DAVID': Pope-Hennessy, *A Lonely Business*, p. 223.
'ONLY HALF A COAT': Duke of Windsor, *A Family Album*, p. 58.
SHEPHERD'S PLAIDS/TWEED: *Ibid*, p. 126.
BY SUTHERLAND FAMILY: *Vogue USA*, November 1967.
UNHEATED HOUSES: Duke of Windsor, *A Family Album*, p. 121.
HAT CHECK GIRLS/DISCARDED FUR COATS: *Ibid*, p. 120.
EXPENSIVE FUR: Duchess of Windsor, *The Heart Has its Reasons*, p. 204.
'I BOUGHT WITH $200': *Wallis & Edward Letters*, p. 122.
'LIVE WITHOUT WINTER SPORTS': *Ibid*, p. 134.
TWEED SPORTS JACKETS: archive Metropolitan Museum.

Page 125
OLD REGIMENTAL BUTTONS/DUKE KEEP QUIET: The Duke of Windsor, *A Family Album*, p. 117.
PROVOST MARSHAL'S . . .: Sotheby's, *The Duchess of Windsor's Jewels*, p. 268.
'CHIC FATIGUE': Katell le Bourhis, Metropolitan Museum, to the author, 9 December 1986.

Page 126
TROUSERS MADE IN NEW YORK: Duke of Windsor, *A Family Album*, p. 103.

Page 127
SCHOLTE RIGID STANDARDS/OXFORD BAGS: *Ibid*, pp. 99/107.
'UNFORTUNATELY I HAD FORGOTTEN': *Ibid*, p. 100.

Page 128
A SOFT HAT DISGUISED/TWO BOATERS AFLOAT: *Ibid*, p. 132.
'MY BROTHER AND I': *Ibid*, p. 109.
FRED ASTAIRE: *Ibid*, p. 111.
HAWES AND CURTIS/ORIGIN OF THE MYTH: *Vogue USA*, November 1967.
'ONCE IN WASHINGTON': Duke of Windsor, *A Family Album*, p. 115.

Page 130
'TOGGED UP IN ROYAL STEWART': Hastings, *Nancy Mitford*, p. 185.
FATHER'S TARTAN SUIT: Duke of Windsor, *A Family Album*, p. 129.
'UNIQUE AND ZESTY': *Vogue USA*, November 1967.
'APPEARANCE WAS MAGNIFICENT': Donaldson, *Edward VIII*, p. 344.

Page 132
'I ADORE TO SHOP': Duchess of Windsor in *Woman's Home Companion*, 1953.

Page 134
DOWN AVENUE MONTAIGNE: Claude Laurent to the author, 20 November 1986.
'TELL ME . . . ABOUT SAINT LAURENT': Pope-Hennessy, *A Lonely Business*, p. 217.
FLEUR COWLES/PLAY WITH THE CLOTHES: *Harper's Bazaar*, May 1966.
WHITE FANTAIL PIGEONS: *Woman's Home Companion*.
DUMMY MARKED EDITH PIAF AND FOLLOWING: Dior exhibit Musée des Art de la Mode, Paris, March 1987.

Page 135
'IMMACULATE WAS . . . HALLMARK': Romanones, *Vanity Fair*, May 1986.
'WELL, I'LL BUY THAT DRESS . . .': Pope-Hennessy, *A Lonely Business*, p. 217.
'WITH A BLANK BOARD': *Harper's Bazaar*, May 1966.
TWO OR THREE HUNDRED PATTERNS: *Ibid*.
THE BLOUSE OF ONE: *Ibid*.
MAINBOCHER BLOUSE: Kerry Taylor, Sotheby's textiles, to the author.

Page 138
GREAT CHRISTIAN DIOR/ONE OF YOURS: Dior archive, Paris.
IN VELVET SMOKING JACKET: Danielle Porthault, YSL, to the author.
SO THIS IS THE GREAT DRESS: Beaton, *The Wandering Years*, p. 311.
MAKE-UP ARTIST OVERHEARD: Hebe Dorsay to the author, October 1986.

Page 139
BEATON RECALLS A NIGHTMARE: Vickers, *Cecil Beaton*, p. 521.
'A GREAT COMPLIMENT': Alexandre to the author.
THE DUCHESS VERY DARK . . .: Bryan and Murphy, *The Windsor Story*, p. 590.
CLOSET ON THE LANDING: Windsor archive, Paris.

Page 140
HAS HIS FATHER'S EYES: Pope-Hennessy, *A Lonely Business*, p. 210.
'EYE OF WINDSOR BLUE': Nicolson, *Diaries and Letters*, p. 238.
'CHARMING AS THE BOY KING': Diana Cooper to the author.
HAIR NICOTINE-COLOURED: Pope-Hennessy, *A Lonely Business*, p. 210.
CHARLES TOPPER OF MAYFAIR: Henry Manton to the author.

Page 141
'BLOWN OUT IN TUFTS': Pope-Hennessy, *A Lonely Business*, p. 210.
'HERE COMES MY ROMANCE': Anne Slater to the author, NY, December 1986.

Page 142
'IT WAS A FREEWAY': Hubert de Givenchy to the author.
DOWDILY LADYLIKE/WIDE JAW/JAPANESE LADY: *Beaton in Vogue*, p. 126.
'I HAD NEVER STAYED . . .': *Vanity Fair*, June 1986.
'ETHIC OF LIVING': Edouard in *Point de Vue, Images du Monde*, 2 May 1986.
SMOOTHED OFF THE BROW: Nicolson, *Diaries and Letters*, p. 351.
WINDS CANNOT DISHEVEL: Bloch, *Duke of Windor's War*, p. 182.

Page 144
BOYISH YOUNG KING: Channon, *Chips: Diaries*, p. 55.
'INTENSELY YOUTHFUL': Bloch, *Duke of Windsor's War*, p. 168.
'WALLIS IN WONDERLAND': *Wallis & Edward Letters*, p. 120.
NOT A MANNIKIN: Pope-Hennessy, *A Lonely Business*, p. 210.
'HE LIKE A BALLOON': Hastings, *Nancy Mitford*, p. 192.
'FOUR POUNDS IN WEIGHT . . .': *Wallis & Edward Letters*, p. 65.

Page 147
WEIGHED THIS MORNING: Duke of Windsor, *A Family Album*, p. 64.
'MY THINNESS': *Ibid*, p. 63.
'I CAN'T BEAR THEM': Sale of letters, Phillips, London, 28 January 1987.
'NAME OF THAT FACE WOMAN': *Wallis & Edward Letters*, p. 283.
'WHAT A LOT WE HAVE TO DO': *Ibid*, p. 283.
CONVERSATION WAS DEVOTED: Noël Coward, *Diaries*, p. 399.
'LIKE A MAD GOYA': Vickers, *Cecil Beaton, Diaries*, p. 559.
'SPENT . . . ENTIRE DAY': *Wallis & Edward Letters*, p. 36.
'FROM . . . FEMININE SIDE': *Ibid*, p. 277.

Page 149
RICHARD AVEDON PUBLISHES: Nancy Spain, *She*, December 1960.
'SHE WAS A COQUETTE': Edouard, *Point de Vue, Images du Monde*, 2 May 1986.

CHAPTER 4   OBJECTS OF DESIRE

Cartier details before the abdication in December 1936 are taken from Cartier London archives. All subsequent references to dates and purchases from Cartier, and details of design or re-setting of jewels, come from the Cartier archives in Paris, with grateful thanks to Madame Betty Jais. All Van Cleef details are from Van Cleef & Arpels, Paris, courtesy M. Canavy. Sotheby sale references are to their catalogue, *The Duchess of Windsor's Jewels*, Geneva, Thursday and Friday, 2 and 3 April 1987.

Page 151
Quotation: George Eliot, *Middlemarch*, p. 35.
THE PANTHER BRACELET: Cartier, Paris.
OTHER NATURALISTIC TRINKETS: Cartier, Paris.
'I LOVE THE NEW FROG': *Wallis & Edward Letters*, p. 274.
ENAMEL FROG BRACELET: Sotheby's catalogue, p. 45.
'TWO OLD PEOPLE': Beaton, *The Parting Years*, p. 112.
SEX URGES OF YOUTH: *Ibid*, p. 111.
PRINCE CHARMING/SEM: See illustration p. 176.

Page 152
'PRESSED AN EMERALD . . . CHARM': Duchess of Windsor, *The Heart Has its Reasons*, p. 197.
'OH! SO MANY HAPPY RETURNS': *Wallis & Edward Letters*, p. 148.
'MY WALLIS FROM HER DAVID': Sotheby's catalogue, p. 88.
'NOTHING A MAN IN LOVE': Van Cleef & Arpels slogan.
'MRS SIMPSON WAS GLITTERING': Channon, *Chips: Diaries*, p. 43.
'DRIPPING WITH EMERALDS/WEARING NEW JEWELS': *Ibid*, pp. 77/85.
'HOLD TIGHT': Sotheby's catalogue, p. 87.
'SMOTHERED IN RUBIES': Channon, *Chips: Diaries*, p. 73.
BRACELET OF LITTLE CROSSES: *Beaton in Vogue*, p. 127.
'ON THE LINE FOR HOURS': Donaldson, *Edward VIII*, p. 311.
'KEEP ONE'S SANITY': *Wallis & Edward Letters*, p. 282.

Page 154
ARMISTICE DAY: *The Uncrowned Jewels*, BBC TV, March 1987.
'AN EANUM NEW YEAR PRESENT': *Wallis & Edward Letters*, p. 264.
WOMEN DRESSED TO NINES: Beaton, *The Wandering Years*, p. 304.
'GOD BLESS WE': *Wallis & Edward Letters*, p. 209.

Page 158
OUR BUTLER TELEPHONED/DUCHESS'S BEDROOM: Laura, Duchess of Marlborough to the author, 28 April 1987.
'FOR OUR CONTRACT': Sotheby's catalogue, p. 70.
EXOTIC JEWELLED FLOWERS: Cartier archives.
WITH HIM FOR FIVE DAYS: Oonagh Shanley to the author, 18 May 1987.
FLOWER PIN: Sotheby's sale, 21 May 1987.
FROM NEW YORK'S HARRY WINSTON: Sotheby's catalogue, p. 95.
ADMIRER OF JEWELLERY/LITERALLY COVERED: Laurence Krashes, Harry Winston archives, New York, 12 December 1986.
'IT IS OFTEN MEN': Joseph Allgood to the author.
NO LONGER CARES FOR PEARLS: Wilson, *Her Name was Wallis Warfield*, p. 91.
'I CAN'T THINK . . .': Sotheby's catalogue, p. 91.

Page 159
'WE ARE OUR NOW': *Ibid*, p. 81.

BELONGED TO GRAND MOGUL: *Ibid*.
'WHEN I NEGLECT . . .': *Ibid*, p. 95.
WALLIS HAD LOVE AFFAIR: Laura Marlborough to author.
ANYTHING SO LOVELY: *Wallis & Edward Letters*, p. 186.
'THOSE WERE BETTER DAYS': Kenneth J. Lane to the author, 13 December 1986.
DUKE AND DUCHESS THEFT: Bryan and Murphy, *The Windsor Story*, p. 586.

Page 163
'WHY THEY'RE IN LOVE!': *Ibid*, p. 582.
'SHE WAS MESMERIZED': Laura Marlborough to the author.
'GAVE HERSELF WILLINGLY': Grace, Countess of Dudley to the author.
'DUKE A . . . SAD PERSON': Bryan and Murphy, *The Windsor Story*, p. 588.
'LEARNED TO DRILL': *Ibid*, p. 597.
LOVELY DIAMOND CLIPS: *Wallis & Edward Letters*, p. 143.

Page 164
TIARA NEVER HAVE: Channon, *Chips: Diaries*, p. 81.
'WE'VE HAD ENOUGH OF YOU': Bryan and Murphy, *The Windsor Story*, p. 598.
SEVEN ITEMS: Sotheby's catalogue, pp. 41, 107, 128, 148, 175, 251.
ORIENT EXPRESS: Duchess of Windsor, *The Heart Has its Reasons*, p. 296.
'OUR REUNION AT CANDE': Sotheby's catalogue, p. 44.
CHRISTMAS 1953: *Ibid*, p. 107.
DIAMOND ENCRUSTED HEART: *Ibid*, p. 26.
CURRENT TRENDS IN CLOTHES: Beaton, *The Parting Years*, p. 111.

Page 165
HIPPIE CAFTAN/GARLAND OF SUNFLOWERS: Sotheby's catalogue, p. 146.
DUCHESS AT MOULIN: Joanne Cummings to the author, 11 December 1986.
NECKLACES BARBARIC: Nicholas Haslam to the author, 13 May 1987.
'CHIC JEWELS': Jacqueline de Ribes to the author, 13 April 1987.
TONY DUQUETTE: Nicholas Rayner, Sotheby's Geneva, to the author.
SUZANNE BELPERRON: Raulet, *Art Deco Jewelry*, p. 331.
STAINED CHALCEDONY: Sotheby's catalogue, p. 123.
SENSUOUS WRIST-PIECE: *Ibid*, p. 101.
EMERALD ANKLETS: *New York Times* magazine, n.d.
'MY APPROACH TO ART': *Woman's Home Companion*, October 1954.
DRESSMAKERS' JEWELS: Thornton, *Royal Feud*, p. 80.
BALL AT VERSAILLES: Nino Caprioglio to the author, 28 April 1987.

Page 166
LATTICE NECKLACE/BREASTPLATE/SEAMEN SCHEPPS: Sotheby's catalogue, pp. 46/51/18.
'BUYING AN AQUAMARINE . . .': *Wallis & Edward Letters*, p. 50.
'GORGEOUS STONES': Wilson, *Her Name was Wallis Warfield*, p. 86.

Page 168
'I HATE TO ADMIT IT': *Harper's Bazaar*, May 1966.
BOXES OF 1960s CHAINS: Windsor archive, Paris.

Page 169
WORKING ZIP FASTENER: Van Cleef archives.
'A FOOL WOULD KNOW': Thornton, *Royal Feud*, p. 235.
FULCO DI VERDURA/LIZ WHITNEY: *Connoisseur* magazine, NY.

Page 170
'MINERALOGY ISN'T JEWELLERY': *The Daily Telegraph*, 18 December 1986.
'WITH MY JEWELLERY . . .': CHANEL: *Ibid.*
HEART-SHAPED COMPACT/PEARL EARCLIPS: Sotheby's catalogue, pp. 103, 23.
CAN'T EXCHANGE IT: *Connoisseur* magazine, NY, n.d.
DAVID WEBB: Sotheby's catalogue, p. 5.
DARDE ET FILS: *Ibid.*, p. 10.

Page 172
MADAME BELPERRON MADE: Vreeland to author, 10 January 1985.
'WE HAVE BOTH BEEN TARTS': Gautier, *Cartier the Legend*, p. 210.

Page 173
HER FLAT A SECRET: *Ibid.*, p. 210.
WINTRY WREATH OF SAPPHIRES: Sotheby's catalogue, p. 71.
FLAMBOYANT FLAMINGO: Menkes, *The Royal Jewels*, pp. 76/77.
'I LIKE BIRDS': Gautier, *Cartier the Legend*, p. 222.
EXOTIC BIRD OF PARADISE: Menkes, *The Royal Jewels*, p. 87.

Page 174
'MY FAVOURITE JEWEL': Gautier, *Cartier the Legend*, p. 237.
BUNCH OF WISTERIA: *Ibid.*, p. 238.
FLOWER BOUQUET BROOCH: archives Van Cleef.
NEVER SAW BROOCH: Ofelia Sanègres to author, January 1985.
BANGLE PEACOCK PLUME: Menkes, *The Royal Jewels*, p. 99.

Page 176
HEAVY BRACELETS TINY ARMS: Schlumberger to author.
CHIMAERA BANGLE: Sotheby's catalogue, p. 30.
MARCHIONESS CASATI/DISCOURAGE THIEVES: Gautier, *Cartier the Legend*, p. 192.

Page 177
SIGHT OF STUFFED PANTHER: *Ibid.*, p. 193.
GOLD AND ENAMEL PANTHER: Menkes, *The Royal Jewels*, p. 84.
FASHION FOR SKINS: Nadelhoffer, *Cartier*, p. 229.

Page 178
THE FAMOUS TORSADE: *The Uncrowned Jewels*, BBC TV, March 1987.

Page 179
'OVER ALL THOSE BEADS': *Harper's Bazaar*, May 1966.
'SLIM TRIM DUCHESS': Bryan and Murphy, *The Windsor Story*, p. 619.
'VERY NICE AND SAD': Lawford, *Letters*.
CHRISTMAS CAROLS/HARD BRILLIANCE: Mosley, *The Duchess of Windsor*, p. 197.

Page 180
ONE WAS A HEART: Aline de Romanones to the author, 30 April 1987.
ON THE RIGHT WRIST: Spain, *She*, December 1956.
'OUR MARRIAGE CROSS' AND FOLLOWING INSCRIPTIONS: Sotheby's catalogue, p. 31.
WATCHED THE PRINCE: Duchess of Windsor, *The Heart Has its Reasons*, p. 204.
'DREADFUL BIRDS': Bryan and Murphy, *The Windsor Story*, p. 139.

Page 181
PRINCE AND BROTHER GEORGE: Joseph Allgood to author.
BOTH WORE CRUCIFIXES: Diana Cooper to author.
HIS CROSSES CARRY: Sotheby's catalogue, p. 38.

Page 182
GEM-SET CIGARETTE CASE: Sotheby's catalogue, p. 32.
'THE KING SITUATION': Channon, *Chips: Diaries*, p. 85.
HEALED ULCER SCAR: *Wallis & Edward Letters*, p. 211.
'OH THELMA . . .': *Wallis & Edward Letters*, p. 103.
'NO ACCOUNT TO BE SENT': Cartier archives, London.
'MANY HAPPY RETURNS': *Wallis & Edward Letters*, p. 90.
INTIMATE MESSAGE: Sotheby's catalogue, p. 15.
FAMILY BIRTHDAYS: Duke of Windsor, *A King's Story*, p. 421.

Page 184
'THEY LIKED THIS BRACELET': *Wallis & Edward Letters*, p. 194.

'HALLO EANUM PIG': Sotheby's catalogue, p. 78.
'PLEASE-PLEASE': *Wallis & Edward Letters*, p. 258.
STUFFED TOY PIGS: Windsor archive, Paris.
A CAIRN PUPPY: *Wallis & Edward Letters*, p. 124.
'OUR MR LOO': Sotheby's catalogue, p. 164.
'HAPPIER NEW YEAR': *Ibid.*, p. 112.
'IS THERE SCOPE . . .': Bloch, *The Duke of Windsor's War*, p. 142.
'ALL THE THINGS I SAID': Sotheby's catalogue, p. 155.
ON THE GOLD HEART: *Ibid.*, p. 39.
MOTHER SON RELATIONSHIP: *Wallis & Edward Letters*, p. 130.
'HAVEN'T GROWN UP': *Ibid.*, p. 141.
KING CROSS: Sotheby's catalogue, p. 31.
'THAT LITTLE KING': *Wallis & Edward Letters*, p. 90.

Page 185
GOLD NOTEBOOK COVER: Windsor archive, Paris.
'KING'S CROSS, WHAT SHALL WE DO?': Farjeon, *Nursery Rhymes of London Town*.
ORDER TAXI CAB: Channon, *Chips: Diaries*, p. 79.
QUEEN MARY . . . 90 OBJECTS: Pope-Hennessy, *Queen Mary*, p. 613.
ALL BEAUTIFUL OBJECTS: Pope-Hennessy, *Queen Mary*, p. 411.
TABLES WERE LADEN: *Ibid.*, p. 613.
'I AM CARESSING IT . . .': Rose, *King George V*, p. 284.

Page 186
FRUITS OF COLLECTING: Pope-Hennessy, *Queen Mary*, pp. 611–13.
PRECISE POSITION: *Ibid.*, p. 414.
IMPOSSIBLE TO REMOVE: *Ibid.*, p. 524.
'MAY I GO BACK': Rose, *King George V*, p. 284.
EXQUISITE BOX: Musée National de Céramique, Sèvres.
'SMALL OVERCROWDED . . . ROOM': Beaton, *The Parting Years*, p. 111.
COLLECTION LUCKY ELEPHANTS: Wilson, *Her Name was Wallis Warfield*, p. 74.
IN NEGLIGEE RESTING/HER SOFT VOICE: Duke of Windsor, *A King's Story*, p. 26.

Page 188
SETS ORNAMENT IN PLACE: Bryan and Murphy, *The Windsor Story*, p. 600.
WE ARE BOTH TERRIFIC COLLECTORS/OLD SHOPS LEFT BANK: *Woman's Home Companion*.
SENT OFF ANTIQUE-SPOTTING: Marchioness of Cambridge to the author, 12 December 1984.
DIFFICULT TO PICK UP: Pope-Hennessy, *Queen Mary*, p. 411.
'DAVID FROM MAMA' AND FOLLOWING INSCRIPTIONS: Sotheby's catalogue, pp. 218–23.
'DUKE BROKE DOWN': Bloch, *The Duke of Windsor's War*, p. 273.
'SINCE I HARDLY EVER . . .': Duke of Windsor, *A Family Album*, p. 59.

Page 191
GOLD HANDBAG SUITE: Sotheby's catalogue, p. 166.

Page 192
THE CHARMING FRAME: Pope-Hennessy, *Queen Mary*, p. 412.
'WINSTON'S LITTLE EFFORTS': Grace Dudley to the author.
'HIS ROYAL HIGHNESS TELLS': Sotheby's catalogue, p. 79.

Page 193
DUKE OF WINDSOR DENIED: Maître Blum to the author.
ROBBERY AT EDNAM LODGE AND FOLLOWING PARAS: Laura, Duchess of Marlborough to the author.
RICHARD TIPTOE DUNPHIE: Michael Nash to the author.
THE STOLEN GEMS: Menkes, *The Royal Jewels*, p. 84.
'DIAMONDS . . . AS PLENTIFUL': *Ibid.*, p. 38.
ROPES OF WONDERFUL PEARLS: Ponsonby, *Recollections of Three Reigns*, p. 340.

Page 196
'DUKE INHERITED': Ghislaine de Polignac to the author.
'I FEEL SO SORRY': Pope-Hennessy, *Queen Mary*, p. 614.
FLUIDS IN HER VEINS: Bloch, *The Duke of Windsor's War*, p. 241.
'MAMA, MAMA, MAMA, MAMA': Sydney Johnson to the author.

ILLUSTRATION CREDITS

CHAPTER 1

p. 10 Horst; p. 12 Gérard Maré, Paris; p. 13 Rex Features; p. 14 Horst; p. 15 Gérard Maré; p. 18 & p. 19 Horst; p. 20, p. 21 & p. 24 left Gérard Maré; p. 24 right Syndication International; p. 25 left & bottom right Horst; p. 25 top right Musée National de Céramique, Sèvres; p. 26 top & bottom & p. 27 Gérard Maré; p. 28 top & bottom Musée National de Céramique, Sèvres; p. 28 centre & p. 29 Horst; p. 32 left Syndication International; p. 32 top Private Collection; p. 33 & p. 36 top & bottom, p. 37 & p. 40 top & bottom Gérard Maré; p. 41 Horst; p. 42 left & right & p. 43 Gérard Maré; p. 46 top Derry Moore/Sunday Times; p. 46 bottom, p. 47 top & bottom & p. 49 Gérard Maré

CHAPTER 2

p. 50 Life/Colorific!; p. 51 Punch magazine; p. 54/55 Life/Colorific!; p. 55 right Private Collection; p. 58 left courtesy of Sotheby's, London; p. 58/p. 59 Dominique Beretty/Hillelson; p. 60 left & right & p. 61 Patrick Lichfield; p. 62 & p. 63 Hillelson; p. 64 top & bottom & p. 65 top & bottom Private Collection; p. 68 top Hillelson; p. 68 centre & bottom Musée National de Céramique, Sèvres; p. 69 Hillelson; p. 70 top Patrick Lichfield; p. 70 bottom Hillelson; p. 71 & p. 72 Patrick Lichfield; p. 73 top & bottom By kind permission of the Baron de Cabrol; p. 74 Cecil Beaton, courtesy of Sotheby's, London; p. 77 Robert Hunt Library; p. 79 By kind permission of the Baron de Cabrol; p. 80/p. 81 BBC Hulton Library; p. 83, p. 84 & p. 85 By kind permission of the Baron de Cabrol; p. 86 Rex Features; p. 87 Popperfoto; p. 88 courtesy of the Waldorf Astoria, New York; p. 89 Horst; p. 93 Popperfoto

CHAPTER 3

p. 94 Horst; p. 96 Cecil Beaton, courtesy of Hugo Vickers; p. 97 Cecil Beaton, courtesy of Condé Nast; p. 100 Cecil Beaton, courtesy of Sotheby's, London; p. 101 Man Ray © DACS 1987; p. 102 top Private Collection; p. 102 bottom Camera Press; p. 103 Life/ Colorific!; p. 104 left Author's Collection; p. 104/p. 105 Cecil Beaton, courtesy of Sotheby's, London; p. 106 Author's Collection; p. 107 Cecil Beaton, courtesy of Sotheby's, London; p. 108 & p. 109 top Windsor Archives, Paris, by generous permission of Mohamed Al-Fayed; p. 109 bottom Private Collection; p. 110 photograph by Dorothy Wilding/National Portrait Gallery, London, courtesy of Tom Hustler; p. 111 Horst; p. 112 top & main picture Dorothy Wilding/National Portrait Gallery, London, courtesy of Tom Hustler; p. 113 Gérard Maré; p. 114 & p. 115 Cecil Beaton, courtesy

of Sotheby's, London; p. 116 left Private Collection; p. 116 right Cecil Beaton, courtesy of Sotheby's, London; p. 117 Gérard Maré; p. 118/119 Gérard Maré; p. 122 Private Collection; p. 123 Popperfoto; p. 124 Rex Features; p. 125 left & right Gérard Maré; p. 126 top & bottom left courtesy of Sotheby's, London; p. 126 right & p. 127 left Patrick Lichfield; p. 127 right Horst; p. 128 Popperfoto; p. 129 left Rex Features; p. 129 top right Derry Moore/Sunday Times; p. 129 bottom right courtesy of Sotheby's, London; p. 130 Patrick Lichfield; p. 131 Camera Press; p. 132 & p. 133 Cecil Beaton, courtesy of Sotheby's, London; p. 136 left Private Collection; p. 136/p. 137 drawings & photograph courtesy of Christian Dior, Paris; p. 138 BBC Hulton Library; p. 139 Rex Features; p. 140 left & right Maison Givenchy, Paris; p. 141 left L. de Raemy/Hillelson; p. 141 right Yves Saint Laurent, Paris; p. 142 Alexandre de Paris; p. 143 & p. 144 left Patrick Lichfield; p. 144 right Rex Features; p. 145 Patrick Lichfield; p. 146 Central Press; p. 147 Patrick Lichfield; p. 148 top & bottom & p. 149 Dorothy Wilding/National Portrait Gallery, London, courtesy of Tom Hustler

CHAPTER 4

p. 150 © Kenro Izu 1987; p. 152 & p. 153 inset Cartier, Paris; p. 153 © Kenro Izu 1987; p. 154 Paris Match; p. 155 Cecil Beaton courtesy of Sotheby's, London; p. 156 left Windsor Archives, Paris; p. 156/p. 157 © Kenro Izu 1987; p. 160 Hoyningen-Huene © Horst; p. 161 © Kenro Izu 1987; p. 162 Cecil Beaton, courtesy of Sotheby's, London; p. 163 inset & main picture courtesy of Stephane Graff; p. 164, p. 165 & p. 166 Sotheby's, London; p. 167 Horst; p. 168 Courtesy of Van Cleef & Arpels; p. 169 Sotheby's, London; p. 170 Rex Features; p. 171 & p. 172 Sotheby's, London; p. 173 Karsh of Ottawa/Camera Press; p. 174 Van Cleef & Arpels; p. 175 By generous permission of Mohamed Al-Fayed; p. 176 left & right Cartier, Paris; p. 177 Sotheby's London; p. 178 left Van Cleef & Arpels; p. 178 right & p. 179 left Condé Nast; p. 179 right Private Collection p. 180 Nino Caprioglio; p. 181 © Kenro Izu 1987; p. 182 top & bottom & p. 183 inset Sotheby's, London; p. 183 main picture Camera Press; p. 184 top & bottom, p. 185 middle & bottom Cartier, Paris; p. 185 top & p. 186 left Sotheby's, London; p. 186 top Musée du Louvre, courtesy of Cliché Musées Nationaux, Paris; p. 187 Horst; p. 189 Cartier, Paris; p. 190 © Kenro Izu 1987; p. 191 Horst; p. 192 Sotheby's, London; p. 194 Stephane Graff; p. 195 Cecil Beaton, courtesy of Sotheby's, London; p. 195 inset Courtesy of Ghislaine de Polignac; p. 196 left Private Collection; p. 196 right Sotheby's, London; p. 197 Dorothy Wilding/National Portrait Gallery, London, courtesy of Tom Hustler